Migration, Incorporation, and Change in an Interconnected World

Written in engaging and approachable prose, *Migration, Incorporation, and Change in an Interconnected World* covers the bulk of material a student needs to get a good sense of the empirical and theoretical trends in the field of migration studies, while being short enough that professors can easily build their courses around it without hesitating to assign additional readings. Taking a unique approach, Ali and Hartmann focus on what they consider the important topics and the potential route the field is going to take, and incorporate a conceptual lens that makes this much more than a simple relaying of facts.

Syed Ali is Associate Professor of Sociology at Long Island University in Brooklyn, NY. He is currently the co-editor of *Contexts Magazine* and is the author of *Dubai: Gilded Cage* (Yale UP, 2010). He is also an Ultimate Frisbee player and a potter.

Douglas Hartmann is Professor of Sociology at the University of Minnesota. He is the author of *Race, Culture, and the Revolt of the Black Athlete: The 1968 Olympic Protests and Their Aftermath* (University of Chicago Press, 2003) and co-author of *Ethnicity and Race: Making Identities in a Changing World* (Pine Forge Press). Hartmann is also co-editor and publisher of the award-winning TheSocietyPages.org.

Contemporary Sociological Perspectives

**Edited by Douglas Hartmann, University of Minnesota and
Jodi O'Brien, Seattle University**

This innovative series is for all readers interested in books that provide frameworks for making sense of the complexities of contemporary
social life. Each of the books in this series uses a sociological lens to
provide current critical and analytical perspectives on significant social
issues, patterns, and trends. The series consists of books that integrate
the best ideas in sociological thought with an aim toward public education and engagement. These books are designed for use in the classroom
as well as for scholars and socially curious general readers.

Published

Political Justice and Religious Values by Charles F. Andrain

GIS and Spatial Analysis for the Social Sciences by Robert Nash Parker
and Emily K. Asencio

*Hoop Dreams on Wheels: Disability and the Competitive Wheelchair
Athlete* by Ronald J. Berger

The Internet and Social Inequalities by James C. Witte and Susan
E. Mannon

Media and Middle Class Mom: Images and Realities of Work and Family
by Lara Descartes and Conrad Kottak

*Watching T.V. Is Not Required: Thinking about Media and Thinking about
Thinking* by Bernard McGrane and John Gunderson

Violence Against Women: Vulnerable Populations by Douglas Brownridge

State of Sex: Tourism, Sex and Sin in the New American Heartland
by Barbara G. Brents, Crystal A. Jackson & Kate Hausbeck

Sociologists Backstage: Answers to 10 Questions About What They Do
by Sarah Fenstermaker and Nikki Jones

Migration, Incorporation, and Change in an Interconnected World

Syed Ali and Douglas Hartmann

Routledge
Taylor & Francis Group

NEW YORK AND LONDON

First published 2015
by Routledge
711 Third Avenue, New York, NY 10017

and by Routledge
2 Park Square, Milton Park, Abingdon, Oxon, OX14 4RN

Routledge is an imprint of the Taylor & Francis Group, an informa business

Library of Congress Cataloging-in-Publication Data
Ali, Syed, 1968–
  Migration, incorporation, and change in an interconnected world / by Syed Ali, Doug Hartmann.
     pages cm. — (Contemporary sociological perspectives)
  Includes bibliographical references and index.
  1. Emigration and immigration—Study and teaching. 2. Assimilation (Sociology)—Study and teaching. 3. Social change—Study and teaching.
I. Hartmann, Douglas. II. Title.
  JV6013.5.A45 2015
  304.8—dc23
  2014029689

ISBN: 978-0-415-63740-4 (hbk)
ISBN: 978-0-415-63739-8 (pbk)
ISBN: 978-1-315-73303-6 (ebk)

Typeset in Adobe Caslon and Copperplate
by Apex CoVantage, LLC

For Eli, Sami, and Noura
(Syed)

~~~

For Teresa, Ben, and Emma
(Doug)

CONTENTS

PREFACE

This book is and is not a textbook. It has the look of a textbook, in that it covers the bulk of material a student should need to understand to get a good sense of the empirical and theoretical trends in the field of migration studies. But it is not really a textbook in that it is not comprehensive. We planned it that way. We wanted the book to be short and cheap and conceptual so that the professor could use it to build a course around, and not feel too guilty assigning students additional materials to read. Wasn't that nice of us?

Because the book is purposefully short, we had to make stark choices as to what to put in and what to leave out. If you compare our book to other migration textbooks, you will find that much of what they discuss is missing from here. Conversely, much of what is in here you won't find anywhere else. Again, that is on purpose. A lot of what's in the book is our take on what is important in the field, where we think the field is going, and to a degree is a matter of taste. The chapters on Muslim immigrants in the West, low-end migrant workers (including lengthy sections on marriage migration, sex work, and human trafficking), and high-end expatriate workers are indicative of this. While you may not find the breadth of topics you could get elsewhere, we try to make up for it in depth and readability, especially with topics that others do not deal with, or only touch upon. (And for the professors out there, this lends itself easily to assigning short and long essay questions. If any students are reading this preface, please stop groaning.)

Much of the material in the book is based upon our own research on migration, multiculturalism, and race and ethnicity. Though we have both written on these topics, we are outsiders to the migration field, in the sense that we don't have the personal network connections to the "big players," and our approach in our published work is quite different from that of the bulk of researchers in the field. Ali's studies of assimilation in multiple contexts (United States, Europe, India, Dubai) have led him to a theoretical stance at odds with mainstream conceptions of assimilation, theories that draw largely on the American experience. His studies of migrants in India and Dubai also shape his notions of why migrants leave and the different ways in which they adapt and are incorporated (or not). Hartmann approaches the topic of migration a bit differently, more from the perspective of his interests in race and ethnicity on the one hand, and social solidarity, diversity, and belonging, on the other. In current research, both of us have closely linked the concept of race and ethnicity to incorporation, and in ways different from how others have.

Being outsiders has disadvantages of course. But it also has advantages. The biggest is that we can "see the forest for the trees." That is, we make the claim that *because* we are outsiders, we can evaluate the field (what's interesting, what's not, what's dead, what's hot) better than others who are players in the field, who may have vested interests in certain theories or studies, or who will insist on incorporating as much research as possible. We chose to go another route—to make the book reader-friendly. You will immediately get a sense of that from some of the material we choose to foreground, the storytelling approach we use, and our writing style.

The writing style that we use is unique for a textbook. We have both written and worked for *Contexts* (Ali is currently an editor and Hartmann is a former editor), a sociology magazine dedicated to bringing insightful research that is written for the lay reader. So we wrote this book in a very simple, easy-to-read style, intended for undergraduates of all levels (and for non-Western students who often get lost in dense writing styles), graduate students (because they don't want to read dense academic-y material any more than undergraduates do), and any journalists and other nonacademics who might be interested in the topic.

The question we ask ourselves when writing is, "Will my mother-in-law read this?" Your mother has to read it, but your mother-in-law is under no such obligation. But don't be put off or fooled by our writing style—simple is not simplistic! The theories and ideas in the book are often complex. We have done our best to explain in clear English what they mean. Some professorial types might not like our writing style (they'll call it "journalistic," as if that is some kind of insult). But from our experiences teaching undergraduates (and as life-long students and readers ourselves), we believe that students will greatly appreciate it, will pay more attention, and will actually read it! And in the end, they will likely learn more. Isn't that what it should be about?

INTRODUCTION

Why do people leave their homes for a new land? Where do they go, and how do they get there? What do they do once they get there? And what about their children, what happens to them? These four linked questions about movement and incorporation are the building blocks for the field of migration studies. They are also the backbone of this book and constitute the core preoccupations of the chapters that follow.

The book will provide a broad, sociological introduction to migration, migrants, and incorporation in a rapidly changing and increasingly interconnected world. Each chapter and case will be based upon (and thus highlight) classic works, key concepts, and the newest, most innovative research and thinking in the field. We will show how these various concepts are intimately connected and place them in a global context. We will do this by presenting a series of stories of the experiences of different groups of migrants in the contemporary world to give a general overview and synthesis of the most important ideas and recent findings about both international movement and immigrant incorporation in the field. We hope this book will serve as a starting point for clear thinking, further research, and informed discussion on all these matters.

It is important to see the underlying points and patterns that each case represents and that organize a sociological approach to the topic and material. As sociologists, we go a bit further in framing migration and incorporation than many scholars in the area. What this means, generally, is that we place these core concerns in the broader social contexts that drive and determine the movement of people and that shape their experiences in new circumstances.

Context is an important word and a big concept for sociologists. In the sociological imagination, why migration happens and how migrants fare is not just about their culture and resources and hard work (or lack thereof). It is not just what they bring or do. The experience of migration and incorporation is more importantly driven and determined by the conditions that migrants encounter, the very social and cultural situations that motivated their movement in the first place. This is core sociological territory.

There are at least four contexts of the migration experience that we focus on. One is economic—the need that nations have for workers on the one hand, and that migrants have for work. Another is cultural. It is under the general heading of culture that we would call attention to the social dynamics of gender, class, and race, both in terms of movement and incorporation. Across all of the chapters of our book, we will highlight the powerful ways in which gender, class, and race shape, distinguish, and stratify the immigration experience all over the world.

A third contextual factor crucial to understanding migration and migrants is legal and political. This includes the laws and public policies that govern immigration, citizenship, and naturalization, as well as those that dictate the conditions of work. Laws and policies also determine access to social services like education and health care that shape the experience of migration in a new place and that affect movement in the first place. There is a big difference, for example, between the experience of migrants who are undocumented workers (that is, lacking a valid visa for work or residence, or having no visa at all) as compared with those who are refugees from war-torn states who have been granted the benefits and protections of political asylum, or as contrasted with those who work in an industry that has been targeted by a government for economic growth (thus bringing with it favorable tax policies and worker visa programs).

A fourth context is globalization itself. Our emphasis on globalization speaks to the truly international dynamics of movement and migration, and how these dynamics play out differently in different parts of the world. We are also interested in how globalization is driving the incorporation of migrants' into their new societies, the impacts that migration is having on race and ethnic relations, citizenship and multiculturalism, and national politics in societies all over the world. Ultimately, we are interested in what the evolving dynamics of migration and incorporation can teach us about globalization and the contemporary global world itself.

In addition to our emphasis on context, another distinctive aspect of this book and the sociological orientation to migration and incorporation more generally is a focus on the broader social impacts and cultural significance of migration. Our premise is that migration not only changes things for the lives of migrants and their children, but it changes things for the societies they move into, the natives and other foreigners they come into contact with, and those they leave behind. Indeed, the final chapter of the book will discuss explicitly the transformations that immigration leads to in countries and societies all across the world.

We don't intend this to be a particularly long book, or a completely exhaustive one. Rather, our goal is to produce a volume that will—in an engaging, accessible way—introduce readers to the classic works, key concepts, and original new research and topics that together constitute the unique, broad vision of and orientation to migration that is cultivated in sociology. It is an invitation—or perhaps challenge—to think sociologically about migration and be able to apply that orientation and basic set of facts and concepts to the unfolding world around us.

American Migration as Starting Point

Although migration is fundamentally a global phenomenon, it operates very differently for different people in different societies over the world. But you have to start from somewhere in order to begin to grasp all of this complexity and variation. Since we are from the United States, and many of our students and readers will be American, that's where we will start.

The United States offers a very important, if somewhat particular starting point for thinking about migration and migrants. The United States is one of those rare societies that think of itself as a nation of immigrants. The country's history has been thoroughly shaped and determined by migrants (though also by the colonization, imperial conquest, and the displacement of Native Americans). Moreover, the country has been, and still is, the most popular destination for immigrants globally. According to the US Census, there are approximately 40 million foreign-born people in the United States.[1] That is to say, about 12–13 percent of the total population was born in and comes from a country outside of the United States.

These are quite remarkable numbers. To put them in some perspective, consider that this is the highest *raw* number ever in American history, though not the highest proportion of immigrants, which was in the 1890s–1910s when about 15 percent of the population was foreign born. And it has all happened very quickly. In the 1970s, after a long hiatus brought about by various restrictions following the world wars, the percentage of persons born outside of the nation's borders was only 4.7 percent. So from the 1970s to 2013, the percentage of foreign-born residents had more than doubled to about 13 percent.

There are not only a lot of immigrants in the United States, but they are also an extremely diverse group. About one-third of the foreign born—13 million—who live in the United States are legal permanent residents, with close to half being citizens. Around another 11 or 12 million are undocumented, the most controversial group. And no matter what their legal status, migrants come from many different countries. By far, the largest number of foreign born is from Mexico (about 12 million), more than five times the next two largest groups of Chinese (2.2 million) and Indians (1.8 million) respectively. About half of all legal residents live in four states: About 25 percent live in California (3.5 million), while another quarter of all legal residents live in New York, Texas, and Florida.[2]

Immigrants and residents are diverse in terms of economic status and education. Though public discussion often focuses on poor and undocumented immigrants, the fact is that American immigrants taken as a whole are far from the poor, huddled masses they are sometimes imagined to be. For example, a large number of immigrants in recent years have been political refugees—people who come to the United States because the political situation in their home countries has deteriorated so much that their rights and freedoms have been taken away or their lives put in jeopardy. They come with varying amounts of economic resources and education, but also typically receive special recognition and assistance from the governments and communities that they settle into. Other American migrants are actually sought out for the scientific or technological skills that they have, or the wealth they possess. Many migrants in the United States are highly educated and fairly well off, and migrants and their children also incorporate themselves into American society at rates and levels, from second to third generations, far more quickly and smoothly than is often imagined. The acquisition of English happens particularly quickly, even for first-generation migrants.[3] The exceptions to these general patterns tend to be immigrants who are darker skinned and seen as culturally different. In fact, a recent book on anti-immigration sentiment in the United States suggests that those who have been here the longest and have the most experiences with racism and discrimination are the least likely to think of themselves as Americans.[4]

It is important to place American migration patterns and settlement experiences in some historical and global context. A century ago, the bulk of global migrant flows was to the United States. Migrants came from Southern and Eastern Europe, including the Irish, Italian and Polish. In the early mid-1800s, large numbers of German, British, and Canadian migrants also made their way to the United States. In fact, if you look at Map 0.1 comparing where immigrants to the United States were born in 1910 and 2010, you see that in 1910, the biggest immigrant population in individual states was of Germans, British, and Canadians, whereas by 2010, the largest immigrant population in most states was of Mexicans.[5]

These patterns have been shaped by both economics and governmental policies—or, more accurately, how these two dynamics affect each other. The Mexican case is illustrative. From 1942–1964, the United States had a temporary labor program, the Bracero program, which brought 450,000 temporary Mexican laborers to the United States yearly. An additional 50,000 Mexicans arrived with permanent residence. These numbers changed with the Immigration and Nationality Act of 1965 (also known as the Hart-Celler Act) that limited permanent resident arrivals to 20,000 overall annually. Also in 1965 the United States shut

2010

1910

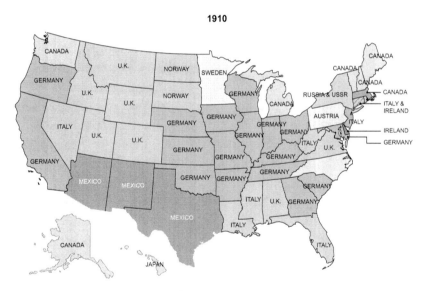

Map 0.1 Top nation of origin by US state

Source: Pew Research Center, "From Germany to Mexico."

down the Bracero program. So the number of legal, permanent residents declined significantly. But temporary workers, who used to come legally, in the 1970s started to come without proper documentation. (In the United States today, there are around 12 million undocumented migrants—more than half of which are Mexican. Of these, around three million or more entered as minors and grew up in the United States.[6]) In fact, Mexico-United States migration is the greatest flow in the world. Almost 10 percent of Mexican citizens live in the United States, and this flow constitutes 6 percent of all global migrants.[7]

In recent years, increased border controls (walls, patrols, drones, etc.) between the United States and Mexico have made migration more difficult and more costly. This has changed the nature of undocumented migration. Before the 1990s, when the United States became stricter about undocumented migration, migrants often went back and forth. But by the 1990s, it became more difficult to enter, which made migrants more likely to stay, and have children and raise them in the United States.[8] In fact, there are a great number of families where the parents and some children are undocumented, while other children are born in the United States and are citizens.[9] But while the undocumented population of Mexicans has increased dramatically, so has the documented population. In recent years, large numbers of Mexicans have naturalized—between 1990 and 2010, 2.1 million naturalized. US citizens are allowed to sponsor direct relatives (spouses, minor children, and parents and adult siblings subject to certain numerical conditions). Because so many Mexicans have naturalized, they are sponsoring relatives—in 2010, two-thirds of all Mexican immigrants, about 170,000 a year, arrived as permanent residents. The number of legal, temporary Mexican workers has quietly risen also—in 2008 there were 361,000, the most since 1959.[10]

But what about the rest of the world? The high percentage of foreign-born residents in the United States as well as the extreme range and variation in terms of their experiences can give us a skewed sense of the scope and significance of migration worldwide. Only 3 percent of people around the world live outside of the country that they were born in, and half of those live in just 28 countries (see Map 0.2).[11]

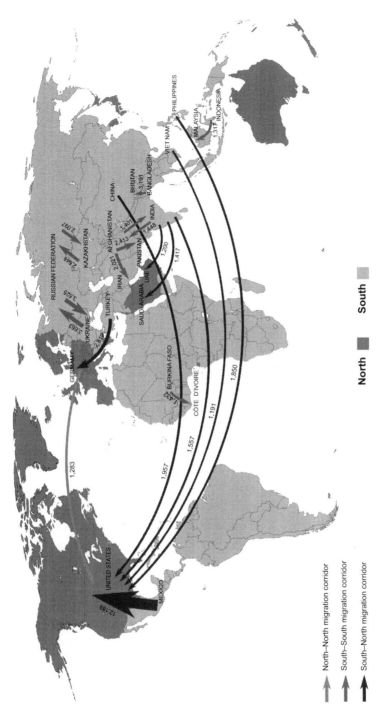

Map 0.2 Top twenty migration corridors worldwide (migrant stock in thousands)

Source: International Organization for Migration, *World Migration Report 13*.[12]

Global Stocks and Flows

Western European countries have also seen a jump in immigration over the past half century. Immigration there was driven by the need to rebuild after World War II, and because of the long economic boom in the 1960s. Most of the immigrants that came as temporary guest workers were from Muslims countries—Turkey, Algeria, Tunisia, and Morocco sent the most. In the mid-1970s most Western European nations shut down avenues for labor migration, but many of these workers, who it was assumed would just go home, didn't. They settled and started families. Migration since then has been mostly through family reunification and to a lesser degree of refugees. (We will have more to say about Muslim migrants in Western Europe in Chapter 5.)

While the United States and other Western countries are the most popular destinations for migrants, they only account for about 45 percent of the total stock of global migrants. So less than half of all migrants have gone from developing to developed countries. Migrants going between developing countries account for another 35 percent of the total, those migrating between developed countries are 17 percent, and three percent have gone from developed to developing countries (see Table 0.1).[13] Migrants moving West will often travel long distances (like Filipinos to Canada to work as maids), but those moving between developing countries tend to go to neighboring countries, like Zimbabweans to South Africa, or Bangladesh to India. For some developing countries, refugees make up more than 10 percent of the total number of migrants.[14]

In much of the world, working-class migrants come on temporary visas, such as individuals from former USSR countries to Russia; Indians, Pakistanis, and Bangladeshis going to the resource-rich Persian Gulf countries; Chinese, Indonesians, and Vietnamese to Singapore, Hong Kong, Japan, and South Korea; and so on. There are also some countries that migrants recently have started going to that few people would even guess would be attractive destinations. For example, Kazakhstan became an important destination for low-skilled migrants from central Asia and to a lesser extent from Russia and China after the Russian financial crisis in 1998, and since 2000 as Kazakhstan's economy has grown considerably due to its recently acquired oil and natural gas wealth.[15] All of these differences matter—and our task in

Table 0.1 Top five migrant corridors on each of the four migrant pathways

S-N	Origin	Destination	Number of migrants	% of total S-N migrants
1	Mexico	United States	12,189,158	12.8
2	Turkey	Germany	2,819,326	3.0
3	China	United States	1,956,523	2.1
4	Philippines	United States	1,850,067	1.9
5	India	United States	1,556,641	0.7
N-N	*Origin*	*Destination*	*Number of migrants*	*% of total N-N migrants*
1	Germany	United States	1,283,108	4.0
2	United Kingdom	Australia	1,097,893	3.5
3	Canada	United States	1,037,187	3.0
4	Korea, Republic of	United States	1,030,561	2.8
5	United Kingdom	United States	901,916	2.5
S-S	*Origin*	*Destination*	*Number of migrants*	*% of total S-S migrants*
1	Ukraine	Russian Federation	3,662,722	4.9
2	Russian Federation	Ukraine	3,524,669	4.7
3	Bangladesh	Bhutan	3,190,769	4.2
4	Kazakhstan	Russian Federation	2,648,316	3.5
5	Afghanistan	Pakistan	2,413,395	3.2
N-S	*Origin*	*Destination*	*Number of migrants*	*% of total N-S migrants*
1	United States	Mexico	563,315	7.8
2	Germany	Turkey	306,459	4.3
3	United States	South Africa	252,311	3.5
4	Portugal	Brazil	222,148	3.1
5	Italy	Argentina	198,319	2.8

Source: International Organization for Migration. *World Migration Report 13.*

the chapters that follow will be to try to understand and explain how and why this is the case.[16]

The figures we gave above regarding migration numbers are for the *stock* of migrants. The total stock of global migrants is about 3 percent, or 214 million people. This includes people who have just migrated, and people who migrated when they were infants who have lived in those countries all their lives. A quick glance at these numbers may give a reader the sense that these numbers are similar over time, that is, the percentages of where people go to and from are the same over time. They are not. These stock numbers don't give us a dynamic sense of what is happening recently.

A better way to examine recent migration is by looking at *flows*. Getting a comprehensive picture of migration flows around the world has been difficult, because the sizes of flows between countries cannot be directly compared using existing datasets. The problem is that countries vary widely in the amount and quality of data they collect on migration. Most countries collect information on the size of their immigrant population (the migrant stock), but less than 50 countries provide data on incoming and outgoing migrants over a specific time interval (the migrant flow).

A new study presents for the first time ever data on the flow of people over five-year periods, from 1990–1995 to 2005–2010.[17] It captures people who changed their country of residence over a five-year period and allows for comparisons between 196 countries. But the data aren't perfect. The coverage of refugees is uneven, and undocumented migrants and seasonal workers can't be captured. So for instance, it will underestimate migration flows to the United States, which has a sizeable population of undocumented workers.

Data on human movements have traditionally been visualized with lines or arrows overlaid on a world map (like the previous map). Circular migration plots created by the migration scholar Nikola Sander and her colleagues make the complex and dynamic patterns of flow data more easily accessible und understandable. The shading tells the direction of each flow: The flow has the same shade as the origin and a different shade as the destination. The width of a flow shows its size, and every tick mark on the plots represents 100,000 migrants.

The next four circular plots show migration between seven world regions, to and from the United States and Canada, Western Europe, and the Persian Gulf for the period from 2005 to 2010. Overall, 41.5 million people, or about 0.6 percent of the world's population, migrated during this time, and this five-year flow amount hasn't changed much from 1995 to 2000.[18]

Plot 0.1 Migration between seven world regions, 2005–2010

One thing that stands out in all of these plots is that migration is overwhelmingly from "transitional" countries—not the poorest developing countries, but those with some level of economic development and education. The plots do show some migration within the West, and some from the West to the Persian Gulf, but mostly it is within and from the developing world. This contrasts with the data in Table 0.1, for instance, where we see a great deal of migration within the West. But that is misleading, as the number of German, Canadian, and British migrants in the United States, and British migrants in Australia are mostly settled, that is, they are not recent migrants. Similarly, Russians

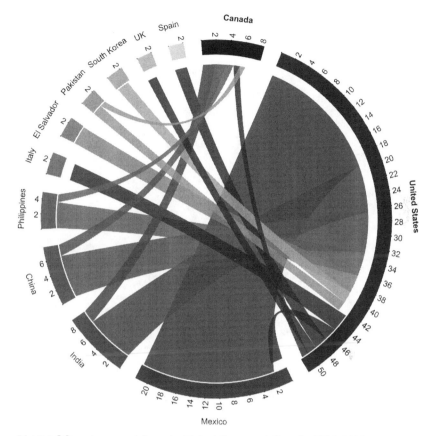

Plot 0.2 Migration to and from the United States and Canada, 2005–2010

in Ukraine (and Ukrainians in Russia) date largely to the early 1990s when the Soviet Union collapsed.

Chapter Summaries

The first chapter, "Leaving Home," will look at the why's, how's, and where's of people leaving their homes. It may seem obvious why people leave their homes to seek out a new society, but there are actually many reasons, and how they get from point A to point B (and for many on to point C) is a rather complex process. Here, we explore the main sociological explanations and contexts of emigration: economic factors,

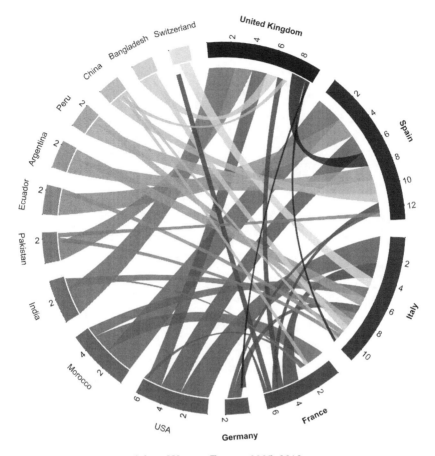

Plot 0.3 Migration to and from Western Europe, 2005–2010

networks, political and legal systems, cultures of migration, and the importance of remittances migrants send home. We also examine how migrants travel back and forth and sometimes split their time and mental energies between countries, a process dubbed "transnational-ism." Many of the most important theories of emigration answer why people go, but do not adequately show how people go. We try to answer the question "how do migrants get to where they are going?" by look-ing at under-examined mechanisms in migration such as the role of middlemen—agents and smugglers. This consideration of why and how people move not only sets the stage for the rest of the book, but it

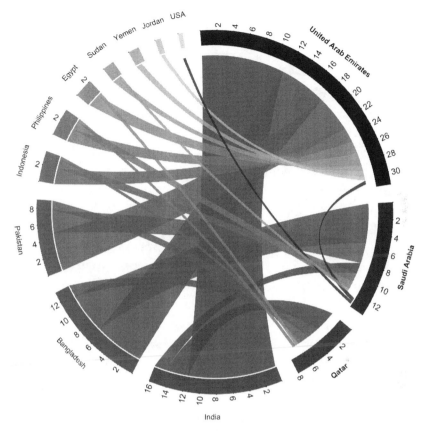

Plot 0.4 Migration to and from the Persian Gulf, 2005–2010

provides a lens onto the organization and complexity of the contemporary, global world.

Economic forces are obviously one of the chief drivers of international migration, but economics works in different ways for different groups of migrants. The second chapter of the book will examine the international migration of workers at the lower ends of the labor market—maids, service workers, construction workers, hawkers, sex workers, and so on. Specifically, we will explore the migration of these types of workers in the context of a globalized world where goods and services flow freely across national borders. But these people, whose labor is needed in these destination countries, face greater barriers. We examine labor migrants who go to their new countries with the understanding that they are merely workers, not immigrants, that is, they go knowing they are temporary (and sometimes undocumented) and in many places have no rights of permanent residence, let alone citizenship. Unlike yesteryear's migrants who were mostly European (and went mostly to the United States) and arrived with legal rights of permanence, today's migrants are darker skinned and often arrive with temporary visas, if they have proper documentation at all.

This chapter also examines the controversy over human trafficking and introduces gender as a key variable shaping the migration and incorporation experience. In recent years, it has become an accepted truth put forward by some scholars, politicians, nongovernmental organizations and activists, that millions of workers have been trafficked and enslaved, mainly women forced into sex slavery, and to a lesser degree men and children forced into various kinds of labor. This may be exaggerated. We look at arguments by some scholars that the focus on trafficking and slavery is one that is morally driven by an aversion to prostitution generally, and greatly inflates the degree to which slavery exists, thus moving the focus away from more pertinent issues of discriminatory visa practices and labor exploitation.

Chapter 3 will look at workers at the other end of the global labor market—professional migrant workers, or "expatriates," who typically have a greater degree of freedom of movement and choice of what to do and where to go. This chapter concentrates on the working and lifestyle experiences of three types of expatriate workers: Westerners going East; non-Westerners working and living in the East; and non-Western expatriates in the West. In many ways the freedoms and economic benefits enjoyed by these groups of migrants stand in contrast to the experience of the much poorer migrants that are the focus of Chapter 2. However because of government policies restricting their political rights and ability to naturalize, expatriates are also usually short-term migrants and know they will return home at some point. We will show how this status greatly affects their work and lifestyles in their temporary abodes and helps bring into focus the political and legal conditions that structure the migrant experience, whether by setting the laws for citizenship or by structuring the economic policies that shape economic and corporate markets.

Some of the most familiar, and perhaps most important questions that arise in the study of immigration today involve the adult children of immigrants, the so-called second generation. How does this second generation adapt to their family's new societies, and how and why does this adaptation vary and change across contexts and communities? To what degree do they achieve upward or downward economic mobility? What various governmental policies, cultural conditions, and historical forces affect these outcomes? The most contentious theoretical debates over assimilation rage here, especially through the dominant paradigms of segmented and new assimilation theories. This is the focus of the fourth chapter of the book. We examine a range of second-generation immigrants in the United States and Europe, and contrast these diverse experiences with the case of second-generation immigrants in non-Western settings.

The debates between the different theoretical camps, and the criticism of American theories from Europe, have centered on the degree to which immigrants assimilate or do not assimilate, and the degree of downward assimilation. A contribution that we make will be to point out that while these theories do explain assimilation at the group level, they do not do so at the level of the individual. Therefore they do not explain assimilation, but rather why some *groups* have greater or lesser degrees of assimilation. We will propose and justify an approach centering on peers that looks at how and why individuals assimilate.

The fifth chapter of the book will explore the varied experiences of arguably the most despised and maligned immigrants in the West today: Muslims. We compare the experiences of American with European immigrants. European Muslim immigrants are largely working-class North Africans and Turks in continental Europe and South Asians in the United Kingdom. They came to Western Europe largely as "guest workers," but became permanent simply by not leaving. Their children have improved upon the parents' educational and occupational status somewhat, but by and large trail their native European peers. The experiences of American Muslim immigrants are quite different. For one, there is a very large native-born (that is, whose parents are also native born), mostly African American contingent. Another major difference is the Muslims who migrated between the 1960s and 1980s were largely professionals, as these people had visa preferences, though by the 1990s the educational, occupational, and country backgrounds began to vary greatly.

What is the meaning and significance of migration for non-migrants? How does all of this affect those who do not migrate, or natives in the countries that migrants are moving into? This is the focus of the sixth and final substantive chapter of the book. We again examine the economic impacts of migration and remittances for migrants and their kinfolk and others back home.

This chapter will also address a range of demographic issues, focusing on overall patterns of population growth as it is driven by migration as well as how race and ethnicity are affected by these demographic shifts. We end by discussing multiculturalism and nativist backlash to the rise of multiculturalism.

In the final, concluding chapter, we will revisit some of the main trajectories and future questions revolving around migration and immigration globally, and try to show the utility of the key concepts and insights of the works discussed in the book. We will also try to suggest some of the historical forces and social factors that are most likely to be decisive in determining the future patterns of migration, incorporation, and change in an increasingly interconnected world.

Notes

1 US Bureau of the Census. "B05005. Year of Entry by Nativity and Citizenship Status in the United States—Universe: Population Born Outside the United States." *2011 American Community Survey 1-Year Estimates.* Washington, DC, US Bureau of the Census: 2012. http://factfinder2.census.gov/faces/tableservices/jsf/pages/productview.xhtml?pid=ACS_11_1YR_B05005&prodType=Table. <retrieved October 9, 2014>

2 Rytina, Nancy. "Estimates of the Legal Permanent Resident Population in 2012." *Population Estimates* (July). Washington, DC: Office of Immigration Statistics, US Department of Homeland Security, 2013.

3 Alba, Richard, and Victor Nee. *Remaking the American Mainstream: Assimilation and Contemporary Immigration.* Cambridge, MA: Harvard UP, 2003.

4 Massey, Douglas, and Magaly Sanchez. *Brokered Boundaries: Creating Immigrant Identity in Anti-Immigrant Times.* New York: Russell Sage Foundation, 2010.

5 Pew Research Center. "From Germany to Mexico: How America's Source of Immigrants Has Changed Over a Century." May 27, 2014. www.pewresearch.org/fact-tank/2014/05/27/a-shift-from-germany-to-mexico-for-americas-immigrants/ <retrieved June 2, 2014>

6 Massey, Douglas. "America's Immigration Policy Fiasco: Learning from Past Mistakes." *Daedalus* 142.3 (2013): 5–15, p. 13.

7 Alba, Francisco. "Mexico: The New Migration Narrative." *Migration Information Source.* April 24, 2013. www.migrationpolicy.org/article/mexico-new-migration-narrative/ <retrieved May 12, 2014>

8 Massey, Douglas, Jorge Durand, and Nolan Malone. *Beyond Smoke and Mirrors: Mexican Immigration in an Era of Economic Integration.* New York: Russell Sage Foundation, 2002.

9 Gonzales, Roberto, and Leo Chavez. "Awakening to a Nightmare." *Current Anthropology* 53.3 (2012): 255–281.

10 Massey, 2013, pp. 10, 12.

11 Waldinger, Roger. "Crossing Borders International Migration in the New Century." *Contemporary Sociology: A Journal of Reviews* 42.3 (2013): 349–363.

12 International Organization for Migration. *World Migration Report 2013.* Geneva: International Organization for Migration, 2013, p. 61.

13 International Organization for Migration, 2013, p. 55. These numbers are from the World Bank, and estimates from other organizations differ, sometimes greatly. So take them as indicative, but not definitive.

14 International Organization for Migration, 2013, p. 68.

15 Anderson, Bridget, and Blanka Hancilová. "Migrant Labour in Kazakhstan: A Cause for Concern?" *Journal of Ethnic and Migration Studies* 37.3 (2011): 467–483.

16 International Organization for Migration, 2013, p. 62.

17 Abel, Guy, and Nikola Sander. "Quantifying Global International Migration Flows." *Science* 343 (2014): 1520–1522; Sander, Nikola, Guy Abel, and Ramon Bauer. "The Global Flow of People." www.global-migration.info/ <retrieved July 8, 2014>

18 All four plots were made for us by Nikola Sander. We're greatly thankful and indebted to her for making these plots, and writing the description for them. You should go to her website, www.global-migration.info/, to see more detail about global migration flows for different periods and for specific countries. They show how flows change over time, and how some countries get more while others get less. For instance, between 1995 and 2010, the flow of migrants to the United Arab Emirates increased dramatically, whereas immigration to Saudi Arabia was higher in 2000–2005 than in 2005–2010. Her plots are interactive and fantastic. What we present here is just a glimpse of the data.

1

LEAVING HOME

As we saw in the introductory chapter, there are clearly identifiable patterns and paths of international migration. There are specific places that send off greater numbers of migrants, and specific places that are more likely to receive them. And the places they go to have shifted over time. Some countries that were net exporters of people have become net importers, and vice versa.

Here, we explore the main sociological explanations of why people emigrate, or leave their home countries: economic reasons, networks, and cultures of migration. We will also look at how migration affects migrants' kinfolk and others back home through remittances, money, and ideas that migrants send home. Remittances shape future migration patterns, and thus are theoretically very important. We further examine how migrants travel back and forth and sometimes split their time and mental energies between countries, a process called "transnationalism."

Many of the most important theories of emigration answer *why* people go, but do not adequately show *how* people go. We try to answer the question "how do migrants get to where they are going?" by looking at under-examined mechanisms in migration such as the role of middlemen—agents and smugglers. This consideration of why and how people move not only sets the stage for the rest of the book, but it provides a lens onto the organization and complexity of the contemporary, global world.

Economic Arguments

The basic economic argument for why people migrate is twofold: Migrants make a rational decision to leave home because job prospects and pay are poor, and they choose to go to a place because job prospects and pay there are better. This is known as the "push-pull" model and is the basis for "neoclassical" economic arguments for why people migrate. In this view, the broad migratory trend will be from developing world countries to developed countries. The migration trend will be in this direction because there is a great demand for labor in the richer, developed countries, and the wages are greater there.[1] Essentially, the individual does a cost-benefit analysis. If the financial costs of migration are outweighed by the benefits of a higher salary, the person goes. The motives for migration then are economically rational and individualistic.[2]

This economic framework is sensible but, in itself, has not proven to be a good explanation for why people migrate. If it were true, we would expect a lot more people to migrate than actually do, especially from poorer countries, and we would expect the poorest to go. In reality, the bigger sending countries, like India, Mexico, and China, are not the poorest countries. And within the sending countries, it is not the poorest generally who migrate. Further, this line of argument ignores social aspects of migration. It assumes that decisions are made by the individual and are made for purely monetary reasons.

A revised version of the neoclassical approach is the "new economics of labor migration." Here the emphasis is not on the individual making a rational economic decision to migrate, but rather it is the household that makes the decision.[3] Migration of a family member is an opportunity for the family to enhance its income base through the remittances sent home by the migrant family member and is also a hedge against economic risks at home. Families can protect against risk by the migrant sending home economic remittances. This theoretical approach in fact puts forward the idea that remittances are a central motive for migration.

While this is a marked improvement over the more simplistic "push-pull" model, there are multiple problematic assumptions. One is that everyone within the household shares the same interests and there is little conflict or inequality within the family. Another assumption is the possibility that no matter how long the migrant is abroad, he or she will keep sending remittances, and send the same or more. It also assumes the would-be migrant goes where the family wants him or her to go, and stays if they want him or her to stay.

But people are funny sometimes and do what they want, even going against their family's wishes, not going along with the family game plan. For instance, Salman, a civil engineer, was being pressured by his parents and siblings in the late 1990s to leave Hyderabad, India, to get a job in Saudi Arabia, where he could make much more money. His sister's husband lived in Saudi Arabia and remitted substantial amounts and built a three-story addition to the joint family compound for his nuclear family. His brother lived in Iran for ten years and also sent substantial remittances, and when he came back, built himself a large, fancy house. Salman, his wife, and three children lived in one room off the kitchen. His parents and siblings insisted, pretty much demanded, that he *must* go, that it was his moral duty to migrate to support his family. But he didn't want to go. His nonmigration was a source of family tension for many years.[4]

So while this added emphasis on the family and remittances is an improvement over the neoclassical model, it still leaves much unanswered about the process and dynamics of international migration, and still suffers from the assumption that the sole reason to leave is monetary.

Networks

In the early 2000s, Germany tried to recruit high-tech workers, specifically from India. They expected a flood of migrants. What they got instead was a trickle.[5]

Germany's assumption was that if you gave the opportunity to professionals in a developing country like India to come to a developed country with much higher wages, they would jump on it because it is the economically rational thing to do. Basically, they were operating under the "push-pull" model. It is true that a great number of migrants move initially for economic reasons—whether due to trouble at home or better opportunities abroad. But this is only a partial explanation of why people move, since migrants often dismiss opportunities abroad, as was the case with Germany. Basically, there are non-economic factors also at play.

Another way to look at this case is to put yourself in the potential Indian migrant's shoes and ask, "Why would I go to Germany?" Your answer would likely be, "It's cold and I don't speak German. In fact, I don't know anything about Germany or anyone there." Indeed, that is a good question and those are good points. For the most part, migrants are going to places that already have links with their country. These could be colonial (India was a British colony, so it shouldn't be surprising that there are large numbers of Indians in the United Kingdom) or military (the United States has had a military presence in countries like Philippines and Vietnam, and this helped spur migration). There are of course economic links. Firms need workers, and one way to get them is to go to the source and recruit them directly. (We'll have more to say on recruitment and agents later.) Another type of economic link is indirect and unintended. Many firms instead of bringing workers back take their workplaces to them, for instance with US firms setting up in China, Haiti, Mexico, etc. Many people thought this foreign investment would deter migration, but paradoxically, it may actually increase it.[6]

The dominant theoretical explanation today looking at why people migrate examines personal networks. The basic idea here is that once these links between places are made, as more people from certain groups—family, village, ethnic group—start migrating, the financial and psychological costs for each succeeding migrant within the network decrease. And as more migrants go, it becomes easier and easier, and the migration flow will become self-perpetuating. This is known as "chain migration" or "cumulative causation."[7]

One of the more important aspects of this approach is the insistence that interpersonal ties drive international migration, and that these networks provide various kinds of aid—information, money, housing, and so on.

Maritsa Poros expands on network theory, while also criticizing it, by introducing more network possibilities beyond the standard "strong" personal network ties, which result in chain migration where family and friends encourage other family and friends to migrate.[8] Her criticism of network theory is that it only looks at one kind of network—the interpersonal network. To that she adds "weak" ties through organizations and institutions, that is, relations with co-workers, employers, bureaucrats, or community leaders.[9] They provide other sources of information and opportunities to migrate through intracompany transfers, study abroad programs, and direct potential migrants to particular destinations that are often different than those where people who migrate through interpersonal ties settle. Then there are composite ties made up of interpersonal and organizational ties. These ties differ from those above because the interpersonal and organizational aspects of these ties are inseparable, for instance with certain Indian family firms involved in the global diamond trade.

Poros's approach to networks is quite interesting. She says we should see networks as variable—she uses the term "relational"—in strength, and we need to understand that individuals have multiple networks. Given that, we should try to understand why and how they vary, and when one rather than another network will be important for a migrant.

Studies of migrants generally look at them through geographical origins—Mexicans, Gujaratis, Dominicans, and so on—and assume that the strong interpersonal connections based on these places are the network, and are important for migration patterns. In fact, if you look at the titles of important empirical scholarly work on migrants, nearly all look at migrants from specific places, and they assume (to greater or lesser degrees) that ethnicity or nationality is a basis of solidarity, that, say for instance, Turks in the Netherlands will aid each other because they share nationality. Poros acknowledges that is often the case, but she then wonders about those who are not helped by "their people." Why and on what basis are they excluded? Why do some get resources from co-ethnics while others do not? Not everyone is equally loved by their co-ethnics, and some people don't want to be around their co-ethnics or to get help from them, as taking help can put you into financial or social debt, which can lead to more problems than it's worth.

Poro's suggests that we look at the number and quality of the network connections of migrants, and what actually happens between people in these networks. Some networks provide help and resources; others do not. We also have to get away from the assumption that just because people share the same nationality/religion/ethnicity that they will provide assistance to others who share those characteristics. Sometimes they do; sometimes they don't. It is important to see when and where they do or don't. By looking at migrant networks as variable, and by looking at the broad types of networks (interpersonal, organizational, composite), we can see more clearly and with greater focus more exactly how migration happens.

Another major criticism of migrant network theory is that it concentrates too much on the supply side. That is, it puts too much emphasis on the actions of migrants themselves and the activities within their networks. It ignores the role that employers, the demand side, have in driving migration.[10] If there were no employer demand, then a lot of migrants, perhaps the vast majority of migrants, would never bother going to those places, and the networks might shift location, or wither away.

This has immediate policy implications concerning migration generally, but undocumented migration specifically. Today in most countries concerned with undocumented migration, policing efforts center on finding, punishing, and deporting the migrants themselves. But if migration is largely demand-driven, then it might be more practical and more effective to focus on employers (who are fewer in number than undocumented migrants and often concentrated in certain types of jobs and industries). In the United States, for example, migrant employers are in very high numbers in restaurants, sweatshops, agriculture, meat-processing plants, and construction. If governments gave harsher financial penalties and jail time for employers, it's possible they would not take the risk and would refuse employment to undocumented workers, and there would be less reason for these migrants to come. Currently under US federal law, an employer only faces relatively small fines for hiring undocumented workers, even if the employer is a repeat offender.[11]

Culture of Migration and Remittances

In spite of the above criticisms, networks are a useful way to understand migration chains that have already occurred. But people don't migrate just because they are connected to others who have migrated, which is essentially the story of migrant network theory, or because there are better jobs available, the basis of economic theories of migration. They have to learn that migration, which is often scary and lonely, is a good thing to do, and they have to have the desire to do it. Or at the least they have to overcome their fears or desires not to do it. Some scholars call this the "culture of migration."[12] This culture of migration, once developed, has the effect of reinforcing and even expanding the migrant networks. We should point out that this is usually a local, not a national phenomenon. When we talk of emigration from Mexico or India, it is from specific areas like Oaxaca or Hyderabad where migrants disproportionately leave from, and it is in those areas that a culture of migration is most developed.

We can define the culture of migration as ideas, practices and "cultural stuff" that reinforce the celebration of migrants and the process of migration. These include beliefs, desires, symbols, myths, education, and stories about migrants. Simply put, migration is a learned behavior. People have to learn to migrate, and learn to desire to migrate. Ali saw this in simple things in daily life, like young men in Hyderabad putting American/Canadian/Australian flag stickers on their motorcycles. He also found young men of working age sitting in cafés sharing a cup of tea, studying, gossiping, and waiting for agents to process their visas—anything but building a life in Hyderabad itself. Though they physically lived in Hyderabad, in their minds, they had already left.

Wanting to leave in a culture of migration becomes the norm; wanting to stay is deviant, even though only a small minority actually leaves. Salman, the engineer in Hyderabad we met earlier, was perfectly happy to stay. He had his own business and didn't want to be away from his wife and kids for 11 months out of the year. He had siblings who had gone off and made a lot of money, come back and built large houses. His siblings and parents insisted to him and his wife that he *must* go to Saudi Arabia or Canada (or anywhere in the West or Persian Gulf). The not-so-subtle implication was that by staying with his family, he was being a bad husband; the good husband goes away to send money back.

The culture of migration likely emerges after migration has already begun. Once a chain of migratory behavior has started, once networks have started to flourish, this culture emerges to reinforce the desire among those directly affected by migrants—family, friends, neighbors—and extends out beyond those networks to intensify the desire among even nonmigrants to migrate.

How does this happen? A big part of the story is remittances. Remittances are things that migrants—usually first-generation migrants—send home to family and sometimes to others in their communities. Usually this is economic or material—cash, electronics, clothes, etc. The amount of remittances sent by individuals varies due to many factors: where the migrant has gone to and how long they've been there, what their visa status is in their new country, how strong their family ties are back at home, and whether they think they'll return home or not.

Some countries receive more in remittances from their migrants than others. (See Table 1.1 and Map 1.1.) India and China receive far and away more in remittances (USD 71 and 60 billion in 2013, respectively) than for any other country, not surprising given that both have populations well over one billion people. The next largest recipient nations are Philippines, Mexico, Nigeria, Egypt, Bangladesh, and Pakistan. But in terms of shares of gross domestic product (GDP), nations that are critically dependent upon remittances often have small populations and high unemployment, and many are suffering from effects of wars and natural disasters, and they usually have little other high-income–generating

Table 1.1 Top ten recipients of remittances

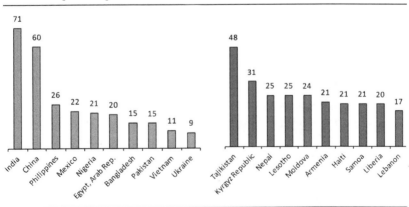

Source: Dilip Ratha et al., "Migration and Remittance Flows," p. 5.

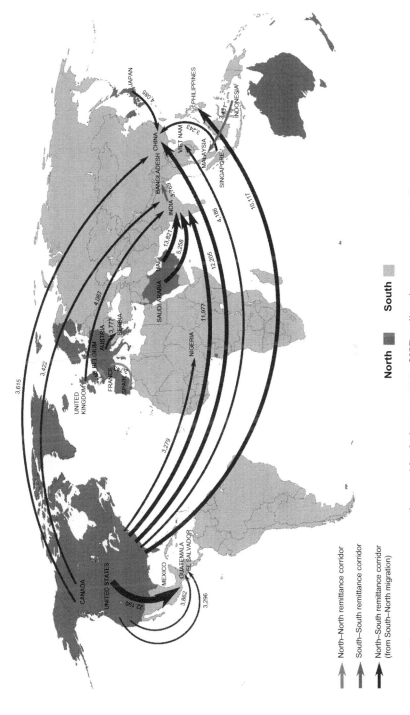

Map 1.1 Top twenty remittance corridors worldwide (remittances in USD millions)

Source: International Organization for Migration, *World Migration Report 13.*

North   South

economic activities. These include countries such as Tajikistan (which gets half of its GDP from remittances), Kyrgyz Republic, Nepal, Lesotho, Moldova, Haiti, and Lebanon.[13] For places like these, anything that slows down the pace of remittances can have disastrous ripple effects on the broader economy, as remittances pay for construction, school fees, marriages, and support local businesses. Not surprisingly, many governments, like the Philippines, Mexico, and Sri Lanka actively encourage and facilitate the sending of remittances.

In addition to financial resources, some migrants send "social" remittances that benefit their localities beyond just family and friends. Migrants who go back and forth between Dominican villages and towns in Massachusetts in the United States learn political strategies and "send" them back to the Dominican Republic where people then take those lessons learned and apply them locally.[14] Similarly, Mexican villagers in New York City set up organizations to send money back and administer funds for public works projects.[15,16]

These remittances are important because they transform how the families of migrants live their lives at home. Obviously the money and material stuff makes life easier. Economic remittances for families in places like India, Lebanon, Mexico, and so on are essential for maintaining and improving their standards of living, making the poor less poor, and making the rich much richer.

These financial and material remittances have no meaning in and of themselves—they're just useful things. But people give meaning to these things, and that is important here in understanding the culture of migration. This also takes us beyond the simple financial family calculations we see in the new economics of labor migration theory. Remittances greatly affect how people think about *status*, or honor or social prestige. Families of migrants who were poor and low status can quite quickly become wealthy, even wealthier than the local economic elite is. This can change the ways they interact with others.[17]

This status transformation is most obvious when looking at the one place where status matters the most—marriage. Who is good marriage material in many places has become the person who has migrated or is willing to migrate. Those who can't—or won't—go abroad are seen as lacking. A 19-year-old woman in Beirut said, "The guys that remain in

Lebanon are the stupid ones! You start to feel that the men who stay in Lebanon are the ones with no ambition in their work, and so you wonder, why are they still here?"[18]

For many people who find their marriage ambitions stunted at home, migration provides the possibility of remaking themselves because the opportunity to make more money can increase their social status dramatically. In fact, being a migrant *in and of itself* has become a status marker in many places. Ali found that in Hyderabad, for men, and often women, going to the West or to the Persian Gulf to work changes the ways they are perceived in Hyderabad itself. The identities they are born with, such as caste or nobility (Hyderabad was a kingdom until 1948) or the class background of their parents, become secondary or irrelevant. Even educational achievements, so important as status markers throughout the world, can lessen in importance. These migrants become highly prized commodities because they have that valued social marker—a foreign visa or citizenship. And these people can demand better—better-educated spouses, better quality families, and better (that is, bigger) dowries. Those who get abroad are victorious, and to the victor go the spoils.[19]

Because migrants and migration are socially valued, people in the sending societies take keen interest in the lands to which they may migrate. They become familiar with how people live their lives there through doing things like watching satellite TV and hearing the stories (and seeing the results) of migrants who come back to visit or settle permanently. Essentially there is a cultural presocialization that goes on, sometimes well before a migrant even decides to migrate.

To facilitate migration, many learn the languages of the places where they intend to migrate, often even before it becomes clear they have a chance to migrate. At higher educational levels, students often choose their courses of studies based on perceptions of what is in demand in the countries they would like to emigrate to. So for instance, in the late 1990s, there was a great demand in Hyderabad for software training in programs like Oracle, Java, and C++. Many did not do this to work in Hyderabad, which was certainly possible, as international firms such as Microsoft, Texas Instruments, and many others had set up operations there. Rather, they were trying to get to the United States, United

Kingdom, Canada, and Australia—places that had visa preferences for IT workers.

The possibility that they may migrate affected how these young people thought about working at home. For many, they didn't bother, as they were receiving remittances from family abroad, which was more money than they could make working. So why work? Many educated young men sat around and chose not to work, instead putting their efforts into securing a visa to go abroad, to do anything. Many highly educated young men in Hyderabad would sit idly and not work at low-paid, low-status jobs. But they were more than happy to do menial jobs once abroad, like working at a gas station in Chicago or Melbourne. Why? Because they saw work abroad as inherently higher status than work at home.

The above examples all focus on status mobility—or changes in the relative social ranking within their communities—of individuals and, by association, their families. But remittances have social effects that go beyond the individual and family. Take for example a study of the effects of migrant remittances on caste (hereditary status groups that tend to marry amongst themselves) in three villages in the coastal Indian state of Kerala.[20] In a Hindu village, migration by lower-caste members led to an inversion of rank of the two major castes; in a Christian village, the high castes took advantage of migration, leading to greater caste polarization; but in a Muslim village, the economic success of the low castes served to erode the caste differences, and broke down traditional patterns where marriages were arranged within castes. What's interesting here is that patterns of social inequality that took hundreds of years to build up were so strongly affected by remittances sent home over merely a few decades.

Transnationalism

Arguably the most prominent paradigm that scholars use today to study the flows of migrants between countries is transnationalism. Transnationalism does not try to directly answer the question of why or how people migrate as the above theories do; rather it shows how people maintain connections across multiple countries. Most scholars of transnationalism, though, just look at how migrants maintain such connections between their home and host countries.

Scholars generally see transnationalism as a process where individuals and families and/or ethnic, nationality, or religious communities maintain varying degrees and types of social, economic, and political ties across two or more nations. Additionally, some scholars put forward the idea that actual mobility across borders is not even required, that living within a "transnational social field" where others participate in transnational activities encompasses both those who move and those who stay behind.[21] The ability to be transnational is made easy through fast and cheap transportation, email, texting and video chatting, ease and speed of sending remittances, and so on.

While some scholars argue that transnationalism is a recent product of globalization, it's not actually new. We can see examples of transnational behavior among 19th and early 20th century Italian and Russian Jewish immigrants in the United States. They sent letters home, and perhaps more importantly, money orders. Russian immigrants set up hometown associations in New York to send aid back to war-ravaged home communities. And many returned back to Russia and Italy, often to build houses. Many Italians were "birds of passage" flitting back and forth between the United States and Italy. Even among Russian Jews who faced political oppression and an incredible degree of anti-Semitism in Russia, as many as 20 percent of those who came between 1880 and 1900 returned. More broadly, for every 100 migrants that came to the United States in the first two decades of the 20th century 36 returned. That's actually a higher rate than later in the 20th century, when between 1971 and 1990, 21 of every 100 migrants returned.[22]

The earliest theoretical writings on transnationalism in the 1990s cast a very wide net.[23] They defined transnationals as migrants who maintained any kind of personal, political, or cultural link to the homeland. This would conceivably include, say, a second-generation Irish American who likes to drink Guinness beer.

While earlier scholars made it seem that nearly all immigrants were transnational, more recently other writers have begun to emphasize that not all international migrants are transnationals.[24] Many if not most migrants—especially those in Western countries—have little, if any, qualitative or quantitative connection with their home countries outside of close family. Even where one finds the greatest numbers of first-generation immigrants who are engaging in transnational behavior, the absolute numbers are still few relative to the total population of migrants.[25]

One understudied element in the field is of adult, second-generation migrants, who, not surprisingly, tend to have fewer and less intense transnational connections than their parents with their parents' country of origin.[26] However, many scholars assert that the children of migrants do engage in transnational activities, even if not to the same degree as first-generation immigrants.[27] Some of these young adults choose, for economic and/or cultural reasons, to return to their parents' homeland, laying claim to it as theirs.[28] But again, transnationalism is not common among the first generation; it is far less common among the second generation.[29]

Most studies of transnationalism look at migrants in countries where there is a chance of permanent settlement, which partially explains why rates of transnationalism are so low. Instead, let's look at a place where there is no chance of permanent settlement. In his research on Dubai, Ali found a situation where *all* second-generation migrants, like first-generation migrants, regardless of country of origin, must at some point consider leaving Dubai.[30] This is very different from second-generation migrants in the West. The key factor that makes these migrants in Dubai different from immigrants in other countries is the structured impermanence they live under as a direct result of the state defining them as temporary migrant contract workers, rather than as immigrants. All non-citizens in Dubai are on temporary visas. Even if they're born in Dubai, hardly any will ever get citizenship, and there is no such category as permanent residency. Their passports and citizenship are those of their fathers, even if they have never been to those countries.

For most global migrants, conscious decisions have to be made to leave one's home and engage in transnational behavior. For second-generation migrants in Dubai, however, their transnationalism is compelled by the state and is their default strategy. Alejandro Portes makes the point that "the ways immigrants are incorporated in the host society [affects] their propensity to engage in transnational initiatives."[31] In Dubai and throughout the Persian Gulf, migrants are barely incorporated into the host society beyond their economic activities; indeed they are not even considered immigrants.

One of Ali's more interesting findings was not simply how common transnational behavior was for these people, but rather, how these migrants accepted their reality of going between multiple countries to live and work with such mental ease. They live with the possibility that their visas could be cancelled, and they may find themselves deported. But at the same time, in a way they are untethered from Dubai, as they do not legally belong. For these people in Dubai, transnational behavior is something they all engage in, or will necessarily engage in, as they have no choice. Since Dubai is not really their "home," their attachment to it is much less than, say, for second-generation migrants in London or New York City who do have legal permanence and are socially recognized as belonging, even if they do experience forms of exclusion such as garden-variety racism. It should be no surprise, then, that second-generation immigrants in the West so rarely engage in transnational behavior.

Government Regulations and Migration

At this point we should make clear, if it's not already obvious, that we feel laws and governmental actions are possibly the most important, and least theorized, factors affecting international migration. Governmental action shapes who migrates, where, and how. Sometimes migration happens the way the government intends; at other times it does not. Migrants react to the actions of governments, by abiding by their rules or figuring out ways to get around them. On occasion migrants are able to mobilize to get governments to change the rules; sometimes they're successful, though usually they're not. While it is true that economic compulsions, network connections and a culture of migration are important, it is governments that set the rules of the game—migrants either follow the rules or they cheat (which can be another way to get governments to change the rules if the cheating is widespread and successful). However, ultimately migrants cannot ignore these rules, nor can they make their own.

Nation-states issue passports and visas, and go to great lengths to regulate who comes in and out and who is able to stay and for how long—from short-term tourist and work visas to permanent residency visas to granting citizenship. Those without visas—or undocumented persons—are subject to prosecution and deportation. Most states have very stringent controls and detailed bureaucratic processes. Migrants have to do the things that need to be done to get them admitted legally, or figure out ways around border controls to get there illegally. For instance, as the United States has stepped up border controls and built a border wall with Mexico, migrants have to work harder to get to the United States, often crossing through the Arizona desert, where deaths have skyrocketed in recent years. Again, governments set the rules here, and migrants react by either following them or figuring out how to get around them.

This should be an obvious point, but somehow it is one that does not get as much attention as it deserves in theories of why people migrate. Migration theorists, while they often acknowledge that the state is important, usually don't put it theoretically front and center. That is to say, the state seems to be for many writers the *context* in which migration happens, rather than a *cause* of migration. They instead emphasize that the important causes of migration are economic reasons, networks and cultures of migration. But the state is an active player in migratory flows, and, again, can be an active cause that affects people's decisions to leave, and affect the destinations they go to.

How People Actually Migrate: Middlemen

Given that a passport is almost universally required for international travel, and that nearly all countries have visa requirements for visitors, students, businesspeople, workers, and noncitizen residents, the would-be migrant has to be able to navigate a massive bureaucratic maze if he or she wants to come legally. And if they want to migrate without documents, they have to figure out how to get there without getting caught—either by illegally crossing a border, or by arriving on a short-term visa then overstaying, an increasingly popular option. These are not easy for an individual to do, no matter how good their network connections are.

There is a movement among some scholars outside of these theories we discussed above to pay more attention to *how* people actually get to where they're going. They focus on middlemen—legal and "kind of" legal brokers, smugglers, and traffickers—who are central to migration.[32] Middlemen are important for many people as countries make the process of getting a visa more difficult, and as countries increasingly police their borders. The state is important to whether or not brokers are important. Lax borders and easy admissions and visa policies mean individuals can navigate the holes in border enforcement or bureaucratic processes by themselves. But in the past forty years or so, migration controls have been proliferating throughout the world. At the behest of the US government and its obsession with the possibility, no matter how remote, that terrorists might try to enter their land, in nearly every country these controls—visa requirements, border checks, body and luggage scanning—have become far more stringent and intrusive since 2001.

The importance of brokers is not new. In the 17th century, people were "spirited" from English ports to the Americas to become indentured labor through a combination of persuasion, alcohol, money, and kidnapping. British and "native" brokers sent Indian and Chinese migrants to various parts of the British Empire in the 19th century as indentured labor. The conditions of indentured Chinese migrants and the bad reputation that Chinese brokers developed as exploitative were crucial to the rise of anti-Asian immigration laws throughout the West in the late 1800s. Chinese exclusion laws in North America and Australia in the 1880s gave rise to a form of migration control focused on borders, and where migrants came from.[33] Brokers were also important for transporting women to be married. The novelist Anna Solomon, in her lovely book *The Little Bride*, describes how young Jewish girls from Odessa used marriage brokers to fulfill a dream in the 19th century to go to America.[34]

Today, in the popular imagination, brokers are usually thought of as smugglers and traffickers who bring undocumented workers to the West. Mexican coyotes, Chinese snakeheads, and various organized crime syndicates who smuggle men, women, and children in cargo containers, the holds of ships and in the back of trucks are the stories we get from journalists. And these highly organized smugglers are important. For instance, undocumented Mexican migrants to the United States increasingly use smugglers—73 percent used them in 1975, and by 2005, this number went up to an astonishing 96 percent as the United

States increased the stringency of border controls and the number of border guards.[35]

Like other forms of international trade, smuggling requires cooperation with numerous intermediaries, often through multiple countries. One of the most famous cases of human smuggling that came to light was in 1993 when the *Golden Venture*, a 150-foot tramp steamer ran aground on Rockaway Beach in New York City with a cargo of nearly three hundred smuggled Chinese workers.[36] Cheng Chui Ping, a middle-aged New York City Chinatown businesswoman also known as Ping Jia, or Sister Ping, masterminded the smuggling operation. Sister Ping was a snakehead, described by authorities as the "mother of all snakeheads." She worked with middlemen in China (small-scale snakeheads in Fujian province recruited migrants to bring to larger-scale snakeheads there), Hong Kong, Thailand, Belize, Kenya, South Africa, Guatemala, Mexico, and Canada from the early 1980s to bring thousands of undocumented Chinese migrants to New York City's Chinatown. In the early years, it was a family-run business. One of her sisters would meet the migrants in Hong Kong, a brother would meet them in Guatemala, and Sister Ping would meet them in California and fly with them to New York City.

As demand for her services grew in the early 1990s, she expanded her network of associates, including the very violent Fuk Ching gang, whose leader Ah Kay was also a snakehead, and was one of her partners for the *Golden Venture*. (At that point in time, snakeheads started to prefer ships to air travel, as they could move more people that way, thus increasing profits, and it diminished the necessity of using forged travel documents.) The *Golden Venture*'s itinerary started in Bangkok, Thailand, picking up ninety Chinese passengers. The *Golden Venture* sailed with a Panamanian flag, and then changed in international waters to a Honduran flag. (Its original name was *Tong Sern*, changed at the same time as the flags.) The ship stopped in Pattaya, Thailand, and then made its way to Mombasa, Kenya. It then spent months at sea. Before the ship made its way to the Atlantic coast, there was an internal fight within the Fuk Ching gang that left several of the gang members dead, including the leader's brother, sending Ah Kay into hiding. More importantly, no one was going to be able to meet the ship to offload the passengers into

smaller boats at sea. A Taiwanese snakehead, who was another partner in this smuggling operation, told the boat's crew that no one was
coming to meet them, at which point the crew decided to run the ship
aground. Many of the passengers were deported; of these, some came
back to the United States later with the help of other snakeheads. Others were arrested and spent nearly four years in jail in the United States.
Upon their release, several were approached by snakeheads demanding
their payments.

Sister Ping fled the United States, continuing her smuggling operations from China, and was caught in Hong Kong and brought back
to the United States in 2003 to face trial. Her former snakehead associates testified against her, and she was found guilty in 2005 "of conspiracy
to smuggle aliens and take hostages, money laundering, and trafficking
in ransom proceeds." But still, she performed a valuable service for the
migrants she smuggled. One of the *Golden Venture* migrants upon his
release from prison said of Sister Ping, "She's a very nice lady. Even if
some of her customers died by accident, it's not her fault."

The point of this lengthy description of Sister Ping's networks and
enterprise is to show how global and intricate smuggling can be. As
it has to be, given the degree of international policing, and given the
amounts of money involved. And while the methods they use may be
violent and exploitative, the would-be migrants are desperate to go
abroad. The tens of thousands of dollars spent, the possibility of being
caught or even dying is well worth the risk.

While smugglers like Sister Ping are quite important to moving
around the estimated 50 million undocumented migrants globally, most
smuggling is likely done on an ad hoc basis, on a smaller scale, and
through more loosely organized networks. Still, whether large or small
scale, they are not the most important middlemen moving migrants.
The vast majority of global migrants move legally, and likely most brokers operate legally. A recent special issue of the journal *Pacific Affairs*
was dedicated to examining the poorly understood role of brokers who
make possible the mobility of migrants throughout Asia.[37] The edi-
tors of this issue argue that focusing on migrant brokers, rather than
migrants themselves, shows us very concretely how migration happens.
Looking at brokers illuminates the infrastructure that makes migration

possible and is an improvement on other theories of migration that largely assume that if migrants want to go somewhere, they will just go.

Legal brokers are indispensable for marriage migration, student migration, unskilled labor migration and sex work. It may seem that it is only the poor, or those whose bonafides are questionable, who would need the assistance of brokers to spruce up their applications and perhaps provide bribes (where applicable). This is not the case. Even highly educated workers often need the help of brokers, such as Indian IT workers trying to make their way to the West.[38]

Who are these legal brokers who are so critical to the flow of migrants? They are sometimes state officials, some are legally licensed, and others are themselves migrants. Some work alone, while others are engaged in complicated networks. Most are men, though the numbers of women are increasing. Some are professionals, other are amateurs who become recruiters by accident. Some work the brokering angle in multiple ways, such as Indian computer programming schools that also provide visa assistance and job placement promises abroad for their students. More generally, the brokers *make migration possible* by organizing the recruitment process. In the past few decades, there has been an increase in formally licensed private recruitment across Asia, but the line between formal and informal brokering is not hard and fast.

Brokering arises from complex institutional arrangements that depend on the relations between countries, on the demands of receiving countries and the policies of sending countries. For instance, the Chinese state is central in the rise of broker networks in China. Since the 1980s it created complicated structures and licensing policies for international migration brokers. But these large brokers also rely on a large network of unlicensed agents to recruit migrants at the local level, in spite of the government trying to stamp them out.[39]

In Indonesia, it is informal brokers who actually recruit people. Because migration here relies on informal, unregulated brokers, this requires a great deal of trust on the part of would-be migrants. These brokers are often themselves migrants, and their brokering careers are often short term.[40]

Another wrinkle to this point on informal brokers comes from a study of anti-trafficking (particularly sex trafficking) programs along the Laos-Thailand border. Many international organizations want to stem the "problem" of undocumented migration and trafficking by creating "safe migration," that is, legally documented and registered brokers, or informal, intimate networks that are thought to be safe because they are personal. The assumption is this will put an end to the need for undocumented migration and dry up trafficking because the middlemen are "safe." But trafficking may continue because of high costs of getting legal documents, which increases the likelihood of debt bondage. And further, it is often these "safe" intimate brokers, sometimes sex workers themselves operating within their social networks, who are recruiting others to be sex workers. So creating and enhancing "safe migration" may in the end be counterproductive and not so safe.[41]

A careful reader—you!—would have noticed by now that there's probably risks involved with going through a broker. And you're right. Sometimes brokers try, but fail to get their clients visas. But you don't get your money back. And sometimes the broker is a scam artist. Ali has a cousin in Hyderabad, a middle-class kid who had recently graduated from university in the mid-1990s and wanted to go abroad as the pay in the United States was far greater than in Hyderabad at the time. He gave a broker USD 10,000 in 1998 to get him a visa to go to the United States. The broker disappeared with his passport and money. But the cousin didn't give up; the influence of the culture of migration on him was too strong. A couple of years later, he went to Saudi Arabia where he got a job as a computer programmer. His uncle who was working in Saudi Arabia helped him to get a visa. He stayed there for a few years and then went back to Hyderabad and found work with a large transnational corporation making a very comfortable salary. After a few years, he got antsy and applied for a visa to the United Kingdom, which had just changed its visa allotment system in 2008. As he now had many years of experience as a high-level professional, he was easily granted a Tier 1 visa as a "high-value migrant." He stayed there for a few months looking for work, but didn't find the weather or the United Kingdom quite agreeable, so he returned to Hyderabad. He recently joined an American firm with an office in Hyderabad that has a practice of sending workers from India to the United States for projects. He came to the United States in 2013 on an H1-B temporary (three years) visa for professionals. But he has no intention of staying. In fact, he had planned to return to Hyderabad after a few months in San Francisco, but the company sent him to work on a project in Boston.

Conclusion

How and why people cross international borders to live and work are fascinating questions and the answers are complex. We have outlined some of the most important and prominent theories that try to answer these questions and have promoted a newer approach that emphasizes the central role that middlemen play in the process of international migration. While economic motivations, migrant networks, and cultures of migration are certainly important as reasons why some rather than others migrate, to us, it seems these are necessary, but on their own not sufficient to account for migration. Similarly, the idea that people can be transnational, living their lives across multiple countries begs the question of how they got to where they were going in the first place. Over the last few decades, as border controls and visa regulations have become more stringent, it becomes more difficult for individuals to navigate the process on their own. While some people are able to get visas directly themselves, for many others middlemen have become more important.

In the next chapter, we look at the global working class, or as we indelicately, but accurately describe them, meat for the global market. We continue the theoretical discussions from this chapter by looking at the forces that allow and, in some cases, compel individuals to go to such magnets for disposable, low-end labor, such as the United States, Dubai, Hong Kong, Western Europe, and so on.

Notes

1 Borjas, George. *Friends or Strangers: The Impact of Immigrants on the American Economy*. New York: Basic, 1990.
2 Arango, Joaquin. "Explaining Migration: A Critical View." *International Social Science Journal* 52.165 (2000): 283–296.
3 See for example Stark, Oded. *The Migration of Labor*. Cambridge, MA: Blackwell, 1991. Hein de Haas (de Haas, Hein. "Migration and Development: A Theoretical Perspective." *International Migration Review* 44.1 [2010]: 227–264) provides an excellent summary of this line of argument.

4 Ali, Syed. "'Go West Young Man': The Culture of Migration among Muslims in Hyderabad, India." *Journal of Ethnic and Migration Studies* 33.1 (2007): 37–58, pp. 51–52.

5 Poros, Maritsa. *Modern Migrations: Gujarati Indian Networks in New York and London.* Stanford, CA: Stanford UP, 2011, p. 66.

6 Sassen, Saskia. *A Sociology of Globalization.* New York: W.W. Norton, 2007.

7 Massey, Douglas et al. *Worlds in Motion: Understanding International Migration at the End of the Millenium.* Oxford: Clarendon, 1998.

8 Poros 2011, op cit.

9 It's rather strange that migrant network theory largely ignores or downplays weak ties, as weak ties are such a central, important idea in sociology. The article "The Strength of Weak Ties" by Mark Granovetter (written in 1973) is one of the most cited sociological articles ever. See, Granovetter, Mark. "The Strength of Weak Ties." *American Journal of Sociology* 78.6 [1973]: 1360.

10 Krissman, Fred. "Sin Coyote Ni Patrón: Why the 'Migrant Network' Fails to Explain International Migration." *International Migration Review* 39.1 (2005): 4–44.

11 A first offense is punishable by a fine ranging from USD 275 to 2,200 for each undocumented worker. A second offense can lead to fines between USD 2,200 and 5,500 per worker, and a third offense between USD 3,000 and 10,000 per worker.

12 Ali 2007, Cohen, Jeffrey. *The Culture of Migration in Southern Mexico.* Austin: U of Texas Press, 2004. Cohen, Jeffrey, and İbrahim Sirkeci. *Cultures of Migration: The Global Nature of Contemporary Mobility.* Austin: U of Texas Press, 2011. Kandel, William, and Douglas Massey. "The Culture of Mexican Migration: A Theoretical and Empirical Analysis." *Social Forces* 80.3 (2002): 981–1004.

13 International Organization for Migration. *World Migration Report 2013: Migrant Well-being and Development.* Geneva: International Organization for Migration, 2013.

14 Levitt, Peggy. "Social Remittances: Migration Driven Local-Level Forms of Cultural Diffusion." *International Migration Review* 32.4 (1998): 926–948; Levitt, Peggy, and Deepak Lamba-Nieves. "Social Remittances Revisited." *Journal of Ethnic and Migration Studies* 37.1 (2011): 1–22.

15 Smith, Robert. *Mexican New York: Transnational Lives of New Immigrants.* Berkeley: U of California, 2006.

16 Ratha, Dilip et al. "Migration and Remittance Flows: Recent Trends and Outlook, 2013–2016." *Migration and Development Brief* 21 (2013): 2.

17 International Organization for Migration 2013, p. 74.

18 Zoepf, Katherine. "Where the Boys Are, at Least for Now, the Girls Pounce." *New York Times.* November 2, 2006. www.nytimes.com/2006/11/02/world/middleeast/02beirut.html <retrieved January 2, 2014>

19 Ali 2007, p. 66.

20 Kurien, Prema. *Kaleidoscopic Ethnicity: International Migration and the Reconstruction of Community Identities in India.* New Brunswick, NJ: Rutgers UP, 2002.

21 Levitt, Peggy, and Nina Glick Schiller. "Conceptualizing Simultaneity: A Transnational Social Field Perspective on Society." *International Migration Review* 38.3 (2004): 1002–1039.

22 Foner, Nancy. *From Ellis Island to JFK: New York's Two Great Waves of Immigration.* New Haven: Yale UP, 2000, pp. 171–173.

23 For example, Basch, Linda, Nina Glick Schiller, and Cristina Szanton Blanc. *Nations Unbound: Transnational Projects, Postcolonial Predicaments, and Deterritorialized Nation-States*. Staten Island, NY: Gordon and Breach, 1994.

24 Portes, Alejandro. "Conclusion: Theoretical Convergencies and Empirical Evidence in the Study of Immigrant Transnationalism." *International Migration Review* 37.3 (2003): 874–892.

25 Levitt, Peggy, and B. Nadya Jaworsky. "Transnational Migration Studies: Past Developments and Future Trends." *Annual Review of Sociology* 33.1 (2007): 129–156, p. 129; Waldinger, Roger, and David Fitzgerald. "Transnationalism in Question." *American Journal of Sociology* 109.5 (2004): 1177–1195.

26 Levitt and Jaworsky 2007: 134, op cit.

27 Levitt, Peggy. "Roots and Routes: Understanding the Lives of the Second Generation Transnationally." *Journal of Ethnic and Migration Studies* 35.7 (2009): 1225–1242; Levitt, Peggy, and Mary Waters. *The Changing Face of Home: The Transnational Lives of the Second Generation*. New York: Russell Sage Foundation, 2002; Smith 2006.

28 See for example, King, Russell, and Anastasia Christou. "Of Counter-Diaspora and Reverse Transnationalism: Return Mobilities to and from the Ancestral Homeland." *Mobilities* 6.4 (2011): 451–466.

29 Fokkema, Tineke, Laurence Lessard-Phillips, James Bachmeier, and Susan Brown. "The Link Between the Transnational Behaviour and Integration of the Second Generation in European and American Cities." *Nordic Journal of Migration Research* 2.2 (2012): 111–123.

30 Ali, Syed. "Going and Coming and Going Again: Second-Generation Migrants in Dubai." *Mobilities* 6.4 (2011): 553–568.

31 Portes 2003: 879, op cit.

32 This is not to say that migration theorists have completely ignored middlemen. But they find the importance of middlemen to be secondary, at most, to other causes. For instance, Douglas Massey writes: "Over time individuals, firms, and organizations become well known to immigrants and institutionally stable, constituting another form of social capital that migrants can draw on to gain access to foreign labor markets. Recruiting agents can at times be active in creating new flows of migration from areas of labor surplus to areas of labor scarcity." (Massey, Douglas. "Why Does Immigration Occur? A Theoretical Synthesis." In Charles Hirschman, Philip Kasinitz, and Josh DeWind, *The Handbook of International Migration: The American Experience* [New York: Russell Sage Foundation, 1999], p. 45.) While this is on the face of it true enough, more recently scholars are proposing that middlemen *drive* migration. In this formulation, personal networks can be important, but are not completely necessary, and definitely not sufficient.

33 Mckeown, Adam. "How the Box Became Black: Brokers and the Creation of the Free Migrant." *Pacific Affairs* 85.1 (2012): 21–45.

34 Solomon, Anna. *The Little Bride*. New York: Riverhead, 2011.

35 Kyle, David, and Rey Koslowski, "Introduction." In David Kyle and Rey Koslowski, *Global Human Smuggling: Comparative Perspectives*, 2nd ed. Baltimore: Johns Hopkins UP, 2011, p. 8. This may be an overestimate, however. The Migrant Border Crossing Study found that 72 percent of people they surveyed who had crossed the border clandestinely used a smuggler. See Slack, Jeremy, Daniel Martinez, Scott Whiteford, and Emily Peiffer. "In the Shadow of the Wall: Family Separation,

Immigration Enforcement and Security." Center for Latin American Studies, The University of Arizona, March, 2013.

36 The narrative that follows is from Keefe, Patrick. "The Snakehead: The Criminal Odyssey of Chinatown's Sister Ping." *The New Yorker*. April 24, 2006. www.newyorker.com/archive/2006/04/24/060424fa_fact6?currentPage=all <retrieved June 19, 2013>

37 Lindquist, Johan, Biao Xiang, and Brenda Yeoh. "Opening the Black Box of Migration: Brokers, the Organization of Transnational Mobility and the Changing Political Economy in Asia." *Pacific Affairs* 85.1 (2012): 7–19.

38 Xiang, Biao. *Global "Body Shopping": An Indian Labor System in the Information Technology Industry*. Princeton, NJ: Princeton UP, 2007.

39 Xiang, Biao. "Predatory Princes and Princely Peddlers: The State and International Labour Migration Intermediaries in China." *Pacific Affairs* 85.1 (2012): 47–68.

40 Lindquist, Johan. "The Elementary School Teacher, the Thug and His Grandmother: Informal Brokers and Transnational Migration from Indonesia." *Pacific Affairs* 85.1 (2012): 69–89.

41 Molland, Sverre. "Safe Migration, Dilettante Brokers and the Appropriation of Legality: Lao-Thai 'Trafficking' in the Context of Regulating Labour Migration." *Pacific Affairs* 85.1 (2012): 117–136.

2

CHEAP MEAT FOR THE GLOBAL MARKET

In 1980, Emmet Comodas, a Filipino pool maintenance man got on a plane to Saudi Arabia. He grew up an orphan, selling cigarettes on the streets in Manila as a child, then had a job at a government sports complex for many years. But his monthly salary of USD 50 did not do much more than keep his family barely fed and housed in a one-room shanty.

But fortune smiled. His boss offered him a job cleaning pools in Saudi Arabia thousands of miles away in a theocracy where foreign workers have little rights and are regularly abused. He immediately accepted. His wife Tita went with him to the airport, waved at the plane from the departure lounge, went home, and cried.

Two years later, Emmet came home with chocolates for the kids and earrings for Tita. His two-year-old son looked at him like he was a stranger and cried when he touched him. Emmet threw himself a party, fixed the walls and roof of his house, and three months later, left again. This was a cycle he would repeat for two decades. His monthly salary in Saudi Arabia was USD 500—he made more in those two years than he would have in two decades in Manila. He sent two-thirds of his salary home. All five of his children, young when he started but grown by the time he finished migrating, followed his lead and became overseas workers. His initial desperation became his, and his children's, way of life. In order to live at home, they had to leave it. Even if it means your son cries when you come home and thinks you're a stranger.[1]

This chapter looks at the experiences of global, migrant laborers like Emmet. We examine the global market in cheap, disposable, temporary labor crossing international borders. These laborers are maids and nannies, houseboys and gardeners, construction workers, agricultural workers, factory workers, staff in restaurants, bars and hotels, taxi drivers, security guards, store clerks, and sex workers, among others. And, as these categories suggest, gender really matters here, as we will illustrate by paying particular attention to the experiences of working-class female migrants.

The title of this chapter might seem somewhat flippant, but it was chosen with the utmost care. From the perspective of many of the firms and individuals who employ these global working-class migrants and the countries where they reside, these people are not people—they are merely labor, cheap meat to be used, chewed up and eventually spit out. Emmet's story is a relative success and highlights the typical working-class migrant's hopes and dreams and desires. He overcame poverty through migration, and his remittances helped his family have a better life. For every story like Emmet's though, there are darker stories of deportation, getting fired, heavy debts due to the initial expense of migration, cheated wages, physical and mental abuse, and even death. In the Philippines, workers going abroad don't say they're going to make their fortune. Rather, they say they're going to try their luck.[2]

Unfortunately for unlucky workers, enforcement of labor laws is regularly lax, even in the West. For undocumented migrants, and even for documented migrants in countries where residence permits are tied to their jobs, migrants live with the constant threat of deportation. The slow, or no, response of governments to violations of workers' legal rights contrasts with how quickly many governments move to punish workers who violate terms of their visas or who are undocumented.

In spite of such real and potential problems, people still go. And while work and living conditions may be horrible, it must not be all that bad. Otherwise a very large number wouldn't go, right?

Why They Go

So why do labor migrants go? For the same reason that Emmet went—the pay abroad is far greater than the pay at home. In richer countries, firms and individual employers generally need these labor migrants because there is not enough local, cheap, low-skilled or unskilled labor to meet demand (for example, construction work in the Persian Gulf). Another reason is because local labor is relatively expensive and, perhaps more importantly, many employers see no reason to pay more for local citizen or permanent legal resident workers when temporary or undocumented migrant labor is cheaper (such as agricultural workers in the United States and Western Europe). Related to that, many citizens can't or won't do the backbreaking work for low pay that migrants do (like, again, agricultural work in the West).[3]

This is the economic "pull." But workers can't be enticed to go somewhere if they're happy enough where they are. There are economic factors at home that "push" workers out—such as poor agricultural conditions for rural residents, poor and poorly paid work opportunities in the cities, and high unemployment and underemployment generally. The economic push and pull, as we pointed out in Chapter 1, are in and of themselves insufficient to account for why people migrate. We must also look at how many migrants are tied into broader networks of people who have migrated and to those who can facilitate migration (like Emmett's boss) and come from places where there is a culture of migration. Most important for the working class is the possibility of remittances, which improves their lives *back home*.

But it is not enough that potential migrants want to go to those places and that employers want to hire cheap labor. Employers are able to hire migrants in part because the state devises policies to let such workers in, like with temporary guest worker visas, sometimes favoring particular nationalities over others. Another reason is because the state does not or cannot strenuously enforce border controls, which allows workers to come to these countries without documents, or often on temporary visas, like tourist visas, which many workers then overstay. Other workers are able to buy or rent various documents, such as passports, residence cards, social security cards, and so on.[4]

States where migrants often go tend to prefer temporary workers—and actively encourage or even recruit them—because they are not a financial or social burden on them. These workers are generally prohibited from staying permanently in many states, and some, like Singapore, forbid marriage of maids to citizens. They come, work, and then leave. There is no cost of raising them, or taking care of them when they are old or if they get injured or so ill they cannot work anymore. In many countries, if you lose your job, you lose your visa (which is tied to one employer) and get deported.

Sending states also often prefer temporary guest worker programs. As the workers know they will return, their mental focus remains back home, so they essentially earn to remit—though it's important to point out that not all workers send remittances.[5] Sending states like the Philippines invest a lot of ideological work to secure the loyalty of their overseas citizens so that they send remittances. Many states have special tax breaks for remittances, and make sending remittances easy.[6] Why? In part because remittances supplement and often substitute for government welfare and development programs, which many states either don't want to or can't afford to fund adequately, or at all.

Then there is also the role that brokers play, reacting to the actions of governmental regulations, in making migration happen for these workers. As we emphasized in the last chapter, brokers are essential for a great number of people to move between countries.

How Do They Get There?

Some individuals in the global working class are able to move somewhat freely between particular countries where visa regulations are fairly easy to deal with. But entry requirements and immigration laws for most countries are generally more stringent for the working class. As we saw in the last chapter, brokers are becoming indispensable for moving a great number of migrants from one country to another. Brokers make it possible for workers to move into those countries, legally or not. But they of course don't work for free, and the price is usually borne by the workers themselves.

For instance, in 2009, Human Rights Watch did a study of workers at Abu Dhabi's Saadiyat Island, future home of the Louvre, Guggenheim, and New York University. Almost all the 94 workers HRW interviewed paid recruiting fees to brokers of up to USD 4,100 to obtain their jobs—a king's ransom for poor workers from South Asia. They should not have had to pay these fees, as it is illegal under United Arab Emirates (UAE) law for companies or recruiters to charge workers recruiting fees.[7] But they do it anyway. The result is these workers are stuck working for companies who regularly switch contracts they signed in the country of origin for contracts that stipulate much lower pay when they arrive in the UAE. They can of course quit, but then they still owe the moneylenders back home for the loans to cover those fees. And if they quit, their visas are immediately cancelled, as they are tied to specific employers, and they will be deported. So they stay, and their income for the first year or so goes largely toward paying off those fees.

Brokers play a similar critical role for migrants coming to Taiwan. Wages offered there are higher than most anywhere else in Asia. Placement agencies in Taiwan as well as recruitment agencies in sending countries are major gatekeepers—few migrants are able to negotiate getting a job in Taiwan on their own. The fees are generally very high, and the first year of employment mostly goes to paying down their debts.[8]

What Do They Do Once They Get There?

While higher wages is obviously a driving force, migrant networks and a culture of migration are also critical aspects for observing and understanding migrant flows. For instance, working-class Mexicans go the United States and Indians go to the Persian Gulf in large numbers, and from specific places. A disproportionate number of Mexicans come from a handful of states (such as Guanajuato, Veracruz, and Oaxaca), and about half of all Indian migrants in the UAE come from the tiny coastal state of Kerala, with large numbers also coming from Hyderabad and Punjab.[9] In both, migrants have established strong network connections, where family and friends help each other to get to their destinations and get jobs. And in both, a strong culture of migration has developed to reinforce migration flows.[10]

A critical driving force behind the network ties and culture of migration of working-class migrants is the desire to remit to their families. Though many also remit to villages and communities for things like public works projects, baseball fields, etc.[11] According to the World Bank, migrants in developed countries sent USD 414 billion in 2013 to their homes in poorer countries (out of total global remittances of USD 550 billion), and this is projected to rise to USD 540 billion by 2016.[12] These numbers are likely gross underestimates, as it only includes money sent through official channels. The actual amount is likely much higher.

A typical remittance story comes from an interesting study of the Chunking Mansions in Hong Kong, a densely packed, lower-end business area. Indian workers who come on tourist visas are the bulk of the labor force of Chungking Mansions. They are touts, waiters, dishwashers, cleaners, and goods transporters. They arrive at Hong Kong airport on 14-day visa free entry, which is renewable twice, and can stay in Hong Kong for a maximum of 180 days in a year. Because it is illegal to work without Hong Kong residence and identity card, they earn considerably less than people with legal residency—around 3,500 HK dollars (about USD 450) per month. And the pay, meager though it is, is far and away more than they could earn at home, and enables these workers to remit large sums. One man paid for his and his two sisters' weddings, bought a motorcycle, and was financing the reconstruction of his extended family's house.[13]

In fact, workers regularly endure pay that is much lower when compared to natives, and put up with harsh working conditions and brutal living conditions, just so they can remit money. Many die trying. For instance, the migrant labor population in Qatar (in the Persian Gulf) has come under increasing pressure at work as construction activity has gone into fever pitch preparing for the 2022 football (soccer) World Cup. Around 900 Indian and Nepalese workers—among the largest contingents of foreign workers in Qatar—died while working between 2012 and early 2014, as safety at worksites is not of paramount concern for Qatari officials.[14] Again, they are treated as meat, fully disposable. If some die, there are many more willing to migrate to take their places.

Not surprisingly, the working and living conditions for the bulk of the global working class are rather poor, though this varies from place to place, and job to job. A common story is that of construction workers in the UAE. Their passports are regularly confiscated by their employers (an illegal action that even government departments engage in), their wages are usually lower than what was promised when recruited in their countries of origin, and they live in labor camps where they are packed into rooms and share bathrooms that are often filthy beyond description, and sometimes have raw sewage running in the alleys.[15]

And they are the lucky ones. Unlucky workers who cannot get housing in the camps live in rundown villas lacking basic amenities, illegally sharing rooms with the ever-present threat that housing authorities will evict and even deport them. Deportation of course means you lose your job, your ability to remit, and if you weren't there long enough, your ability to pay off your debts to the moneylender back home.[16]

These conditions are not unique to the UAE. In a survey of migrant workers throughout Kazakhstan, 20 percent had their passports kept by employers and 20 percent had to borrow money to get to Kazakhstan. Sometimes their wages were less than their expenses in Kazakhstan, leading to a situation of debt bondage with their employers. For some workers "not being beaten too much, having enough to eat, and a roof over their head were 'enough.'" Though Kazakhstan has an 8-hour-day/40-hour-week labor law, most of the workers worked far longer days and had hardly any days off in the month.[17]

While the typical story of migrant workers is that of working-age men going abroad to earn money to send back home, the landscape of migrants is changing. An interesting development over the past few decades has been the migration of women independent of their husbands and families. As women in the developed world have entered the labor force in large numbers, there has been an increasing global transfer of traditional wifely duties of childcare, care for the elderly, household maintenance, and sex work from developing to developed countries.[18]

Female Migration

Working-class female migrants are often more vulnerable than men at work. Migrants in "visible" jobs, that is, those in the public eye, have it good relative to "invisible" maids, especially those who are live-in workers in private households. Maids are often subject to a great deal of physical and mental abuse, rape, wage theft, and sometimes nonpayment of wages. Part of this vulnerability is because they are women, and part of it is due to their work being behind closed doors (in the UAE, maids and nannies are not even covered under their labor law).

Take for example the vulnerability, and paradoxical freedoms, of overseas contract worker (OCW) maids in Taiwan.[19] For one, their time off is extremely limited. One Filipina worker's employer only gave her two days off each month and didn't want her to mingle with other Filipinos; the employer preferred she work and pay her overtime. Actually many workers themselves also prefer to work on their days off to earn extra income and minimize expenses. (She's lucky to get overtime though; in many countries while maids may legally be eligible for overtime, they rarely get it.) But her pay was so low that this woman ran away from her employer, which immediately nullified her legal status. The upside though was that as she was no longer a live-in maid she could work as a freelancer, earning twice what she did before.[20]

One of the crucial principles of the OCW program is the strict prohibition of permanent settlement. OCWs can only work in Taiwan for up to six years, and can only work for one particular employer during their stay. Basically, they have no freedom in the market. If they do not like their employer, their only legal option is to leave. This contrasts with professionals who are subject to different rules. For professionals, there is no limitation on their length of stay in the country, and they are eligible for permanent residence after working legally for five years.[21]

The structure of the OCW program in some ways encourages workers to go underground, like the woman above, in part because they cannot leave bad employers for other opportunities. Some workers become undocumented to avoid abuse. Others don't want to go home and have to go through another round of debt associated with return migration and fees toward a new work contract. This explains why many workers become undocumented toward the end of contracts, or when an employer breaks or refuses to renew a contract.[22]

Undocumented workers in Taiwan become quite free in the labor market and, ironically, have greater bargaining power. Besides being able to choose their employers, they are able to dictate their terms of work (in a way that undocumented workers in other countries cannot) because it also illegal for employers to hire them. As a result, pay and working conditions are better, and social relations are also more equitable. It may seem like a small thing, but the form of address changes. Live-in migrants call their employer "madam," indicating a hierarchical relationship. But undocumented workers who clean and then leave usually use last names. One woman said that many of her employers have the same last name, "So I asked them, 'What is your English names?' They said, 'I don't have any.' I said, 'OK, I will give you a name. You look sexy, so I call you 'Sexy'! When she calls me, I said, 'Who is this?' She said, 'Sexy!'"[23]

This distinction between live-in maid and freelance housecleaner is important. In the UAE, migrant freelance housecleaners also have similar relationships with employers, though perhaps not so egalitarian. But live-in maids are often subject to an incredible amount of wage theft, forced labor, and physical abuse. Maids who run away from abusive employers—in the UAE, they are called "absconders"—often find their visas cancelled by their employers, which immediately means they are undocumented and in violation of the law. To help address the problem of absconding maids, a local newspaper in Dubai gave step-by-step instructions to employers on what to do "just in case your maid runs away."[24]

The governments of many developing countries, such as Sri Lanka, Philippines, and Indonesia actively encourage female outmigration, in spite of abuses they suffer, in large part because of remittances, the value of which far and away exceeds foreign aid.[25] Many countries provide training for women who are preparing to go abroad as household help. As we have seen, many countries are highly dependent on these remittances.[26]

Increasingly over the past few decades, remittances from women are critical to their families back home. A study of Bangladeshi migrant workers in the UAE found that women remit more than men as a percentage of their earnings. Both men and women send money to their spouses, and often women send money directly to their fathers. While women increasingly support their families, female migrants who try to put conditions on how their money is spent are often ignored. This happened to half of all the women interviewed, as opposed to 20 percent of the male migrants. There were also interesting differences in how their monies were spent. Female migrants' remittances were more often spent on savings, education, medical treatment, and loan repayments, while male migrants' remittances were spent more often on businesses and homes. Also, more females were the main economic providers for their families back in Bangladesh than males.[27]

The drive for remittances is also an important motivation for women who migrate to be sex workers. For example, a study of Latin American sex workers in Spain found that while not many women have *macarras*, or pimps, these women often say they have "little macarras"—demanding children or family members generally, with consumerist needs for designer clothes, skateboards, and so on. One woman said, "Today I have to get a client so I can buy Christmas presents."[28] In fact, satisfying the needs of the household back home with remittances is one reason many women who have paid off their debts associated with the cost of migration stay in the higher-paying brothels in Spain.

For the "smarter" women sex work was a higher-paid means to an end. They worked to remit. Some women who were at it for a while were able to bring over their children, and even other family members. At that point, they stopped doing sex work. Others who paid off their debts and did not have to send remittances also opted out of sex work to reduce conflicts between their work and their partners.[29]

Others though are not so far-sighted, and spend their money in Spain on their apartments, boyfriends, and other expenses. One smarter sex worker said, "I know a girl who never sends any money back to Colombia . . . I told her she was stupid; what does she have to show for it all back in Colombia? [I]t really gets them thinking when I tell them I've already paid for my house."[30]

Migration and Marriage

In richer countries, there is a "care crisis." Upper- and middle-class households hire migrants for domestic labor, while working-class households "hire" migrant wives for unpaid domestic as well as reproductive labor (i.e., having children) as local workers are either too expensive or not found in great enough numbers.[31] Foreign maids and foreign brides are parallel solutions to the care crisis in receiving countries.[32]

Again, the conditions of maids varies depending if they are live-in or not, fulltime or not. There is also variation in the conditions of international brides, depending on how they meet their spouse (brokers, pen pals, through relatives or friends, etc.) Many Filipina and Indonesian domestics received marriage proposals from their middle-aged divorced or widowed Taiwanese employers. For some of the employers, it was about love. For others, it was really an extension and solidification of a labor arrangement where these women were taking care of the man's old parents.[33]

The story of "mail-order" brides and other women looking to get married and go to the West is an old one.[34] It is the story of global inequality, that is, women from poorer parts of the world looking to escape poverty, economic stagnation, or to be upwardly mobile by going to a richer country. For many, marriage also means the opportunity to remit. If we think of marriage as labor, sexual labor, it make sense these workers would want to migrate, as so many other types of migrant workers do.

In some countries, many young women try to seek marriages with Western men through sex work.[35] One study of Vietnamese sex workers found this to be a quite common strategy. Among the sex workers interviewed, almost half got married and of those more than a third got visas and emigrated to the United States, Australia, France, and Canada. These women were not looking to move West to work, though most of them ended up being the family's primary breadwinner, largely as their husbands were old.[36]

The men of course wanted something from the arrangement as well. They had gone to Vietnam to deliberately seek a wife, a woman who would be a "traditional" wife. The man would be the breadwinner, and the women would take care of the house. But once in the West, most of the women ended up working to supplement, or in many cases replace, their older husbands' incomes, and to send remittances to family in Vietnam.

Sex work for these Vietnamese women was instrumental. That is, they did it because it paid far and away better than other work such as farming, factory work, or being a maid. None of the women interviewed who made it to the West wanted to return to sex work, though one secretly did work in a massage parlor. But she "drew clear boundaries for herself around the kinds of sexual practices she would perform."[37]

Most of these women thought they would end up in some place exciting, like Los Angeles, or New York. Instead, they mainly went to small towns or the countryside. They also had to take up jobs that were basically a financial step down from the sex work they did in Vietnam. But the women who were interviewed for the study, while they were not pleased with some aspects of their lives, and though they were mercenary about getting a Western husband, they by and large stayed married. Once in the West, their desires, dreams, and attitudes toward their husbands and work shifted.

As many Asian countries are becoming wealthier and are becoming immigrant-receiving countries, the number of international marriages there are on the rise, with brides coming from China, Vietnam, Philippines, and elsewhere in Southeast Asia, marrying men in Hong Kong, Japan, Korea, Singapore, and Taiwan. In South Korea, the number of international marriages jumped from about 5 percent to almost 14 percent in the mid-2000s, mostly of ethnic Korean women from China, but also Vietnamese and Filipinos. In Taiwan in 2005, 20 percent of marriages were international marriages. In Singapore, more than a third of all citizens have foreign spouses. Even in Japan this trend holds. In 1980, less than 1 percent of all marriages were international, but by 2005, nearly 6 percent were. A common thread in all these countries is that working class and rural men are having a hard time finding local wives and are compelled to look elsewhere.[38]

Caren Freeman in her book *Making and Faking Kinship* looks at how a bride shortage in the South Korean countryside in the 1990s led the South Korean government to encourage ethnic Koreans in China (*Chosonjok*) to migrate as brides and to reunify with South Korean kin.[39] This led directly to a rush for these *Chosonjok* to go to South Korea.

The "making kinship" part of her story concerns the brides. Marriage brokers would lead tours to China of South Korean farmers and others who had trouble finding brides there, as women left the countryside in droves, and female city dwellers could marry up leaving many men unwilling bachelors. The brokers would bring the men to China, set up meetings with eligible *Chosonjok* women, deal with Chinese and Korean authorities, and help to seal the deal. Once in South Korea, these women often themselves became brokers. Other South Korean matchmaker/brokers would pester them to help them recruit would-be *Chosonjok* brides in China, and *Chosonjok* women in China would try to enlist them to find husbands in South Korea.

Chinese and South Korean brokers offered a wide range of services, including forging of fictional identities and setting up paper marriages. This is the "faking kinship" part of her story. Many *Chosonjok* women had no real desire to marry, or already were married, so brokers would also arrange bogus marriages. For married women, the brokers would have to get local officials to record a divorce so they could marry these South Korean men. Once in South Korea, these women would go to work in places where the wages were low, conditions were tough, and hours long. Still, the pay was much greater than in China, though it would take a few years to pay off their debts to brokers and often bribe Chinese officials at various levels, and sometimes to bribe South Korean officials in the consulate in Shenyang in northern China, closer to where the *Chosonjok* live.

Still another path was through proving South Korean ancestry, a kinship to the nation. This gave rise to a broader kind of fake kinship, where brokers would forge documents that proved South Korean genealogy. Once the documents were made, would-be migrants would have to go the consulate for their interview. Interestingly, those with fake documents often fared better than those who actually had South Korean roots, as they had to rehearse and memorize all the minutiae of their stories. Those who had real kinship apparently did not rehearse and would sometimes slip up in the interviews.

Another way to get to South Korea, as a corollary to real and fake marriages, was as a "paper parent." South Korea gave visas for parents to attend the weddings of their daughters. An unintended consequence of this was to generate a black market in the buying and selling of parental identities.

Some enterprising *Chosonjok* saw a different kind of opportunity running boarding houses or as brokers' right by the consulate in Shenyang. They realized that the dirty and difficult life that faced migrants to South Korea was not for them. So they set themselves up around the consulate, facilitating the visa process for other *Chosonjok*.

Freeman describes a hierarchy of brokers. The small ones did the legwork for the big ones by traveling back and forth to South Korea looking for citizens willing to give bogus invitations to fictional *Chosonjok* relatives. At the top of the broker chain were those with high-level connections to South Koreans working in the consulate. One broker said, "It is essential that these connections be continually nurtured, by dining and drinking with the South Koreans. It's hard work." Many of these consulate workers, as the gatekeepers, made a lot of money from bribes from would-be *Chosonjok* migrants.

Many married *Chosonjok* couples would go to South Korea together, but more often one spouse went while the other stayed behind. Men and women migrated in roughly equal numbers, but there were more options for women to enter due to the prevalence of fake marriages and more lucrative options on the job market because women could take up work in restaurants that provided housing (male laborers had to pay for their own housing). The splitting of families is of course very stressful, and sometimes led to infidelities by one or the other partner, both in China and South Korea, and sometimes the marriages broke up. Or the partner in China learned of it when the other one stopped sending remittances.

This was the story in the 1990s. By the end of the first decade of the new millennium, many *Chosonjok* had tired of South Korea, as the economic gap had begun to close. They no longer greeted each other in China by saying "When are you going to South Korea?" Instead they said, "You're going to South Korean, again?"[40] The economic compulsion was gone, and the culture of migration to South Korea had waned. Many *Chosonjok* then began aiming to be migrant workers or brides in Japan. Interestingly enough, around this time many South Koreans had begun migrating to China to live the expatriate life (discussed in the next chapter) to try to maintain or exceed the middle-class lifestyle that was beginning to be more difficult in South Korea itself.

South Koreans had also become fed up with *Chosonjok* brides, who they saw as opportunistic, and they were fed up with *Chosonjok* workers in general. Rural men started to look to Filipina and Vietnamese women as better potential partners, as these women are seen as more submissive, and more easily assimilated into the Korean social fabric.

Sexual Labor: Sex Work and Human Trafficking

In the 2008 thriller *Taken*, Liam Neeson plays a former CIA operative. An Albanian human trafficking ring kidnaps his daughter while she's traveling in Paris. The Albanians sell his daughter, a virgin and thus quite valuable, to a French auctioneer. He then sells her to an Arab sheikh who is about to rape her when Neeson heroically climbs aboard the yacht in open water and shoots the sheikh in the head. Thus the day, and his daughter's virginity, is saved.

Taken is one of a growing number of movies and documentaries that focus on human trafficking as one of the great evils of our time. Alongside these films, movie stars, politicians, and NGOs have also worked to raise the plight of trafficking victims in the public eye.

Human trafficking became a highly visible issue with the passage of the US Victims of Trafficking and Violence Protection Act of 2000. This law established the US Department of State's annual Trafficking in Persons Report (TIPR), which ranks countries on their work to end human trafficking. Countries that the US State Department deems not to have done enough to eradicate human trafficking are subject to various sanctions. Around the same time, the United Nations' Transnational Organized Crime Convention in 2000 established a trafficking protocol. It assumed trafficking was a product of organized criminal activity and that trafficking is a result of calculated and organized conduct. Basically, traffickers are evil and powerful, and victims are unaware, innocent, and weak, and in need of saving.[41] (Just like in the film *Taken*.) The saviors are sometimes police, sometimes NGOs like sociologist Kevin Bales' Free the Slaves, and sometimes journalists like Nicholas Kristof of *The New York Times*.

The image we have of the trafficker is that of an evil person intent on treating women badly, and as disposable commodities. While some traffickers are like their characterizations in the mass media, the reality is not cut and dry. Traffickers are often friends or family members. Many are sex workers themselves bringing the women to work with them. But this nuance is lost in the mythology of trafficking and traffickers.

One of the notions that trafficking hinges on is the idea of deception, that women are tricked into migrating and/or tricked into prostitution. One woman from Moldova (one of the poorest countries in Europe) was told by her boyfriend of a year and a half that he could get her a job waitressing in Portugal. He paid for her airfare, drove her to Odessa (in Ukraine), and put her on a plane to Lisbon. There, a friend of his met her at the airport and said the job had fallen through, but that he could take her to Dubai where there was more work. He seemed trustworthy enough to her, so she went. Once they arrived, an Arab man met them, and a woman from Uzbekistan took her to an apartment. The Uzbek woman gave the Arab man money, and she took her passport. Then the Moldovan woman realized she had been sold into prostitution. After a few years as a sex slave, she escaped with two other women.[42]

The example above is horrible, and there are far, far worse stories we could have told. Still, the results of trafficking by deception are not always or necessarily so awful. For instance, a rural Laotian girl's friend from her village recruited her and said she would take her to work in a noodle shop in Thailand. When she got there, she found it was a "beer shop," a place where sex is sold. The madam didn't force her to sell sex, instead letting her do chores and sit and drink with customers. But after a month, she saw how much the other women were earning, and she started selling sex. Basically, this was a socialization process that eased her into sex work.[43]

Often, what looks like trafficking to some is actually not. For instance, Rhacel Parrenas gives the example of Filipina hostesses in Japanese nightclubs who in the mid-2000s were thought to be the largest group of trafficked individuals in the world.[44] Parrenas worked as a hostess and interviewed 55 hostesses (including 11 transgendered hostesses). She made the point that while flirting is central to their jobs, sex is definitely not. They were not forced to migrate, and importantly, their work was not coerced. So in no sense were these migrants trafficked.

However, hostessing was thought by many, most importantly the US State Department, to be a euphemism for trafficked prostitution. In its TIPR the State Department dropped Japan from Tier 1 to Tier 2. Because of this, Japan greatly restricted the number of Filipina hostesses, from about 83,000 in 2004 to under 9,000 in 2006.[45] Again, these migrants went to Japan of their own accord, but faced what Parrenas called "severe structural constraints." Once in Japan, due to the actions of sending and receiving agents and government policy that affected the ways they were paid (the clubs where they worked could not pay them directly, and instead paid their agents), these female and transgendered workers had to survive on tips because they didn't get paid until they were about to leave. They were certainly in a bind, but this made them bonded laborers, not trafficked.

The contrasting backgrounds of these female and transgendered migrants, and how and why they went to Japan are quite interesting. Women went to escape poverty, while the transgendered migrants truly went for the purpose of being entertainers. The transgendered hostesses were for the most part college educated and came from fairly well-off families—they rarely sent remittances. For them, migrating was about professional advancement, something they could not achieve in the Philippines. They were not in it strictly for the money.[46] Most went to fulfill their desire to sing and dance on stage and for a sense of risk and adventure for "sexualized work."

The female migrants were less educated, and went because the money they could earn was far more than in the Philippines. Their brokers had a "fly now, pay later" system, so even the poor could go. This contrasts with migration patterns elsewhere in the world where the poorest of the poor are generally too poor to migrate, that is, they can't afford to make the trip. Some of these hostesses came with entertainer visas, some with tourist visas. None of the women Parrenas interviewed wanted to be domestics. That was beneath them and actually more expensive as they would have had to pay broker fees up front. Also, Filipino domestics often went to the Persian Gulf, an area of the world the people she interviewed had no desire to go to.

Trafficking does not have to be to a geographical location. Some believe that trafficking also occurs around particular events. For years, many in the media have been saying sporting events like the Super Bowl and soccer's World Cup are magnets for sex trafficking.[47] But, like so many supposed instances of trafficking, it turns out to not be true. According to a report by the Global Alliance against Trafficking in Women, there is no increase in prostitution during those events, and no evidence of any link to sex trafficking.[48]

What is the full extent of the trafficking problem? No one really knows, because it's completely underground. The anti-trafficking crusaders—evangelical Christians, anti-pornography activists, journalists, some feminists, and government officials—have an interest in inflating the magnitude of the problem and creating vague and large numbers. Trafficking victims are said to be anywhere from hundreds of thousands to millions per year.[49]

Estimates vary so wildly, and also from year to year, because they are literally all pretty much pulled out of thin air. The Bangkok office of the United Nations Educational, Scientific and Cultural Organization (UNESCO) said that most such statistics are "false" or "spurious," and that "[w]hen it comes to statistics, trafficking of girls and women is one of several highly emotive issues which seem to overwhelm critical faculties."[50] While the US State Department claims there are anywhere between 24,500 and 50,000 people trafficked into the United States (the numbers vary widely year to year, and the estimates have fallen precipitously), not all government departments are convinced. The US Department of Justice in 2005 said, "[T]he government must address the incongruity between the estimated number of victims trafficked into the United States—between 14,500 and 17,500 [annually]—and the number of victims found—only 611 in the last four years."[51]

Some small-scale studies suggest that trafficking is not as big a problem as anti-trafficking activists and many governments make it seem. One study of Vietnamese sex workers in Cambodia who moved through brokers found that only 6 of 100 women were brought over under false pretenses; the rest knew before they left Vietnam they would be working in brothels in Cambodia. Many women who have been "saved" from brothels by rescue organizations returned to the brothels as quickly as they could after obtaining their release through bribes or getting relatives in Vietnam to come get them. Rather than saving them, the rescuers compounded their problems by increasing their debts (due to the paying of bribes) and scaring off customers. This had the effect of reducing their incomes and damaging relations with brothel managers who further restricted their movements.[52]

The same team also surveyed migrant child workers, a secondary preoccupation with anti-trafficking activists, and found of 1000 young migrants in Mali only 4 could be classified as having been deceived, exploited, or not paid for their work.[53]

Again, many migrant women have been deceived by migration brokers/smugglers into thinking that they would be working at some other sort of job—maid, waiter, etc. This deception does constitute trafficking. The results can be devastating, often wrecking these women's and often their families' lives.

And yet, many studies have found that even when migrants feel they have been deceived into going into sex work, their complaints are usually about the working conditions, rather than that the work is sexual. Often they don't mind the work itself, as it pays quite well.[54]

The anti-anti-trafficking scholar and activist Laura Agustin makes the point that migration scholars, especially those studying transnationalism, should be interested in migrant sex workers as, in Europe and elsewhere, many workers tend to stay only a few weeks or months in a place then move on, in a circuit crossing national borders.[55] That is, their multiple movements across country borders should be an important topic for people who study multiple movements across country borders. Instead, she asserts that sex workers have "been disappeared" from migration studies, only to reappear in criminology or feminist studies as victims. Male, transsexual, and transgender sex workers are even more neglected in migration studies and don't reappear anywhere.[56] The idea that women (and others) could *knowingly choose to engage in sex work* rarely makes its way into the scholarly literature or popular press.

Does sex trafficking occur? It does. It's just not clear to what degree it's a problem. More importantly from a policy and humanitarian standpoint, it obscures the broader problem of human trafficking for other forms of trafficked labor, such as factory, agricultural, and domestic work, working in restaurants, etc. And what happens once their trafficking ordeal has ended? Once they've escaped, or been given their freedom, they face still more problems. Denise Brennan, an anthropologist who has worked with trafficking victims for over ten years, found that trafficking victims who've found their freedom in the United States have to rebuild their lives from scratch. They have no money, and often only the clothes on their backs. They don't know anyone, and they stay away from their co-ethnics out of shame and also out of fear of seeing their abusers. So they have to forego the ready-made communities that often give help and emotional support to migrants. Still, many insist if they could survive their abusers, they can survive the mundane struggles of poverty.[57]

Conclusion

Migrants, like people everywhere, have hopes and dreams and desires for better lives for themselves and their children, and they migrate with the intention of fulfilling these. Some migrate to Western countries, like Mexicans to the United States, to make a better life there. Temporary workers like Filipino maids going to Hong Kong or Bangladeshi construction workers going to Kuwait have no chance of settling. For them, they toil and live, sometimes in atrocious conditions, for the chance to make a better life back home through remittances. They willingly go to these places, as the promise of the future is much brighter than the bleakness of the present. For some, it's an empty promise. For others though, the promise gets fulfilled. But it's a risk that they feel they have to take, a risk that millions before them, and millions after them, will take.

For others—employers, natives, and government officials in receiving countries—the hopes and dreams of these people are often invisible. Many see working-class migrants as nothing more than disposable, interchangeable parts, factors of production, and little else. Anne Gallagher extends this idea even further in her writing on trafficking in organs, saying that migrants are desirable *for* their parts.[58] Because we live longer, and because of an organ donor shortage in the West, a black market in other parts of the world has arisen to fill this need. Many of these organs come from migrants from poor countries who are deceived or threatened into "donation." These migrants usually don't make it to the West; their organs are harvested in Cairo, Kosovo, South Africa, and other developing world countries. Then the organs migrate to the West. In this sense, migrants truly are meat.

Notes

1 DeParle, Jason. "A Good Provider Is One Who Leaves." *The New York Times*. April 22, 2007. http://query.nytimes.com/gst/fullpage.html?res=9D04E7D6113FF931A1575 7C0A9619C8B63&ref=jasondeparle&pagewanted=all <retrieved March 30, 2013>
2 DeParle, ibid.
3 Schlosser, Eric. "In the Strawberry Fields." *The Atlantic*. November 1, 1995. www. theatlantic.com/magazine/archive/1995/11/in-the-strawberry-fields/305754/ <retrieved Jan 22, 2013>
4 Vasta, Ellie. "Immigrants and the Paper Market: Borrowing, Renting and Buying Identities." *Ethnic and Racial Studies* 34.2 (2011): 187–206.

5 Ali, Syed. *Dubai: Gilded Cage.* New Haven: Yale UP, 2010; International Organization for Migration. *World Migration Report 2013: Migrant Well-being and Development.* Geneva: International Organization for Migration, 2013.

6 Lan, Pei-Chia. "Legal Servitude and Free Illegality: Migrant 'Guest Workers' in Taiwan." In Rhacel Salazar Parreñas and Lok Siu, eds., *Asian Diasporas: New Formations, New Conceptions.* Stanford, CA: Stanford UP, 2007, p. 256.

7 Human Rights Watch. *"The Island of Happiness": Exploitation of Migrant Workers on Saadiyat Island, Abu Dhabi.* New York: Human Rights Watch, 2009. www.hrw.org/reports/2009/05/18/island-happiness <retrieved June 1, 2013>

8 Lan 2007, op cit., pp. 260, 264.

9 Ali, 2010, op cit., p. 29; Kurien, Prema. *Kaleidoscopic Ethnicity: International Migration and the Reconstruction of Community Identities in India.* New Brunswick, NJ: Rutgers UP, 2002; Terrazas, Aaron. "Mexican Immigrants in the United States." *Migration Policy Institute.* February 22, 2010. www.migrationpolicy.org/article/mexican-immigrants-united-states-0#11 <retrieved July 17, 2013>

10 Ali, Syed. "'Go West Young Man': The Culture of Migration among Muslims in Hyderabad, India." *Journal of Ethnic and Migration Studies* 33.1 (2007): 37–58; Cohen, Jeffrey. *The Culture of Migration in Southern Mexico.* Austin: U of Texas Press, 2004.

11 Levitt, Peggy. *The Transnational Villagers.* Berkeley: U of California, 2001; Smith, Robert C. *Mexican New York: Transnational Lives of New Immigrants.* Berkeley: U of California, 2006.

12 World Bank. "Migrants from Developing Countries to Send Home $414 Billion in Earnings in 2013." October 2, 2013. www.worldbank.org/en/news/feature/2013/10/02/Migrants-from-developing-countries-to-send-home-414-billion-in-earnings-in-2013 <retrieved November 22, 2013>

13 Mathews, Gordon. *Ghetto at the Center of the World: Chungking Mansions, Hong Kong.* Chicago, IL: U of Chicago, 2011, pp. 74–75.

14 Doward, Jamie. "Qatar World Cup: 400 Nepalese Die on Nation's Building Sites since Bid Won." *The Observer.* February 16, 2014. www.theguardian.com/football/2014/feb/16/qatar-world-cup-400-deaths-nepalese <retrieved March 28, 2014>; Gibson, Owen. "More than 500 Indian Workers Have Died in Qatar since 2012, Figures Show." *The Guardian.* February 18, 2014. www.theguardian.com/world/2014/feb/18/qatar-world-cup-india-migrant-worker-deaths <retrieved March 28, 2014>

15 Ali 2010, op cit.; Human Rights Watch. *Building Towers, Cheating Workers: Exploitation of Migrant Construction Workers in the United Arab Emirates.* New York: Human Rights Watch, 2006. www.hrw.org/reports/2006/11/11/building-towers-cheating-workers <accessed June 4, 2014>

16 Ali 2010, op cit.

17 Anderson, Bridget, and Blanka Hancilová. "Migrant Labour in Kazakhstan: A Cause for Concern?" *Journal of Ethnic and Migration Studies* 37.3 (2011): 467–483, p. 474.

18 Ehrenreich, Barbara, and Arlie Russell Hochschild, eds. *Global Woman: Nannies, Maids, and Sex Workers in the New Economy.* New York: Metropolitan, 2003.

19 Lan 2007, p. 257, op cit.

20 Lan 2007, pp. 253–254, op cit.

21 Lan 2007, p. 258, op cit.

22 Lan 2007, pp. 265–266, op cit.

23 Lan 2007, pp. 266, 268, op cit.

24 Ali 2010, pp. 97–98, op cit.

25 Human Rights Watch. *Swept under the Rug: Abuses against Domestic Workers around the World*. New York: Human Rights Watch, 2006. www.hrw.org/reports/2006/07/27/swept-under-rug <retrieved June 1, 2013>

26 Ehrenreich, Barbara, and Arlie Russell Hochschild, "Introduction." In Barbara Ehrenreich and Arlie Russell Hochschild, eds., *Global Woman: Nannies, Maids, and Sex Workers in the New Economy*. New York: Metropolitan, 2003.

27 Rahman, Md Mizanur. "Gendering Migrant Remittances: Evidence from Bangladesh and the United Arab Emirates." *International Migration* 51.S1 (2013): e159–e178.

28 Casas, Laura Oso. "Money, Sex, Love and the Family: Economic and Affective Strategies of Latin American Sex Workers in Spain." *Journal of Ethnic and Migration Studies* 36.1 (2010): 47–65, p. 53.

29 Oso-Casas 2010: 58–59, op cit.

30 Oso-Casas 2010: 4, op cit.

31 Ehrenreich and Hochschild, 2003, op cit.

32 Lan, Pei-Chia. "New Global Politics of Reproductive Labor: Gendered Labor and Marriage Migration." *Sociology Compass* 2.6 (2008): 1801–1815, p. 1803.

33 Lan 2008: 1805, ibid.

34 See Constable, Nicole. *Romance on a Global Stage: Pen Pals, Virtual Ethnography, and "Mail-order" Marriages*. Berkeley: U of California, 2003.

35 See for example Brennan, Denise. *What's Love Got to Do with It? Transnational Desires and Sex Tourism in the Dominican Republic*. Durham, NC: Duke UP, 2004.

36 Kimberly Hoang interviewed 71 sex workers, of whom 30 got married, and 12 moved to the West with proper visas. See Hoang, Kimberly. "Transnational Gender Vertigo." *Contexts* 12.2 (2013): 22–26.

37 Hoang 2013: 24, ibid.

38 Toyota, Mika. "Editorial Introduction: International Marriage, Rights and the State in East and Southeast Asia." *Citizenship Studies* 12.1 (2008): 1–7, pp. 1–2.

39 Freeman, Caren. *Making and Faking Kinship: Marriage and Labor Migration between China and South Korea*. Ithaca: Cornell UP, 2011.

40 Freeman 2011, p. 241, ibid.

41 Molland, Sverre. "'I Am Helping Them': 'Traffickers', 'Anti-traffickers' and Economies of Bad Faith." *The Australian Journal of Anthropology* 22.2 (2011): 236–254, p. 237.

42 Finnegan, William. "A Reporter at Large: The Countertraffickers." *The New Yorker*. May 5, 2008. www.newyorker.com/reporting/2008/05/05/080505fa_fact_finnegan?currentPage=all <retrieved May 30, 2013>

43 Molland 2011: 241, op cit.

44 Parreñas, Rhacel Salazar. *Illicit Flirtations: Labor, Migration, and Sex Trafficking in Tokyo*. Stanford, CA: Stanford UP, 2011, p. 14.

45 Parreñas 2011, p. 4, op cit.

46 Parreñas 2011, p. 19, op cit.

47 Skinner, E. Benjamin. "South Africa's New Slave Trade and the Campaign to Stop It." *Time*. January 18. 2010. http://content.time.com/time/magazine/article/0,9171,1952335,00.html <retrieved March 22, 2013>; Goldberg, Eleanor. "Super Bowl Is Single Largest Human Trafficking Incident in U.S.: Attorney General." *The Huffington Post*. February 3, 2013. www.huffingtonpost.com/2013/02/03/super-bowl-sex-trafficking_n_2607871.html <retrieved Jan 12, 2013>

48 Ham, Julie. *What's the Cost of a Rumour? A Guide to Sorting out the Myths and the Facts about Sporting Events and Trafficking*. Bangkok: GAATW, 2011, pp. 13–14.

49 Weitzer, Ronald. "The Social Construction of Sex Trafficking: Ideology and Institutionalization of a Moral Crusade." *Politics and Society* 35.3 (2007): 447–475, pp. 455–456; Weitzer, Ronald. "Macro Claims Versus Micro Evidence." *Contexts* 13.1 (2014): 24–25.

50 Quoted in Weitzer 2007: 455–456, ibid.

51 Weitzer 2007: 463, ibid.

52 Busza, Joanna, Sarah Castle, and Aisse Diarra. "Trafficking and Health." *British Medical Journal*, June 5, 2004, 328 (7452): 1369–1371.

53 Busza, Castle, and Diarra 2004, ibid.

54 Agustín, Laura. "The Disappearing of a Migration Category: Migrants Who Sell Sex." *Journal of Ethnic and Migration Studies* 32.1 (2006): 29–47, p. 37.

55 Agustín 2006: 32, ibid.

56 Agustín 2006: 30, ibid.

57 Brennan, Denise. "Life Beyond Trafficking." *Contexts* 13.1 (2014): 20–21; Brennan, Denise. *Life Interrupted: Trafficking into Forced Labor in the United States*. Durham, NC: Duke UP, 2014.

58 Gallagher, Anne. "Trafficking for Organ Removal." *Contexts* 13.1 (2014): 18–19.

3
GLOBALLY MOBILE PROFESSIONALS

The counterpart to the globally mobile working class we discussed in the last chapter is the globally mobile professional class. Like the working class, these are people who go to work abroad, usually on short-term work visas, and generally go without the intention of settling down in that country, even if their short stays turn into many years. They include corporate workers (managers, lawyers, engineers, IT specialists, real estate agents, public relations workers, etc.), development and aid workers in NGOs (nongovernmental organizations), English teachers, and so on.

Like the workers in the last chapter, these professionals for the most part are going to locations in the world where capital is concentrated and where employment and advancement opportunities and pay are as good or better than at home. And like the global working class, their labor is increasingly in demand. Many are intra-Western migrants, going from places such as New York to London, or London to Vancouver.[1] (By the West, we mean United States, Canada, Western Europe, Australia, and New Zealand.) Others are going from the West to non-Western global cities, such as Singapore, Hong Kong, Shanghai, Bombay, and Dubai—cities that require global "talent" to continue their economic expansion, as such talent is often in short supply locally. Still others are going from non-Western countries to other non-Western cities, such as from India to Dubai and from Singapore or Taiwan to Shanghai. Lastly, there are many professionals from developing countries who go to developed countries, such as IT professionals from India to Australia and the

United States on temporary work visas, which make them distinct from immigrants who go on permanent visas. They're often desirable because they're usually a lot cheaper than native workers, and like the global meat of the last chapter, they're disposable.

These high-end workers are needed in these various countries to address "talent" shortages (real or perceived—such as in Singapore and Saudi Arabia), and because "native" labor may be more expensive than imported talent (American IT workers). This is the economic "pull," where firms offer these workers salaries and benefits greater than they would get at home, and often governments make it easier for them to get visas.

Skilled migrants do not have to rely on brokers for visas the same way the globally mobile working class does, though it depends on where they're coming from, and where they're going. For instance, Indian IT workers going to the West still usually need help with brokers. Network connections tend to be important to connect these mobile professionals to jobs, and to motivate them to go abroad. The Westerners who go abroad, not surprisingly, also usually have a desire to live in a foreign land. While a culture of migration is also important for non-Westerners, such as Singaporeans and Indians going to China or the Persian Gulf, it is generally not as important as economic concerns.

Here, we are going to examine those high-end workers who not only cross national boundaries, but are also crossing broad social, economic, and cultural boundaries. We start with Westerners going to Asia, and then consider Asians going elsewhere in Asia, and finish by looking at Asians going West.

There are two common patterns of going from the West to less developed places for work. The first way, the "classical" way, is to have a job that takes them to specific destinations. A common example is the intra-company transfer of a (usually) white male sent by his home office on a short-term posting to places such as Jakarta, Beijing, Riyadh, or Bombay. He usually works at a very high level and has to be enticed by his company to go to such places with enhanced salary, free or heavily subsidized housing, household help and driver, club membership, and free schooling for the children at an international school. Alternately, he may seek out such a posting as a way to enhance his upward professional mobility. His wife often gives up her career to support her husband's. Her days are given over to cafes, shopping, and other activities with wives in similar situations, with summers spent back home so the children do not forget from whence they come.[2]

There are of course others who follow a similar pattern as the corporate executives, such as career diplomats, who get many of the perks if not the salaries. More common are those a bit further down the corporate chain who also go on transfers with some, though not all, of the amenities that the higher up executives receive. There is another class of workers that does not follow global financial capital—aid and development workers. They go to where international aid money goes in the developing world—such as to central dispersion points like Kabul or Addis Ababa, or more regional places like Peshawar, down to smaller towns and villages.[3]

The second pattern of migration for the globally mobile Western professional is where individuals migrate *to a place*. In the past 30 years or so, more and more developing countries have abandoned their quasi-socialist economies and embraced, or were forced to embrace, globalization by demands of entities such as the World Bank, IMF (International Monetary Fund) and the WTO (World Trade Organization). Many of the cities in these "third-world" countries have become economically successful, and inviting to foreign companies and recruit foreign "talent" workers to varying degrees. Cities such as Singapore and Dubai have also benefited from increased global trade of goods and services and their attraction as tourist destinations over the past 40 years. They have diversified their economies and are also attractive to foreign workers. These types of cities are alluring to the young, single migrant looking to go abroad for international work experience and professional advancement, but also for the cultural experience and adventure of living abroad. Unlike the executive transferees who are mainly men, here the split between men and women is likely more equitable.

These skilled migrants care about where they live as well as where (and for whom) they work. They want to be in global cities such as Dubai/Singapore/Shanghai, and are often recruited in their home country by employers in those destinations, or apply for jobs in those destinations while still in their home countries. Others go to those places and try to get work once there, though it's often a better financial deal to be hired abroad than going to the place and getting a job once there. Ali was in Dubai in 2006 with one young British man who grew up in Dubai when he received a call from a potential employer on his mobile phone. He was pretending to be having the conversation in London. He explained to Ali later that if the employer knew he lived in Dubai, or even that he grew up in Dubai, then his pay would be that of a "local" employee rather than an international contract, and his terms would be much worse.

These mobile professional workers are called expatriates. The term expatriate is usually used to refer to professional workers, who are generally on short-term visas. These expatriates differ in their degree of "rootedness." Those who are transferred or posted to a place tend to not integrate much into the local social surroundings. They are there to work, and any socializing they do is with coworkers and their families, and often in nationality-based clubs. The people who choose a place are often more rooted there than people who are transferred. But this rootedness, as we will see, is more "shallow" than that of the migrant who can and does stay long-term or permanently in migrant-receiving countries like the United States, United Kingdom, Australia, and so on.

A kind of corollary to the globally mobile professional class is the globally mobile leisure class. One part of the leisure class are long-term tourists, such as all manner of Westerners going to Banaras, India to study dance, classical music, and yoga.[4] Another part of this class is composed of Western retirees moving to cheaper places to live full time or part time, such as Americans moving to Panama, or Britons moving to Spain or France.[5] While fascinating on their own, we limit our focus here to workers.

We will leave aside "permanent" migrants for the next few chapters. Our concern in this chapter is with these expatriates. Where are these people going? Who are they? Why do they want to go there? What do they do once they're there? The answers to these questions not only help us understand these expatriate migrants, they underscore and expand our knowledge of the general dynamics of movement and incorporation that are at the core of this book.

Western Expatriates in Asian Global Cities

Economic globalization has led to the rise of a number of cities becoming important nodes for global trade, culture, and politics. While New York City, London, and Tokyo have been central global cities for decades, more recently many cities in Asia, Latin America, and Africa have become important global cities as well.

In this section we draw upon work that has been done among expatriates in Dubai and Shanghai. There are of course many, many important differences between these places, but one especially stands out: population. In Dubai, well over 90 percent of the population are foreigners, with most of these being the working class—maids, construction workers, etc. Nowhere else outside of the Persian Gulf is the proportion of expatriates so high. Singapore comes closest, with a foreign population of 25 percent.[6] Shanghai has a large expatriate presence—the most numerous are Taiwanese, Japanese, and Americans—though because of its huge population, the percentage of expatriates is small.

The ways expatriates are received varies by place. In Dubai, expatriates are defined by the state as "guest workers" and reside and work on renewable, temporary visas. In Shanghai (and also Singapore, which we discuss later) expatriates are also on temporary visas, but the state allows for expatriates to become permanent residents, unlike Dubai. But still, these expatriates are socially excluded to a degree, and also exclude themselves. For those who choose to make these cities in non-democratic countries their temporary home, they enter into a Faustian bargain, giving up certain Western notions of freedom, like voting and democracy and free speech for the "good life." (One American expatriate in Dubai found himself in maximum-security prison for nine months for making a spoof video of a working-class neighborhood.[7]) For many, other notions of freedom may supersede political ones. The freedom that people have living in Dubai and Shanghai and Singapore is largely economic, as workers and consumers. Expatriates are there to work, and to enjoy themselves for the, by definition, limited time they are in the country. They are economic mercenaries living in "gilded cages."

As we pointed out above, there are many reasons why expatriates go to the places they do. The big draw is of course pay and work opportunities. The pay package, especially when they are recruited in their home countries, is generally better than that for "locals," and the possibility of upward job mobility is also often better and faster than in their home countries. A close second is the style of life that expatriates can expect, often far beyond how they would live at home, with access to cheap household help (maids, nannies, drivers, gardeners, etc.) One of Ali's friends who grew up in Dubai left in 2007 and swore he would never return to live. But London was proving difficult to raise his child, and the "easy" life in Dubai was too strong a draw, so he went back.

Aside from the pay and easy living, these are culturally interesting places to live in, and good jumping off points for local travel. For instance, Dubai is only a two-and-a-half-hour flight to India, and a six-hour flight to most parts of Europe, Asia, and Africa.

For the ever-increasing numbers of young, upwardly mobile professionals, there is another lure to living in these kinds of places—the nightlife. The clubs and drinking are big draws, as is, to be blunt, sex. Sex is a central concern for Western male expatriates in Shanghai. The clubs there are a "sexual paradise" for Western expatriate men who find it relatively easy to engage in casual sex with Chinese women.[8] Professional Chinese women from elsewhere in China also enjoyed going to clubs and hanging out with expatriates, rather than with Shanghainese men, as they essentially share with expatriates a lifestyle and status as outsiders.[9] This was not the case for single Western expatriate women who see themselves as competing sexually with local Chinese women. Some Western expatriate women kept away from the club scene altogether to "avoid the sight of Western men hunting or being hunted by Chinese women."[10]

The story for British expatriates in Dubai is similar. For male and female young, single white professionals, Dubai is a place where "real-life" is suspended. They earn much more than they would in Britain, they drink throughout the week (and quite heavily at that), and see fleeting sexual encounters as their only romantic option as dating is difficult because most expatriates don't stay for very long.[11] Unlike Westerners in Shanghai, Britons in Dubai for the most part preferred the company of others like themselves: young, relatively well-to-do whites.

The British are not alone in enjoying the good life, nor are they even numerically dominant among the well to do in Dubai. Dubai is home to a very large number of upper-middle-class young professional expatriates from outside the West who live their lives similarly, if not to the same degree of excess. In any high-end club or bar you find an international crowd.

Expatriates in these non-Western cities largely live in social bubbles, sealing themselves off from locals, and if their numbers are big enough, as in Dubai, from other expatriates by nationality. In many places expatriates develop an internal hierarchy, a status system, usually based on occupation and wealth. At the bottom in Shanghai are "low-quality" European and North American English teachers who are willing to live on "local" Chinese wages. This should not be surprising as the main requirement to get into that job is simply being a native English speaker.[12] In Shanghai, some older men find it a good place to retire by teaching English and they can still find sexual partners. Higher paid expatriates call the teachers "losers." Even some teachers think of themselves that way. One female expatriate teacher in China said about a male expatriate colleague who'd been doing it too long, "I don't want to be like Dan, he's like what, 40, 45 or something and he's still teaching . . . Dan is just a teacher, and I personally . . . , I'd really be disappointed with myself if I was that age and still floating." And it doesn't take long to become a "floater." The female teacher said you do it for one year and it's exciting. Teach for two years and it becomes difficult to get another job, and then you're trapped.[13]

Another basis for distinction among expatriates is length of residence. In Shanghai, the longer-term residents refer to themselves as "New Shanghailanders" and not as "merely" expatriates, who are essentially sojourners. The New Shanghailanders want to be there, while their companies send other expatriates. One male New Shanghailander said the distinction between New Shanghailanders and other expatriates was "whether your kids are born [in Shanghai], or whether they are going to school with Chinese kids." Having your children in school with local children is certainly a sign of assimilation. But there are limits. For instance, after 15 years of living in Shanghai, the man quoted above still had a preference for Western friends.

While the New Shanghailanders, and other long-term expatriates elsewhere, may think of themselves as belonging to these places and draw a distinction between themselves and expatriates who have not been there as long, they rarely are able to assimilate in the way that immigrants (and especially their children) can assimilate in countries such as the United States, United Kingdom, Canada and other places that have historically received immigrants. Many global cities in the developing world do not have a history of immigration, or often a legal or social mechanism, to incorporate expatriates permanently. Still, "good" expatriates try to culturally assimilate even if they can never fully socially assimilate. (Unlike in migrant-receiving nations, like those we will discuss in the next chapter, the children of expatriates generally will not socially assimilate either.) They may learn the languages and customs—that is, culturally assimilate to a degree—and even live amongst the natives rather than in separate expatriate enclaves. But they usually remain socially distanced from natives. Even the New Shanghailanders, who are fond of showing how immersed in the local culture they are, in the end are not Shanghainese.

For Western expatriates, Dubai and Shanghai and most other cities they go to are places for short-term financial and/or professional gain, and a place to try out a different lifestyle—essentially an extended holiday in a foreign (and in the case of Dubai, not so different) locale where they can also earn money well in excess of what they received back home. But they come knowing they will not stay. Most acknowledge they ultimately do not belong in an Arab/Asian city, even with all the luxury amenities they provide. In the end, family, friends, and their futures ultimately are in the West.

Non-Western Expatriates in Asia

When discussing expatriates, most of the scholarly literature and popular press focus has been on Westerners. Indeed, being Western and having the intention of being a short-term migrant (even if they stay longer) is practically the definition of being an expatriate. But there are a great number of non-Western expatriates who have also made the journey to elsewhere in the non-Western world, such as professional expatriates from South Asia and non-resource rich Arab countries to Dubai, and Singaporean and Taiwanese expatriates in China.

In Dubai, media attention on expatriate living has focused on either high-end, mostly British expatriates, or low-end hyper-exploited labor, such as construction workers and maids. But arguably the backbone of Dubai's economy since the first oil boom of the 1970s has been South Asian (especially Indian) and Arab middle-class workers and their families. South Asians, and to a lesser degree Arabs, have filled the bulk of lower-, middle- and even upper-level professional functions. They are skilled, educated labor, but their wages are often significantly less than their Western counterparts, as many if not most firms in the resource-rich Persian Gulf countries set pay by nationality. Still, their wages are much higher than they would be in their home countries.

While high-end Western professionals may come and go with economic booms and downturns in the Gulf and their home countries, a larger number of these Asian and Arab expatriate workers and their families tend to be longer term, putting their children in schools and putting down roots, tenuous though they may be. A 1982 article noted that early on in Dubai's boom many middle-class Indian migrants expected to remain in the Gulf for many years, possibly for their entire working lives.[14] While there are some Westerners who have been in Dubai long term and have raised and schooled their children there, they are in much smaller numbers than South Asians or Arabs.

These expatriates come with their families to take advantage of two promises that Dubai makes to them—upward mobility and more comfortable family living situations than where they came from, in terms of better housing, better city infrastructure, better schools, less crime, and so on. The biggest portion of the city's population is of Indian origin, and many Indians refer to Dubai as the "best city in India." Indeed, there are many parts of the city where you are hard pressed to find non-South Asian faces.

Again, Dubai promises upward mobility, and it often delivers. Let's compare the experiences of two middle-class brothers from Bombay who came to Dubai in their mid-20s in the late 1970s on transfer postings from multinational corporations. Not too long after arriving, Ahmed decided to follow his wife's family members to the United States, while Ashgar decided he liked the family-oriented lifestyle and business opportunities in Dubai, and the fact it was so close to India. Ahmed went on to live a typical middle-class immigrant success story existence in the American suburbs—a modest house with an above-ground swimming pool, comfortable job, good public schools for the children and the opportunity to send them to professional schools and an upper-middle-class existence. Ashgar, on the other hand, opened up an import firm and became a millionaire and his wife became a prominent lawyer. They hobnob with Bollywood celebrities and own a villa on the famed Palm Jumeirah.

While their lives diverged as they chose different migrant destinations, they both loved their family back in Bombay, though they left them. In fact, it was family obligations that drove them to Dubai in the first place—the need to support family by leaving them. (Contrast this with Salman the engineer from Hyderabad we discussed in Chapter 1 who did not migrate, thus failing to fulfill his family obligations as a provider.) Many Asian and Arab middle-class expatriates (like working-class expatriates) regularly remit large portions of their salaries. When converted into their home currencies their remittances have much more value (in terms of purchasing power) than what it does for a Westerner.

Expatriates, even rich ones like Ashgar, know they must eventually leave Dubai, either to go home or to try to go to the West. Still, they are quite comfortable staying in Dubai for longer stretches of time. Many have been in Dubai their entire work lives, and have raised their children in Dubai. Many of their adult children, second-generation expatriates, live and work in Dubai as adults. Still, Indian and Arab expatriates residing in Dubai know that they do not belong, that they cannot stay. Few think of themselves as permanent—they envision returning to India, or pushing on to the United States, Canada, Australia, or the United Kingdom.[15] For some, the impetus to return is the mandatory retirement age of 60, at which time they usually have to leave. For others, their long-term stays in Dubai are complete when their children finish high school. In any case, no matter how long they are in Dubai, their days by definition are numbered. As a hedge, many acquire Western citizenship or residency, sometimes with more than one country. This is true for other expatriates from non-Western countries as well.[16] This fluid and opportunistic attitude towards passports, nationality, and work opportunities is sometimes called "flexible citizenship."[17]

Unlike Indian and Arab expatriates in Dubai, going to China for Taiwanese and Singaporean expatriates is not a "step up" in terms of living arrangements, and they're not going because their opportunities at home are thwarted. In this sense, they are more like Western expatriates, who go for better opportunities.

Singaporeans started going to China and elsewhere in Asia in the early 1990s due to a top-down government initiated "regionalization drive" to reach out to new markets within a seven-hour flight radius. Companies and individuals were encouraged to embrace a culture of risk taking and innovation.[18] They go to the obvious places like Beijing, Shanghai, and Hong Kong, but also other key areas for investment like Suzhou and Guangzhou. In 2011, it was estimated there were roughly 20,000 Singaporeans (mainly of Chinese descent) in China. They are mainly entrepreneurs, restauranteurs, architects, educators, and other types of professionals.

Singaporean expatriates mainly frame their migration in terms of economic motivations, but secondarily as a "return to roots." Going to China was a chance to discover their "Chineseness" and Chinese culture at the source, which had diminished over generations in Singapore.

But in everyday life, they maintained their distance from local Chinese beyond the workplace; the trailing spouses had hardly any contact socially with Chinese at all. Their social lives revolved around other Singaporean expatriates.[19] Their romantic notions of being in the cultural motherland were quickly, and rudely, put down by the harsher realities of day-to-day living in China. Many Singaporeans thought along the lines of "well, they're Chinese, we're Chinese, so we can get along." But while they may be culturally similar, they are different people, and Singaporeans realized quickly how culturally different they are. Singaporean expatriates of Chinese ethnicity act and react much like the British to being in China. Some act with disdain for locals while others want to absorb Chinese culture. They can act in these varied ways because of their relatively high status vis-à-vis local Chinese.[20]

Singaporeans represent an interesting case because Singapore is a country of both immigration and emigration.[21] Most of Singapore's population growth until WWII was due to migration—largely from China, India, and Malaya. But migration in the 1950s and 1960s was restricted, to the point when Singapore became independent in 1965, nonpermanent, noncitizen residents were only 2.9 percent of the population. In the 1980s, as Singapore started to industrialize, its migrant population increased.

Singapore's population consists of citizens, permanent residents and non-resident migrants (students and foreign workers). By the early 2000s, the nonresident population was 25 percent. The vast majority of those are low-skilled workers—maids, construction, manufacturing, services, and marine industries. About 20 percent of the nonresident population consists of professionals and a small number of entrepreneurs. The professionals/entrepreneurs are eligible to become permanent residents, unlike in Dubai. The majority of skilled workers are from China and India, with smaller numbers from Western countries, as well as Japan and South Korea.

While many expatriates are coming to Singapore, a great number of Singaporeans are emigrating as well—about 200,000 are living abroad, with around 1,200 per year giving up their citizenship, as Singapore does not allow dual citizenship. And thousands a year are possibly applying for permanent residency elsewhere.[22] This combined with very low fertility rates means Singapore is that much more dependent on foreign labor at all levels. Partially as a consequence of this demographic shift, Singaporeans have been encouraged to welcome "talent" (as they call professionals) and "accept the discomfort" of so many more foreigners.

A significant expatriate flow to China, especially Shanghai, comes from Taiwan. In 2011, there were 44,000 Taiwanese in Shanghai (with 29,000 Japanese and 23,000 American expatriates).[23] A good number of Taiwanese expatriates are women.[24] Migration to China for Taiwanese is very much dependent on networks. In one survey, over half the respondents had a relative or close friend in China. Professional Taiwanese can find comparable, or better wage packages in China.[25] Many Taiwanese expatriates go with family as intra-company transfers. Many others go on their own. But even if they go as intra-company transfers, once there, many strike out on their own to find work or start businesses.

Like Singaporeans, Taiwanese tend to live either in areas with lots of other Taiwanese or in gated communities with international expatriates. They generally do not live amongst native Chinese. So while the Taiwanese, like Singaporeans, may be part of the Chinese diaspora, and they may be culturally like the Chinese, they are not Chinese. In fact, they live more like British and other expatriates in China, in the sense that they are spatially isolated, they send their children to international rather than local schools, they socialize with Taiwanese and other expatriates, and few have plans to settle there permanently.

Non-Western Expatriates in the West

The experiences of non-Western expatriates in the West are highly varied. Some come as managers or high-end consultants earning six-figure salaries, no different from high-end Western expatriates. Others come in on the bottom rungs of the professional hierarchy.

Let's focus on one particular group of professional migrants to the West: Indian IT (information technology) workers. What differentiates the Indian IT workers from doctors and nurses and engineers who came to the United Kingdom and United States and other Western countries in especially large numbers from the 1960s–1980s (as a result of changes in immigration policy partially due to the need for such professionals in the West) is permanence. Many of those workers were quickly granted permanent residence. For instance, Ali's father, a medical doctor, migrated to the United States in 1971 with his family and received green cards very soon after. But Ali's cousin, an IT specialist, came to the United States in the late 1990s on an H1-B visa, a three-year temporary visa that you're allowed to renew once, then you have to return to your home country. It is possible to apply for a green card once in the United States, but few people get it. Ali's cousin was lucky; he got one. Hardly any of his cousin's friends, however, got them. Where the United States was once generous in giving permanent residency to professionals during Ali's father's time, in the last few decades, general policy changes in the United States (and United Kingdom and elsewhere in the West) have become more stringent for migrant professionals, promoting temporary migration schemes.

A few years after he got his green card, Ali's cousin went back to India to take care of his ailing mother. After she died, he wanted to go back. But by then it was too late. His green card had lapsed, and he hadn't had his green card for the minimum five years required to apply for citizenship. His two kids though were born in the United States, which makes them citizens. So they may at some point decide to go back. Or not. Who can say what migration trends will be in ten years? It's possible they will not feel the need to migrate for economic, network, or cultural reasons as his father did.

While these children perhaps will not feel compelled to migrate, Indian IT specialists have migrated in droves. Xiang Biao, in his 2007 book Global "Body Shopping" shows how Indian IT workers have taken the greatest advantage of specialized visa programs for IT workers in Australia and other nations since the 1990s (in the United States, more than three-quarters of all H1-B visas for professionals go to Indians, mainly IT workers).

Xiang is especially interested in how these workers arrive through body shopping. A body shop is basically a small international agency that places workers in contract positions in firms for varying lengths of time. Here's how it works: An Indian placement agency in Australia (or the United States or Canada or elsewhere) sponsors a worker (for the most part younger and male) for a visa and brings them over to the country.[26] So the employer is actually the body shop that brings them over, also houses them (usually in group housing where they share rooms), sometimes pays them a small stipend while they are "on the bench," that is, not working (Ali's cousin got a stipend, but Xiang writes that in Australia they do not pay them), and tries to contract them out. Like any temporary placement agency, when they place the worker with a firm, they get a big cut of their paycheck.

The genius of this scheme for large companies who contract with the body shops—or often with larger placement agencies who then subcontract with body shops—is they get workers for cheap when they need them, and send them back when they're done with them. The body shop and larger Indian outsourcing firms like Cognizant and Tata (the top ten firms taking advantage of H1-B visas are multinational, India-based outsourcing companies, with Microsoft at number 11) profit from this arrangement, too.[27] These workers are usually paid substantially less than similarly qualified and experienced local workers.[28] The workers themselves accept this arrangement because they're earning many times more than they would have in India and also hope to move up the ladder, as many success stories before them have done. Many Indian workers believed that the uncertainty of the short-term job contracts was a good thing, as it enabled one to move up quickly and rewarded entrepreneurship. The reality was often different. Basically, everyone wins, except native workers whose wages are often depressed to the level of the expatriate contract worker and are often displaced entirely. For many companies, it's just much cheaper to hire a young, Indian worker on a temporary visa than, say, a native, middle-aged white worker.[29]

Even though Xiang conducted his research among Indian computer programmers in Australia, thoughts of America loomed large. (Remember our discussion of culture of migration in Chapter 1?) Most of his contacts in Australia either had gone to, or wished to go to the United States, which today, like a century ago, is still the numerically most popular migrant destination. To get to the United States, many workers took circuitous routes, often going to the Persian Gulf, South Africa, Singapore, Malaysia, or Canada to then try their luck to get an H1-B to the United States with the eventual hope of the golden ticket, the prized American green card. Many who had gone to the United States returned to Australia when they realized their H1-B visas would not easily convert to a green card, and it was much easier to get permanent residency in Australia. For these Indians, being an expatriate was fine, but being a migrant with permanent residency was much better. Expatriate status, that is, working on a temporary visa, means you will have to go back to live in India at some point. Permanent residency (with the eventual likelihood of citizenship, if one so chooses) on the other hand means you don't have to go back, and if you do, you do so on your own time frame and your own terms.

Cosmopolitan Expatriates

Nearly all of the studies we highlighted above deal with migrants going from one country to one other country, with the notable exception of Xiang's study of Indian IT workers. Even there, his focus was on Indians in Australia, and only secondarily on multiple country migration. But in this globalized world, and with so much academic emphasis on transnationalism—with particular emphasis on the "trans"—we might expect that a substantial number of people would migrate between multiple countries. But there is surprisingly very little research examining this.

One study in particular looked at people who have migrated multiple times. These "serial migrants" have lived in at least three different countries for a minimum of a year each, and so are different from "settler" migrants.[30] It's important to note they are professionals with advanced degrees and highly sought after skill sets who come from developed and developing world countries. Interestingly, they do not have a great attachment to their home countries (they are not nationalistic or patriotic), or to the countries they move to, though once there they do seek to fit in by learning the language, making local friends, etc., which makes them different from most expatriates. Their social ties and norms are not those of their ethnicity or religion, but rather of their professions. It is their achieved professional status that is important to them, not the identities they were born with. They are cosmopolitan individuals who do not look to live in expatriate enclaves with people of the same skin color/nationality/religion, unlike other expatriates we have discussed. They look for good career opportunities in different countries, and once there make a conscious effort of looking to experience the culture and people of these countries—again unlike most other expatriates. They are liberated from the weight of tradition and ethnic identity and keep a distance from their own "culture" (and "people") which might keep them from fully experiencing their new, if temporary, homes. They cross national boundaries multiple times to live and work because of their profession. They claim to have transcended the "tribal" loyalties of national and ethnic group.

Again, these people are very different from the other professionals and laborers we have looked at in this and the previous chapter. For the vast majority of these global workers, where they come from is still important for their identities and orientation. No matter how long an Indian construction worker is in Kuwait, he is Indian. No matter how long a British corporate consultant is in Beijing, she is still British. And they are temporary—they know at some point they will return. While this need to return is in part cultural and social ("I am an American and my family and friends are back in America"), in large part it is legal. Their visas are temporary, and so are they. While the cosmopolitan expatriates are also temporary migrants, they have a distinct advantage: The countries they go to desperately want them for their hard-to-come-by skill sets. So they can come and go easily precisely because those countries want them more than they want to be in those countries. For them, the countries they end up in are just sites where they do their work, and are places to be enjoyed while there, not places they need to be.

Conclusion

The careful reader at this point may be a bit annoyed with our depiction of these low- and high-end global workers as simply temporary workers, as the line between temporary and permanent migrants is not hard and fast. And you'd be right. There are expatriates in Singapore who have permanent residence who will end up not staying. There are Indian workers in the United States on temporary H1-B visas who will get lucky and gain the coveted green card. And some of these same people who gain permanent residency, like Ali's cousin, abandon it. So yes, the line between a temporary and permanent migrant is not a clear one. The distinction, though, is still important because the visa in many ways defines who you are and how the state will relate to you. And that in turn can affect an individual's outlook with regards to the place she lives. Basically, these temporary migrants *cannot* assimilate, though they may stay for decades, while some "settler" migrants *choose not to* assimilate, or even stay.

Another thing you may have noticed over the last two chapters is that no single theory can explain why individuals or groups migrate and where they go. As we stated in Chapter 1, economic pushes and pulls are important, but on their own do not explain migration patterns, and that should be clear by now. Remittances are important, as are networks and cultures of migration. But these all vary by group and individual. Taken together, they help us greatly understand migration. On their own, they help, but leave a lot of questions unanswered. You may be unsatisfied by that, but the social world is messy, and sometimes difficult to explain.

That's just how it is. But scholars keep trying to improve their theoretical models to explain what's happening in the world. Sometimes they're able to do that, sometimes reality shifts so far as to make their theories irrelevant and obsolete.

In the next two chapters, we shift our focus from temporary migrants to permanent migrants (or at least migrants with a legal permanent status). How do they make their place in their new homes when they are pretty certain they will stay? In Chapter 4, we tackle the question of assimilation. We deliberately ignore first-generation immigrants, that is, those who migrate as adults, and examine the adult children of migrants (second-generation immigrants) who are usually permanent residents or citizens. How and why do they assimilate? Chapter 5 is a case study of Muslims in the West that incorporates many of the theoretical and empirical questions of the past few chapters.

Notes

1 On Westerners going West, see for example Beaverstock, Jonathan. "Lending Jobs to Global Cities: Skilled International Labour Migration, Investment Banking and the City of London." *Urban Studies* 33.8 (1996): 1377–1394; Favell, Adrian. *Eurostars and Eurocities: Free Movement and Mobility in an Integrating Europe*. Malden, MA: Blackwell, 2008.

2 Fechter, Anne-Meike, "From 'Incorporated Wives' to 'Expat Girls': A New Generation of Expatriate Women?" In Anne Coles and Anne-Meike Fechter, eds., *Gender and Family among Transnational Professionals*. New York: Routledge, 2007.

3 On aid and development workers, see for example Fechter, Anne-Meike, and Heather Hindman. *Inside the Everyday Lives of Development Workers: The Challenges and Futures of Aidland*. Sterling, VA: Kumarian, 2011; Mosse, David. *Adventures in Aidland: The Anthropology of Professionals in International Development*. New York: Berghahn, 2011; Stirrat, Roderick. "Mercenaries, Missionaries and Misfits: Representations of Development Personnel." *Critique of Anthropology* 28.4 (2008): 406–425.

4 Korpela, Mari. "A Postcolonial Imagination? Westerners Searching for Authenticity in India." *Journal of Ethnic and Migration Studies* 36.8 (2010): 1299–1315.

5 Benson, Michaela, and Karen O'Reilly. *Lifestyle Migration: Expectations, Aspirations and Experiences*. Farnham, England: Ashgate, 2009.

6 On Singapore, see Beaverstock, Jonathan. "Servicing British Expatriate 'Talent' in Singapore: Exploring Ordinary Transnationalism and the Role of the 'Expatriate' Club." *Journal of Ethnic and Migration Studies* 37.5 (2011): 709–728.

7 Cassim, Shezanne. "I Went to Jail for Posting a Comedy Skit on YouTube. Is This the Modern UAE?" *The Guardian*. February 9, 2014. www.theguardian.com/commentisfree/2014/feb/09/shezanne-cassim-jail-uae-youtube-video   <retrieved February 12, 2014>

8 Farrer, James. "Global Nightscapes in Shanghai as Ethnosexual Contact Zones." *Journal of Ethnic and Migration Studies* 37.5 (2011): 747–764, p. 755.

9 Farrer 2011: 758.

10 Farrer 2011: 760.

11 Walsh, Katie. "'Dad Says I'm Tied to a Shooting Star!' Grounding (Research on) British Expatriate Belonging." *Area* 38.3 (2006): 268–278.

12 Farrer, James. "'New Shanghailanders' or 'New Shanghainese': Western Expatriates' Narratives of Emplacement in Shanghai." *Journal of Ethnic and Migration Studies* 36.8 (2010): 1211–228. Pei-Chia Lan ("White Privilege, Language Capital and Cultural Ghettoisation: Western High-Skilled Migrants in Taiwan." *Journal of Ethnic and Migration Studies* 37.10 [2011]: 1669–1693) makes a similar observation about Western expatriates in Taiwan. At the top are intracompany transferees, in the middle are "local" hires, that is, Westerners who get their jobs while in Taiwan, usually at lower salaries and benefits than the transferees, and at the bottom are English teachers in cram schools or kindergartens.

13 Stanley, Phiona. *A Critical Ethnography of "Westerners" Teaching English in China: Shanghaied in Shanghai.* Milton Park, Abingdon and New York: Routledge, 2013, p. 214.

14 Weiner, Myron. "International Migration and Development: Indians in the Persian Gulf." *Population and Development Review* 8.1 (1982): 1–36, p. 6.

15 Leonard, Karen. "Guests in the Gulf: South Asian Expatriates." Perry, Richard Warren, and Bill Maurer. *Globalization under Construction: Governmentality, Law, and Identity.* Minneapolis: U of Minnesota, 2003, pp. 129–170.

16 On Taiwanese and their passport woes, see Wang, Horng-Luen. "Regulating Transnational Flows of People: An Institutional Analysis of Passports and Visas as a Regime of Mobility." *Identities* 11.3 (2004): 351–376.

17 Ong, Aihwa. *Flexible Citizenship: The Cultural Logics of Transnationality.* Durham, NC: Duke UP, 1999.

18 Yeoh, Brenda and Katie Willis, "Negotiating 'Home' and 'Away': Singaporean Professional Migrants in China." In David W. Haines, Keiko Yamanaka, and Shinji Yamashita. *Wind over Water: Migration in an East Asian Context.* New York: Berghahn, 2012, pp. 219–228, p. 221.

19 Yeoh, Brenda, and Katie Willis. "Singaporeans in China: Transnational Women Elites and the Negotiation of Gendered Identities." *Geoforum* 36.2 (2005): 211–222.

20 Yeoh and Willis 2005.

21 Yeoh, Brenda, and Weiqiang Lin. "Rapid Growth in Singapore's Immigrant Population Brings Policy Challenges." *Migration Information Source.* April 3, 2012. www.migrationpolicy.org/article/rapid-growth-singapores-immigrant-population-brings-policy-challenges/ <retrieved June 5, 2014>

22 Yeoh and Lin 2012.

23 Colwell, Jessica. "China Census: Foreign Demographics in Shanghai." *Shanghaiist.* September 23, 2011. http://shanghaiist.com/2011/09/23/china_census_foreigners_make_up_1_o.php <retrieved March 8, 2014>; Yinbi, Ni. "Shanghai Reports 6.7% Rise in Expat Population." *ShanghaiDaily.com.* January 9, 2013. www.shanghaidaily.com/Metro/expat-community/Shanghai-reports-67-rise-in-expat-population/shdaily.shtml <retrieved March 8, 2014>

24 Tseng, Yen-Fen. "Shanghai Rush: Skilled Migrants in a Fantasy City." *Journal of Ethnic and Migration Studies* 37.5 (2011): 765–784, p. 771.

25 Tseng 2011: 769.

26 In Australia, workers come on 457 visas, which allow them to switch sponsors unconditionally. In the United States, though, workers on H1-B visas are tithed to their employer; if they lose their job, they lose their visa, though the worker can search for another employer to sponsor them on the H1-B or attempt to change to an altogether different visa (Xiang, Biao. *Global "Body Shopping": An Indian Labor System in the Information Technology Industry*. Princeton, NJ: Princeton UP, 2007, p. 82).

27 Thibodeau, Patrick, and Sharon Machlis. "The Data Shows: Top H-1B Users Are Offshore Outsourcers." *Computerworld*. February 14, 2013. www.computerworld.com/s/article/9236732/The_data_shows_Top_H_1B_users_are_offshore_outsourcers <retrieved January 17, 2014>

28 Khimm, Suzy. "Do We Need More Skilled Foreign Workers?" *The Washington Post*. March 21, 2013. www.washingtonpost.com/blogs/wonkblog/wp/2013/03/21/do-we-need-more-skilled-foreign-workers/ <retrieved April 1, 2013>

29 Harkinson, Josh. "How H1-B Visas Are Screwing Tech Workers," *Mother Jones*, February 22, 2013. www.motherjones.com/politics/2013/02/silicon-valley-h1b-visas-hurt-tech-workers <retrieved April 3, 2013>; Matloff, Norman. "Are Foreign Students the 'Best and Brightest'?" *Economic Policy Institute*. February 28, 2013. www.epi.org/publication/bp356-foreign-students-best-brightest-immigration-policy/ <retrieved April 3, 2013>

30 Colic-Peisker, Val. "Free Floating in the Cosmopolis? Exploring the Identity-belonging of Transnational Knowledge Workers." *Global Networks* 10.4 (2010): 467–488.

4

ASSIMILATION OF SECOND-
GENERATION IMMIGRANTS

The last two chapters mainly dealt with migrants who either have little chance to stay in their host countries permanently, and/or have no real desire to stay permanently. These next few chapters look more closely at legal migrants and their children who are more likely to stay permanently. These adult, first-generation migrants, and their children, or second-generation immigrants, are more firmly entrenched and have few of the fears or dilemmas that the short-term laborers and professionals we met in the previous chapters experience.[1]

The broad questions we ask here are the following: How do these migrants make their way in a place that legally (at least) is their home? To what degree do they integrate or assimilate to the "mainstream"? And how and why does assimilation vary between individuals?

We pay particular attention to the adult second generation, the children of migrants who were born in or brought to the country at an early age. We focus on adult experiences, and largely ignore children because, well, children change their behaviors and choices over time, sometimes radically. Things are a bit clearer and settled (though not completely) as people enter adulthood. We also largely ignore first-generation migrants who arrive as adults as they are not the true test or focus of assimilation. If they assimilate, great, and if they don't, we shouldn't be surprised since they're spending their time working, possibly speak poor or no English (or French or German, etc.), and probably don't have time to engage in the social aspects of assimilation.

Classical Assimilation Theory

What is assimilation? Most scholars take it to mean two things, especially becoming culturally similar—though not necessarily completely—to "natives" (cultural assimilation, or acculturation), and being educationally and economically upwardly mobile (economic assimilation).

Classical conceptions of assimilation assumed assimilation would follow a straight line, where after a few generations of native-born children, all traces of ethnicity and difference would disappear, and the descendants of immigrants would become like middle-class, white Protestants.[2] That is, they would become proper Americans.

In his landmark 1964 book, *Assimilation in American Life*, Milton Gordon made the important distinction between cultural assimilation (acculturation) and structural assimilation. Structural assimilation "refers to the entrance of immigrants and their descendants into the social cliques, organizations, institutional activities, and general civic life of the receiving society."[3] According to Gordon, two main modes of structural assimilation occur, involving what he calls primary and secondary relationships. The former are "warm, intimate, and personal"—friendships, social clubs, home visits, communal worship, etc. The latter are "impersonal and segmental"—wage labor, schools, political responsibilities—generally instrumental behavior. Acculturation on the other hand, "refers to the absorption of the cultural behavior patterns [by the immigrant] of the 'host' society."[4]

For Gordon, acculturation is essentially inevitable. The key to assimilation, however, is structural acceptance, which is not inevitable. But if and once minority groups enter into the social cliques, clubs, and institutions of the core society at the primary group level, this will inevitably lead to substantial intermarriage. As that happens, the minority group loses its ethnic identity, and they will be fully assimilated and basically indistinguishable.[5]

While assimilation was the dominant means of studying ethnic groups in the United States at the time, it was not the only way. A year before Gordon set out his vision of immigrants and their relationship to the American mainstream in his book, Nathan Glazer and Daniel Patrick Moynihan wrote a nearly-as-influential book, *Beyond the*

Melting Pot: The Negroes, Jews, Italians, and Irish of New York City. In this book, they argued there wasn't really a mainstream to assimilate to, and group identity remained important for these various groups for politics and culture in New York City. Contrary to Gordon, they saw ethnic difference as the primary American pattern, even among white ethnic groups, rather than assimilation.[6]

The discussion around assimilation in the United States up through the 1960s revolved around working-class European immigrants and their children, and that too from a rather limited number of countries. Nathan Glazer, reflecting on *The Melting Pot* almost 35 years after its publication, said that in New York City the problem of immigrants in schools was essentially the "Italian" problem. Glazer's New York compared to today was "a much more homogeneous city, a city of the European immigrants and their children, working class and lower middle class, with a relatively small native elite."[7]

Very soon after the publication of these landmark books, the United States passed the Immigration and Nationality Act (also known as the Hart-Celler Act) in 1965, which revived mass immigration, which had been largely halted by the Immigration Act of 1924. (Though there was a great deal of migration from Mexico from the 1940s to mid-1960s, about 500,000 migrants a year, of which 450,000 were temporary agricultural laborers, while 50,000 were permanent migrants.) So from 1924 to 1965, there was very little new immigration of Europeans to revive the Italian, Irish, Slavic, and other European ethnic neighborhoods and communities in cities and towns around the country. No one expected more than a few thousand Europeans a year would come as a result of the 1965 act. And not that many Europeans came. But, unexpectedly, thousands, then tens of thousands, then hundreds of thousands of new, darker-skinned immigrants from the developing world began to come into the country yearly, and mass migration to the United States reached levels in the 1990s not seen since the late 1800s. While in pre-1965 New York City (and elsewhere) Irish, Italians, and Jews were numerically predominant among immigrants, today immigrants come from all over the world, and no group dominates numerically in such a manner.

Segmented Assimilation Theory

The question that began to develop a quarter century after the publication of Gordon's and Glazer and Moynihan's books and the passage of the 1965 Immigration Act was will the children of the new, darker-skinned immigrants assimilate as easily? By the early 1990s, poor and working-class migrants, especially from Mexico and other parts of Central America and the Caribbean, had become numerically predominant among migrants to the United States.

In 1992, in the midst of a recession, high crime, and the crack epidemic in the United States, Herbert Gans proposed that many second-generation immigrants, specifically the darker-skinned ones, were at risk of downward mobility.[8] Quickly on Gans's heels, Alejandro Portes and Min Zhou built on this idea, publishing their defining statement on what they called segmented assimilation theory.[9] They argued that not all immigrants are upwardly mobile, many immigrants will be downwardly mobile and assimilate to the underclass, and that economic assimilation to the "mainstream" is not inevitable. They also argued that earlier generations of European migrants had it easier because the manufacturing economy at the time allowed for greater upward mobility, as factory jobs, especially in the period between the end of World War II and recession in the 1970s, paid well and there were more opportunities generally, even for people without college or sometimes high school degrees, to move to the middle class as the economy during this time expanded dramatically. Also, these earlier immigrants were white. (Or, we should say, became white. Initially, they were considered racially distinct from established whites of Northern and Western European stock. We examine this in Chapter 6.)

They argue the largely nonwhite children of post-1965 immigrants are more likely to face discrimination based on race or cultural differences. And as the manufacturing economy, with its relatively well-paid factory jobs, gave way to a service-based economy, it became harder to find good paying jobs if one did not have a college education. So the jobs that provided the ladder for vast numbers of the children of pre-1965 immigrants to enter the middle class were not there to provide the same assist for post-1965 immigrants and their children.

Segmented assimilation theorists define and measure economic assimilation by educational and occupational success, or conversely define failure as dropping out of school, low academic performance, arrests or being jailed, and teen pregnancy. They put forward the idea that some people assimilate upwards, some stay in the same economic range as their parents, and some are downwardly mobile into the underclass. Why? Portes and his various colleagues propose a handful of reasons. First are parental effects including parent's education level and occupation (what sociologists call human capital), and family structure (single parent or two parents, multigenerational or nuclear family). Then there is the strength of ties within the ethnic community. Also important is the context of reception for the group in the country, or how the ethnic group is treated socially—for instance, are members of that group more or less likely to face racism and discrimination (Haitians more, Chinese less). Context of reception also refers to how the ethnic group is treated by the government—for instance Cuban, Russian, and Vietnamese refugees from communist regimes got a lot of governmental help, while Salvadorans fleeing US-sponsored violence in the 1980s were treated harshly if they came without documents.[10]

Another critical factor in segmented assimilation theory is acculturating patterns and interactions *between parents and child*. There are three types of acculturating patterns among families across first and second generations: consonant, dissonant, and selective acculturation. For segmented assimilation theorists, acculturation is important to the degree that it affects assimilation. Consonant acculturation occurs when both child and parents gradually abandon the home language and culture and "Americanize" at roughly the same pace. This pattern is likely to occur when the parents have greater resources such as higher income and educational levels, and it usually leads to upward mobility. Dissonant acculturation is where the child learns the English language and American ways faster than his or her parents. This is more likely when the parents' educational and economic resources are limited. Fast and full acculturation of these working-class and poor children will lead to either stagnation or downward mobility. The third type is selective acculturation, where both parents and child are embedded in a co-ethnic community. This promotes partial retention of the parents' home language and norms in such a way that the cultural shift to American norms slows down. Selective acculturation is further associated with having more co-ethnic friends, which they say is dependent upon parents' human capital and the strength of ties within the ethnic group.[11] (We'll have much more to say about the importance of parents later.) Selective acculturation should lead to being bicultural and bilingual, and they find this to be the best approach for upward mobility.

"New" Assimilation Theory

While segmented assimilation theory has dominated for almost two decades, it has come under attack, especially by Richard Alba and Victor Nee's "new" assimilation theory.[12] They did away with classical assimilation theory's idea that immigrants would move toward Anglo-conformity, that is, becoming "white" and middle class and moving to the mainstream. Alba and Nee argue the mainstream changes just as immigrants do, as social boundaries between whites and nonwhites, natives and foreigners shift, get blurred, and get crossed. They define assimilation as "the decline of an ethnic distinction and its corollary cultural and social differences," though they add, assimilation "does not require the disappearance of ethnicity, and the individuals undergoing it may still bear a number of ethnic markers."[13] Here we see clearly their break from the underlying assumption of classical assimilation theory that implicitly linked assimilating with becoming white.

For Alba and Nee, assimilation is the product of immediate causes such as human and financial capital possessed by individuals' parents and ethnic groups. The ethnic groups, especially if they are close-knit, can monitor and enforce norms. (Which members of the group monitor and enforce the norms, they don't say—an important point we will return to later.)

But more important are deeper, institutional arrangements. What they mean is that the assimilating behavior of groups is a result of how they are treated by the government and in the labor market.[14] Before the American civil rights movement and laws of the 1960s, many groups, like the Japanese pre-World War II, had to turn inward and build a parallel society because of racism and segregation laws, such as one that denied Japanese the right to own property. Their "non-assimilation" was forced on them—it was not out of choice. This sounds very much like segmented assimilation theory. Except that Alba and Nee insist that discrimination today, while still prevalent, is nothing like it was until the 1960s, and that laws passed at that time make overt, blanket discrimination impossible. So unlike segmented assimilation theory, which predicts that a negative context of reception, like racism, will affect downward mobility, new assimilation theory is saying racism is actually not as prevalent as before. Therefore assimilation is more likely, and conversely, downward assimilation is not so likely.

Interestingly, their causal variables are similar to those of segmented assimilation theory. Both argue that parents and ethnic group ties are important in understanding assimilation, as is how the state and labor markets treat people. The major bone of contention between these approaches is not *how* assimilation happens, but rather differences in interpreting the degree of actual assimilation. New assimilation theory, unlike segmented assimilation, finds that the second generation is overall doing well, especially when compared to their parents, in terms of educational achievement and income. They feel that segmented assimilation places too much emphasis on the underclass and downward mobility and that segmented assimilation is unnecessarily pessimistic.[15] So new and segmented assimilation theorists largely agree on the causes of assimilation, and they agree on what it means to be assimilated—they just disagree on the degree to which the second generation is actually assimilated.

This question of how well the second generation is doing is difficult to resolve, as is the question of whether they are as susceptible to downward mobility as segmented assimilation fears. Alejandro Portes and Ruben Rumbaut conducted a large-scale longitudinal survey in three stages (1992 at age 14, 1995–1996, 2001–2003) of various second-generation immigrants groups in Miami and San Diego. They found, as predicted in segmented assimilation theory, that some second-generation groups are more prone to downward mobility, like Haitians, Mexicans, and West Indians, and the ones that are upwardly mobile, like Cubans, Chinese, and Koreans, tend to selectively acculturate and have parents with higher levels of human capital.[16] The context of reception for the latter groups is also more positive than it is for the former.

Following Portes and Rumbaut's huge survey, Philip Kasinitz and his colleagues conducted a massive survey of adult second-generation immigrants in New York City in 1998–2000, with respondents whose ages were between 18 and 32, to examine assimilation outcomes.[17] Like Alba and Nee concluded above, they found that whether their parents are poor or professional, the second-generation adult children—Chinese, Russian Jews, South Americans, Dominicans, and West Indians—are generally doing as well or better academically and occupationally than their parents. Unlike Portes and colleagues who don't see much movement to the middle, Kasinitz and his colleagues find that many of these young adults are moving into the middle class, especially among black West Indians, helped in part by affirmative action and other government programs. This seems to refute a central point of segmented assimilation theory that those from groups experiencing discrimination—like West Indians and South Americans—are less likely to experience mobility and indeed more likely to be downwardly mobile. Maurice Crul and his various associates have also found that Turkish and Moroccan second-generation immigrants in Western Europe are doing as well or better than their parents, even though they are doing poorly in terms of education and occupation relative to native-born white Europeans.[18] But Portes and his colleagues challenge such conclusions, saying for some groups the parents' education and income levels are so low that their children have nowhere to go but up, even if they are high school dropouts. So relative to their parents, of course their education levels will be greater.[19]

Well, who is right? Both camps make strong, convincing theoretical arguments, and they draw on solid empirical data. Likely, both are right; it just depends on how you frame your questions, which group or groups you're looking at, and where. (Again, Portes and Rumbaut did their survey in Miami and San Diego starting during the crack epidemic, high crime rates and economic recession of the early 1990s, while Kasinitz and his colleagues did theirs in New York City from 1998 to 2000 when the economy was better, crime was much lower, and the city was much more "livable" than it was in the early 1990s.) This is a hotly contested question that will likely take years to resolve (if ever), and probably awaits the growth of the third generation into adulthood. Again though, we want to stress that while their empirical findings diverge in terms of assimilation prospects for various groups, the variables that they use to understand assimilation are very similar.

Third Generation

And what of the third generation? What will their assimilation trajectory look like? Will they retain their ethnic identity? Herbert Gans, in a 1979 article, developed the idea of "symbolic ethnicity," which he used to describe life situations where the individual makes ethnic choices that have little or no social repercussions. Gans developed this idea with regard to third- and fourth-generation descendants of white, European ethnic immigrants in the United States, who have intermarried so much that there aren't that many "pure" Irish, Italians, Polish, etc. of third or later generations left in the country. This idea of symbolic ethnicity refers to individuals who use ethnic symbols and "feel" ethnic, but are not connected to groups. So, for example, Irishness is no longer about living in Irish neighborhoods (as there are hardly any left in the United States) or having an Irish (or Irish-American) spouse, but rather about celebrating the symbols of Irishness, like St. Patrick's Day and Guinness beer.[20]

What makes this symbolic ethnicity possible? When ethnicity is not a basis of determining life chances, when economic or political resources cannot be acquired or denied based on one's inherited identity, the prominence of group identity will diminish. There are little practical costs or benefits—like being victims of racism or beneficiaries of affirmative action—accruing to white ethnics in the United States by maintaining their particular ethnicities.

It is too early to tell if the third generation of the post-1965 immigrants will show symbolic ethnicity the way third- and fourth-generation European immigrants have, as the third generation is still for the most part quite young. There is one non-European immigrant group, Mexicans, that does have an adult third and fourth generation that provides a good comparison. A study of third- and fourth-generation Mexicans in California found that many are middle class (that is, economically assimilated), culturally assimilated, and live in integrated neighborhoods.[21] Many identify themselves as white. But there is a great range of patterns of assimilation, acculturation, and self-identification. Many others identify as Mexican American or Latino, rather than as just "American." For some, their identity is not "merely" symbolic, as they are still engaged with working-class Mexicans and Mexican Americans of various generations and they also feel the pinch of discrimination and exclusion from whites. The preponderance of first-generation Mexicans of undocumented status may stigmatize all Mexicans in a way that also leads to social exclusion and marginalization of many third- and fourth-generation Mexican Americans.

Unlike Gans's European ethnics, there is a cost to being of Mexican descent that does not allow ethnicity for many to fade. But for others, they are far removed from working-class Mexican communities and networks, and their "Mexicanness" does take on the characteristics that Gans outlines for symbolic ethnicity. Working-class third- and fourth-generation Mexicans on the other hand are more likely to be in Mexican communities and segregated neighborhoods, and thus less likely to have symbolic ethnicity. Their ethnic identity is very real and has repercussions for how they live their lives.

The incoming stream of new Mexican migrants often helps third- and fourth-generation Mexican immigrants to maintain ties to Mexican communities. This differs from the earlier European migrants who had little new blood coming from 1924 on. This meant that for the second and then third and fourth generations, their community ties necessarily weakened as the communities began to disintegrate due to individuals moving out of the neighborhoods and marrying outside their group. This is not the case for Mexicans, or for other post-1965 immigrants, whose oldest third-generation children are largely still quite young. But, if the US Congress were to pass a restrictive law similar to the 1924 act, it could radically change things. You just never know.

Western European Approaches to Assimilation

Like the United States, some Western European nations have long been immigrant-receiving states. For example, from the mid-19th century, great numbers of Irish were migrating to the United Kingdom, and Poles and Italians went to Germany and France, respectively, from the late 19th century.

At the time, these immigrants were seen as dangerous due to their political, religious, and social characteristics and faced social exclusion and xenophobic reactions from natives. Italians in France integrated quickly in the first generation through intermarriage and taking of citizenship, largely "vanishing" as a distinct group. The Irish and Poles took much longer to integrate in the United Kingdom and Germany. They lived in ethnic neighborhoods, developed ethnic subcultures, and had separate churches. They were also highly stigmatized and discriminated against, which encouraged them to further develop various ethnic-based institutions. This separate living situation was true even for the second generation, which began to change only with the third generations. Even for the third generation in the time after World War II, many people were stigmatized and considered alien.[22]

World War II of course devastated Western Europe. As Western Europe was rebuilding and Western European countries' economies started rebounding in the 1950s, they required a much larger labor force to fill unskilled and low skilled manufacturing, construction, and other low-level jobs than was available domestically. Much of the labor for the richer northern European countries came from southern Europe— Italians moved to Switzerland and Portuguese moved to France, among other flows of people. But internal European movement was not enough to fill labor demand. The United Kingdom had a rather open policy toward migrants from its former colonies (especially Jamaica, India, and Pakistan) until 1962, as did France (with Algeria and Morocco), and other Western European states entered into agreements with countries to bring in labor migrants, especially from Turkey.

By the 1960s, as the United States was beginning to open its doors again to migrants, this time from the developing world, Europe already had a sizeable population of migrants. By the 1970s, as European economies contracted, the need for these migrants had dwindled as unemployment rose, and new labor migration largely ceased as these countries stopped their policies of importing labor. It was thought these workers would come, work, and then go home. And a great number of these workers did return home. But many others decided that in spite of the recession European countries faced in the 1970s, they did not want to leave. So they stayed. Many of them brought their wives and children from abroad, or they married women from their homelands and had children and brought them. Today, there is a large second generation of non-European immigrants growing up all over Western Europe.

These second-generation immigrants are today often seen as refusing to culturally assimilate. Also, because the first generation is largely poor or working class, the second generation is seen as economically unable to assimilate and thus a drain upon Europe's resources.[23] But the reality of course is more complex. For instance, a study of professional, college-educated second-generation French whose parents are Muslims from Algeria, Tunisia, and Morocco found that by traditional measures, these people could be considered culturally and economically assimilated as they speak French, consider themselves to be French, were educated in French schools, are French citizens, and have succeeded in their educations and in getting professional occupations.[24] But they have only achieved "partial assimilation," not in the sense of segmented assimilation where they slow the pace of acculturation, but rather because of widespread racism and social exclusion from the majority population. Essentially, these second-generation immigrants, born and reared in France are not, and cannot "really" be French as they are not white.

This study is particularly useful because it focuses on an interesting (and largely ignored) subsection of the second-generation European population, the upwardly mobile ones and shows how assimilation, besides what you do, is also dependent upon how the people you are assimilating to react to you. Yes, segmented assimilation theory also looks at this. But segmented assimilation doesn't talk much about how people with human capital (that is, they're highly educated) can be blocked from assimilation. Their focus on blocked assimilation is of people with lesser degrees of human capital.

As interesting as the above study is, it can't answer the question of how the second generation in France is doing, let alone elsewhere in Western Europe. This is a shortcoming of ethnographies in general, because they focus on the local. There is however a massive Western Europe-wide survey (The Integration of European Second Generation, or TIES) conducted in 2007 that is helping to answer this question. The survey looked at assimilation patterns of second-generation Turks, Moroccans, and former Yugoslavs throughout Western Europe. Just looking at Turks, the first generation is largely rural, and has little formal education—similar to first-generation Mexicans in the United States. But the second-generation Turkish children overall are doing better than their parents. The vast majority across Europe has done apprenticeships or upper secondary schooling, with a great number being university educated. However, an alarming number of Turks drop out of school early.[25] Those with low levels of schooling are not surprisingly largely in unskilled and skilled manual labor. Those who completed an apprenticeship or upper secondary education are for the most part in skilled positions. And then there are those who completed university who tend to be in professional jobs, though an unusually high number of them are in "merely" skilled jobs. This is especially so in Belgium and Sweden, where many Turks are working at jobs far below their educational levels.[26]

The picture of Turks is very complex, and there are too many nations and cities that TIES deals with for us to go into detail here. (And we haven't even said a word on second-generation Moroccans or former Yugoslavs.) The broader point is studies of TIES' results bear out new assimilation theory: The second generation is largely doing alright, especially in comparison with their parents.

In spite of having such a long history with non-European migration, and an even longer history of southern and eastern Europeans moving north and west, European scholars never developed their own independent theories of immigrant assimilation. In fact, few Europeans scholars use the term *assimilation,* which for them has a negative connotation. Many prefer the term *integration,* while some also study first- and second-generation immigrants using the framework of race or ethnic relations. While the terms differ, European scholars are largely concerned with the same things American researchers of assimilation look at—educational achievement and economic outcomes, self-identification, segregation from natives, local language familiarity, etc.[27]

Recently, Maurice Crul (who led the TIES survey) and Jens Schneider have developed what they call comparative integration context theory.[28] Their model seeks to explain differences across countries, for instance, why Turks have better educational outcomes in France than Germany. The idea here is that participating in social organizations and belonging to local communities is dependent on integration contexts, such as institutional arrangements in education, labor markets, housing, religion, and legislation. They argue that differences in social and political contexts—including the reactions of natives, politicians, and the media—are crucial for examining social and cultural participation and belonging. They view "success" of the second generation to be the result of favorable social/cultural, educational, and occupational contexts, while "failure" results from hostile reception and obstacles. Their theoretical statement is still fairly new, and it will be interesting to see how it will shape the research program of immigration scholars in the near future.

The Importance of Peers in the Assimilation Process

There has been an explosion of research on assimilation and acculturation of the second generation in the United States in the past 20 years, and more recently in Western Europe. Broadly, the most influential studies (mostly by survey researchers but also a good number by qualitative researchers), largely guided by either segmented or new assimilation theories, examine differences *between* immigrant groups, and between immigrants and native-born, non-immigrants.

The goal of these scholars is to explain how and why immigrants assimilate, though the way they structure their arguments, they can explain differences between groups, but not within groups. That is, they can't account for how *individuals* assimilate. Few studies of assimilation report *within-group* differences: why for instance some second-generation Jamaican immigrants in New York City or London become doctors while others become high school dropouts. In the most important quantitative and qualitative studies, nearly all the variables usually used to explain variation—including nationality, religion, race, context of reception, and experiences of discrimination for the group—are best at addressing between-group differences, such as why Chinese on average are better off than Hmong in the United States, or why Turks are worse off than Surinamese in the Netherlands. But these variables are not useful for explaining within-group differences, as they are essentially constants when looking within groups. The most common variables in explaining differences in assimilation at the individual level are parents' educational attainment, income, occupational status, and family structure. However, it is unlikely that family effects by themselves can adequately explain assimilation outcomes at the individual level.

To properly explain how individuals assimilate, you need variables that work at the individual level (besides family-level variables), rather than at the group level, and the questions you ask have to reflect that. For instance, how do you explain variation within a family? None of the theories we just discussed can explain why within one family, the oldest son fully Americanizes (or Britishicizes or Frenchifies), the middle daughter mixes some of her ethnic heritage with American culture, and the youngest daughter goes from being highly acculturated to rejecting American culture and only identifying with her parents' culture.

In the above example, all the variables that segmented and new assimilation theories say are important—context of reception, nationality, religion, race, and family-level variables—are constants; that is, they apply equally to all the children. But what about age and gender differences? Ok, those could play a role. So let's take another example. How do you explain the divergent outcomes of two identical twins, second-generation Chinese immigrant brothers, where one becomes a doctor and the other joins a gang? Now age and gender are constants. All the variables that scholars usually focus on are now held constant, so by definition, they cannot explain the variation between these brothers. But there has to be another variable that can account for the divergent outcome of these brothers.

Ali proposes that one's peers—in the past and present—will greatly affect variations in cultural and economic assimilation, perhaps even more than the effect of parents, and that the effects of peers is independent from that of parents. A person's peers affect who they are and what they do—as peers are the ones with whom we spend most of our time from a young age. And they're the ones whose opinions of us really matter into young adulthood (and beyond), in that their opinions are more likely to shape our behaviors and opinions than those of our parents.[29] To phrase it in terms of assimilation, if a person "hangs out" with people who are acculturated or economically assimilated, he or she is more likely to be like them in terms of their behavior (acculturation) and end up in similar economic circumstances (economic assimilation).[30]

Strangely, the effect of peers finds little emphasis in the immigration literature. This is odd because peers are central to the study of outcomes of adolescence and young adulthood such as educational achievement, dating, violent behavior, delinquency, and criminal behavior, substance abuse, obesity, and mental health.[31] These are the same topics that immigration scholars study. Unlike in assimilation theories, peers are often treated as having an independent effect from parents. This is important because, generally, parents don't *directly* affect choices of peers. Parents' education and income affect economic class, the neighborhoods their children live in, and the types of schools they go to, and parents give their children their color of skin, ethnicity, and religion. These characteristics of parents, those they achieve and those they are born with, and the resources they give their children, may shape the *pool* of their children's possible peers, but not whom they actually end up with as peers. A quick thought experiment will illustrate: Are you friends with people because your parents chose them, or told you to be friends with them? Did you ever stop being friends with someone just because your parents told you to? For some of you, yes, but our guess is for the vast majority of readers the answer to these questions is no.

The point here is to show that peers are a necessary part of the explanation of many of the outcomes that segmented and new assimilation theories are concerned with. Given that, it is odd that peers are absent from new assimilation theory, and have at best a secondary place in segmented assimilation theory, where they are seen as reflecting parental and ethnic group effects. In segmented assimilation theory, children who become involved with drugs and gangs are seen as doing so because of a lack of parental and/or ethnic community social capital and control over children, *rather than* being due to peer choices children make independent of parents or ethnic community.[32]

In many landmark qualitative studies of immigration, peer effects are absent from scholars' arguments, but are readily apparent in the stories they tell. Let us give three examples from highly influential studies in the field. The first and most recent is from Min Zhou, one of the developers of segmented assimilation theory. Zhou and her colleagues in a recent study described the plight of Rodolfo, a second-generation Mexican man who joined a gang, got into trouble with the police, was nearly deported for being undocumented, and at 20, worked long hours for low wages. They report that Rodolfo said "if he could turn back time, he would have stayed in school and away from gangs—a path adopted by his older sister, who is now in college and aspires to become an immigration lawyer."[33]

Rodolfo, when talking about gangs is emphasizing the effects and importance of peers. But Zhou and her colleagues' analysis of Rodolfo's woes does not mention peers, and they skip over any analysis of what concretely may have led him to join a gang. They say matter-of-factly: "Alienated, and seeking a sense of belonging, Rodolfo turned to the streets and joined a gang." Why? They don't say. Their overall analysis of his story derives from the standard tenets of segmented assimilation theory: "From the very start, he had numerous odds stacked against him—low parental human and economic capital and unauthorized migration status."[34] But these stacked odds worked against his sister as well, and yet she seems to be succeeding.

Zhou and her colleagues' theoretical stance comes through clearly in the way they ignore the sister, whose life seems to dramatically diverge from Rodolfo's. Rodolfo and his sister share ethnicity and parents—critical variables that segmented assimilation theory sees as central are essentially held constant. They both also came as undocumented migrants with their parents from Mexico. So what differs between them? Gender and peers, the latter Rodolfo himself emphasizes when he says he should have stayed away from gangs. But Zhou and her colleagues ignore how this vignette demonstrates that peers are an important explanatory variable.

The non-importance of peers in the above study is especially interesting here because in Zhou's earlier work with second-generation Vietnamese in New Orleans (work she did with Carl Bankston III), she shows how central peers actually are to the assimilation process. She and Bankston wrote in 1997: "[P]eer groups are more important direct influences on the [cultural] adaptation of young Vietnamese Americans than are individual and family characteristics."[35] This sounds like what we're arguing, right? But, and this is where we differ, they emphatically emphasize that which peers kids choose is *directly* dependent on certain family-level effects, which they say lends support to segmented assimilation theory. We dispute this, as we find it more likely that parents' effects on peer choice is indirect at most. This is an important distinction we will come to in a bit.

Another landmark study in the field that empirically points to the centrality of peers is of Punjabi Sikh high school students in rural California. The conceptual argument in this study stresses the importance of parents and culture upon the children's educational achievement, but much of the empirical data point to the importance of peers. For example, "teachers cited the importance of peer pressure in bringing deviant students back into line. Punjabi students, one shop teacher observed, competed with one another for good grades, teased those who did poorly, *and placed pressure on one another to uphold Punjabi standards of behavior*" (emphasis added).[36] These Punjabi standards of behavior of course originate with the parents. But the shop teacher makes it clear that it's not the parents who are important here. The kids themselves put pressure on each other to get good grades and act Punjabi, not American. This point resonates with much research on the educational outcomes of the second generation. For example, while many Caribbean and Mexican parents have high aspirations for their children, the children often purposely do not succeed as success in school is often seen as "acting white," something unacceptable among their peers.[37] This is a phenomena widely studied among black students in the United States.[38] Conversely, while Punjabi parents may insist on good grades, it is their children who pressure each other and compete to achieve higher grades.[39]

The third example of the importance of peers comes from a study of ethnic identity choices of second-generation black Caribbean immigrant students in New York City, which shows the influence of peers at different points, especially when discussing the idea of "acting white."[40] One student illustrated peer influence beautifully when she said: "When I'm at school and I sit with my black friends and, sometimes I'm ashamed to say this, but my accent changes. I learn all the words. I switch. Well, when I'm with my friends, I say I'm black, black American. When I'm with my Haitian-American friends, I say I'm Haitian. Well, my being black, I guess that puts me when I'm with black Americans, it makes people think that I'm lower class . . . Then, if I'm talking like this [regular voice] with my friends at school, they call me white."[41] While this study gives different examples of the centrality of peers upon behavior of second-generation black immigrants, the interpretation of their ethnic choices focuses on parents, economic class, and generalized notions of race relations in the United States. The idea that who your friends are affects who you are is present in the empirical descriptions, but does not come through clearly in the argument, as peer influence does not figure in the study's theoretical formulation as an important variable that affects behavior.

Ali, taking inspiration from research and theories on peers outside of the immigration literature,[42] conducted two studies that look directly at the effect of peers on acculturation and economic assimilation of adult, second-generation immigrants in the United States and Europe. In the first, he explored how status concerns are useful for understanding acculturation of adult, second-generation South Asian Muslims in New York City. Their peers include immigrants and non-immigrants, co-ethnics and non-co-ethnics, coreligionists and non-coreligionists. These peers have a strong (sometimes, conflicting) influence upon the acculturating behavior patterns of individuals, as there are different status groups the individual is associated with, and each status group may have different norms to which he or she will conform (or deviate from).[43] Also, acculturation is not a "one-time-only" affair. It is continually negotiated, and patterns of self-identification and integration into different groups may vary over the individual's lifetime.

Ali describes three major patterns of acculturation. One is full acculturation along the lines of classical assimilation where individuals largely "Americanize." They tended to have more native rather than co-ethnics friends. A second pattern is partial acculturation, where individuals mix and match their ethnic ways with facets of being American. They tended to have a mix of native and co-ethnic (largely other second-generation, rather than first-generation) friends, often having more co-ethnic than native friends. A third is "de-acculturation," where individuals who are either fully or partially acculturated decide as a result of hanging out with religious Muslims that they will no longer engage in "American" behaviors, like dating, drinking, etc.

A fourth much less common pattern is nonacculturation, where the individual or group decides not to acculturate to American cultural behaviors, and indeed does not engage in any kinds of primary social ties with natives (or primary structural assimilation, in Milton Gordon's terms). One conspicuous group in the United States is Hasidic Jews. They maintain their own institutions, including crucially their own schools, they marry exclusively amongst themselves, work in select occupations and firms, and mainly live in a handful of neighborhoods in New York City and in towns in New York State. They do not socialize with, let alone date or marry, others, even non-Hasidic Jews.

Ali found parents had no effect on these acculturating patterns, and that the strong co-ethnics ties that segmented and new assimilation theory trumpet are only important if these ties are of peers, not of relatives or other adults. Even more interestingly, for the third type, many became increasingly religious *irrespective of* the level of parents' religiosity. Girls and young women who started wearing the hijab (headscarf) or jilbab (full body cloak) generally did so because of the influence of friends, and many did so *in spite of* parental pressure not to do so. On the face of it, these look similar to the patterns of acculturation that Portes and his colleagues spell out. But Ali's "ideal types" are missing their most important causal ingredient: parents.

In the second study, Ali and Tineke Fokkema examined the TIES survey of second-generation, adult Turkish immigrants throughout Western Europe.[44] Ali and Fokkema wanted to see what effect peers have on both acculturation and economic assimilation. They found that parents' economic and educational background was important for both, as segmented and new assimilation theories both predict. But they also found that the more native peers an individual had in the past and present, the more acculturated they were. Further, the more highly educated their friends were, the better off they were economically.

The importance of peers held across countries and cities with different approaches to assimilation and multiculturalism, and where Turks had very different patterns of acculturation and assimilation. This qualifies the assertion made by Crul and Schneider's comparative integration context theory that the country context matters. It does, but just for explaining why some groups do better in one country rather than another, for instance, why second-generation Turks have on average higher educational levels in Sweden than in Germany. So yes, the amount of educational achievement and upward mobility varied between countries. But that doesn't tell us why there would be variation *within* a country. Ali and Fokkema found that for individuals, it doesn't matter which city or country they lived in, but parents and peers were both important for explaining acculturation and assimilation. However, they also believe that the effects of parents on assimilation could be inflated and the effects of peers understated, as the TIES survey didn't have that many or particularly good questions that could address the effects of peers. They felt that if there were more and better questions, the effect of peers would have been stronger.

While studies of peers and social/cultural/educational facets of assimilation are slowly increasing,[45] studies of peers and labor market outcomes are precious few. In addition to Ali and Fokkema's study, one recent study of interest by Frank Kalter found that for second-generation Turks having more German friends greatly raised the odds of obtaining a skilled-market position. On the other hand, a lack of contact with native-born German peers greatly accounted for their disadvantage in the labor market.[46] Kalter examined whether having German friends was cause or consequence of economic mobility. He found strong evidence that it was actually causal—that having German friends led to upward mobility. He then tested the idea that having German friends was a *consequence* of economic mobility. That is, it could be that if you're already an upwardly mobile Turk that would put you in a position to make more native German friends. That sounds reasonable, right? Well, Kalter found little evidence to support this idea.[47]

This last study gives the impression that what's important in determining economic outcomes is having *native* peers. But for economic assimilation, that is, achieving higher levels of education and middle-class economic status, hanging out with second-generation co-ethnics can be beneficial if those peers are high achievers academically.[48] Sometimes native whites, who generally rank higher educationally and economically than other groups in the West, are lower status because they don't achieve to the same degree educationally as second-generation immigrants. This is the case in Cupertino, a town in Silicon Valley in California where three-fourths of the population are professionals, and two-thirds of the town are of Asian origin. Here, native whites are not the "mainstream" reference point for assimilation, other Asians are. The second-generation Asian high school students performed way better in school than the whites, and they define the norms of achievement for everyone. Friendships between whites and Asians are rare. Some white parents have even pulled their kids out of the school because their kids can't keep up.[49]

Again, the important point is not whether your peers are native or not, it's the things they actually do that affect you. For second-generation Turks, having native friends is helpful. For second-generation Asians in Cupertino, native whites could bring them down.

Are Acculturation and Economic Assimilation Inevitable?

The literature on assimilation is very much the story of immigration to the West, especially to the United States. The basic assumption of all these theoretical paradigms discussed is that assimilation is likely. Classical assimilation theory assumed it would happen over time, even if that proved to be a long time. New assimilation theory also predicts that assimilation is the likely outcome for the children of immigrants, though with the twist that they will affect changes in what the cultural "mainstream" is. Even segmented assimilation theory, which protests against the idea that all immigrants will be upwardly mobile, argues that many immigrants will be absorbed into the middle class, others will stagnate in the working class like their parents, or they will be downwardly mobile and be absorbed socially and economically into the lower class. These children of immigrants will eventually become culturally American—the open question is how they will fare economically.

Another idea underlying these theories is about the pace at which group ethnic identity will fade as individuals and groups adapt and assimilate to life in the West. But must it happen this way? Can group identity remain distinct, and individuals truly not assimilate? There are few examples of this in the West (Hasidic Jews in New York being one), but they are relatively rare exceptions. It is better, and more useful, to look at the experiences of groups elsewhere in the world.

There is a separate, distinct literature on diasporas that shows just that. Jews, Chinese, Lebanese, and Indian merchants (among others) throughout the world have maintained distinct communities in places they settled for generations.[50] Partially, this has been because of local laws, for instance those that prohibited Lebanese in Senegal, who have been present there for close to a century, from praying in Senegalese mosques or attending local Islamic schools. After Senegal became independent in 1960, some Lebanese received citizenship. Still, many Lebanese said they "will never feel at home in Senegal," though they are fluent in Wolof and other local languages. Second- and third-generation Lebanese still see themselves very much as Lebanese. There is very little intermarriage between them and other Senegalese by their own choice, and they actively guard against assimilation by reading books from Lebanon in Arabic, reading Lebanese newspapers, listening to Arabic music, and watching Arabic channels on TV. This is very similar to Lebanese in Cote D'Ivoire who, though they may call themselves Ivoirians, think of themselves quite distinct from indigenous Ivoirians, and in fact have a superior sense of themselves and their work habits. They don't seek out social interactions with other Ivoirians and don't intermarry, something that most indigenous Ivoirians resent. They are integrated economically—being businessmen, they are organically linked in the economy—but not socially integrated. They are a part of the society, but live mostly apart.[51]

The situation of Indians in the Persian Gulf is similar to that of Lebanese in Senegal and Cote D'Ivoire. There are many second- and even third-generation Indians in Dubai and Bahrain (and elsewhere in the Persian Gulf) who are still legally foreigners and have Indian nationality, even though some have never been to India.[52] They usually cannot get citizenship in the Persian Gulf countries (except under the rarest of circumstances) and live in these places on temporary visas. Like the Lebanese they are socially excluded in that their children cannot go to schools with citizens, and citizens generally don't socialize with them (and they reciprocate that in turn). Of late, local citizens in Dubai have left many areas where there used to be some residential integration. The result is that where you find Indians (and other foreigners), you will generally not find local citizens.

In spite of such exclusion, Indians are tolerated because they are economically necessary (Indians have been essential traders, shopkeepers, managers, and entrepreneurs in the Persian Gulf since the late 1800s). As a result of their being excluded, they also treat themselves as foreigners. For instance, very few Indians of any generation have even the most basic speaking ability in Arabic. Their children go to school in mostly Indian-run, Indian curriculum schools (though many go to American or British curriculum schools). And most importantly, they do not think of these places in the Persian Gulf as their home, and (recall the discussion of transnationalism in Chapter 1) as a result make plans to leave.

While there are many groups like the Lebanese, Indians, and others who remain socially apart within their societies for generations, there are many examples of individuals and groups assimilating throughout the non-Western world. For example, Yemeni Muslims came to serve in the army of the Nizam (or king) of Hyderabad in the 19th and early 20th centuries. When landlocked Hyderabad was conquered by India in 1948, one year after Indian independence, foreign-born Yemeni soldiers (the local term is *Chawsh*) were deported, but those who were born in Hyderabad (mostly second and third generation) were allowed to stay. They tend to marry amongst each other (though not exclusively), and most live in a few economically depressed neighborhoods, like a great many other Muslims. But in terms of occupation, language, and patterns of socialization, they are largely indistinct from other Muslims. In fact, when *Chawsh* live in neighborhoods with other local Muslims, their neighbors often don't even know they are *Chawsh* until there is a marriage, when they bring out their long swords and Arab drums for the festivities.[53]

Why are people like these not discussed using the language of assimilation? One major reason is the scholars who study these groups in non-Western countries are for the most part anthropologists, and they dislike the concept of assimilation. (There are very few anthropologists studying ethnic groups in the United States who frame their work in terms of assimilation. The most prominent is Nancy Foner, who teaches in a sociology department.) It would be interesting if sociologists, who are the scholars most invested in studying assimilation, were to do research in the non-Western world to systematically see if and where these theories are applicable. It could very well be that the trend in the non-Western world is more exclusion of non-native individuals and groups, rather than assimilation, in which case we would have to admit that assimilation is not a universal process, but rather one more common in the West. Or we might find the concept of assimilation is applicable beyond the West, and that patterns of assimilation and non-assimilation depend on peer effects. But again, the way to figure that out is more research in the non-Western world specifically addressing and testing the concerns of assimilation theories, and comparative research that bridges across disciplinary dividing lines, especially between sociology, anthropology, and history.

Conclusion

The social pressures to acculturate and assimilate to a white, middle-class America are not as strong as they once were. Today, ethnic difference has become more acceptable; it has itself become a sign of "Americanness."[54] But the trend for second-generation immigrants is certainly toward acculturation and economic assimilation, something that is also true in Western Europe and possibly also elsewhere.

In the 1990s, segmented assimilation theory became the paradigmatic approach to examining second-generation immigrant adjustment, which sought to point out and explain that many in the second generation were not succeeding. This then gave rise to a competing theoretical paradigm of new assimilation, which argued that, in fact, most of the second generation was doing quite alright. A third approach we are arguing for looks at the effects of peers to specifically account for how and why individuals, rather than groups, assimilate, and why there is variation in acculturation and economic assimilation within groups. This is something neither segmented nor new assimilation theories ask or are really able to answer, so shackled are they to the idea that parents are centrally important in their children's lives.

But a conceptual question arises that demands to be asked: Are the second generation even really immigrants? Or are they just part of a "minority" group within the broader society in which they live? This is somewhat of a semantic question, as they can be both. And in many countries, even if born there, they are legally and socially treated as foreigners. Still, it is an important question to ask as the answer can affect, and be affected by, the host government's policies toward them, and by how they are treated and perceived by natives. Calling the second generation who are born in the host country immigrants is actually an oxymoron—as a native-born citizen by definition cannot at the same time be an immigrant.[55] This becomes important to the questions and issues we raise in Chapter 6, where we discuss the dynamics of race and ethnicity and multiculturalism in immigrant-receiving countries.

But first, we have to deal with Chapter 5. In this next chapter, we will look at the conditions of first- and second-generation Muslim immigrants in the United States and Western Europe. They will form the key case study, a window through which we will see most of the theories we discussed here and in Chapter 1 play out. We will look at the different ways they went about migrating, the ways the first generation is treated, and how the second generation assimilates.

Notes

1 It's not really legitimate to call immigrants' children second-generation immigrants. As they are born in the "host country," they are usually citizens. Really, in a book on migration, we shouldn't deal with them at all, as they are not migrants. In fact, few scholars use the term second-generation immigrants, preferring "children of immigrants" or just "second generation." That just seems like so much word play to us. So in the interest of less clunky language and clarity, we're going to use the term second-generation immigrant and trust that this will not confuse you.

2 Warner, W. Lloyd, and Leo Srole. *The Social Systems of American Ethnic Groups.* New Haven: Yale UP, 1945; see also Alba, Richard, and Victor Nee. *Remaking the American Mainstream: Assimilation and Contemporary Immigration.* Cambridge, MA: Harvard UP, 2003, p. 4.

3 Gordon, Milton. "Assimilation in America: Theory and Reality," *Daedalus* 90.2 (1961): 263–285, p. 279; Gordon, Milton. *Assimilation in American Life: The Role of Race, Religion, and National Origins.* New York: Oxford UP, 1964.

4 Gordon 1961, ibid.

5 Gordon 1964, p. 80.

6 Glazer, Nathan, and Daniel Moynihan. *Beyond the Melting Pot: The Negroes, Puerto Ricans, Jews, Italians, and Irish of New York City,* 2nd ed. Cambridge, MA: MIT, 1970, p. xxii.

7 Glazer, Nathan. "On *Beyond the Melting Pot,* 35 Years After." *International Migration Review* 34.1 (2000): 270–279, p. 272.

8 Gans, Herbert. "Second-generation Decline: Scenarios for the Economic and Ethnic Futures of the Post-1965 American Immigrants." *Ethnic and Racial Studies* 15.2 (1992): 173–192.

9 Portes, Alejandro, and Min Zhou. "The New Second Generation: Segmented Assimilation and Its Variants." *The ANNALS of the American Academy of Political and Social Science* 530.1 (1993): 74–96.

10 Portes, Alejandro, Patricia Fernández-Kelly, and William Haller. "The Adaptation of the Immigrant Second Generation in America: A Theoretical Overview and Recent Evidence." *Journal of Ethnic and Migration Studies* 35.7 (2009): 1077–1104; Portes, Alejandro, and Rubén Rumbaut. *Legacies: The Story of the Immigrant Second Generation.* Berkeley: U of California, 2001.

11 Portes and Rumbaut 2001: 53–54, ibid.

12 Alba and Nee 2003, op cit.

13 Alba and Nee 2003, p. 11, op cit.

14 Alba and Nee 2003, pp. 38–59, op cit.

15 Alba and Nee 2003, p. 8 op cit.

16 Haller, William, Alejandro Portes, and Scott Lynch. "Dreams Fulfilled, Dreams Shattered: Determinants of Segmented Assimilation in the Second Generation." *Social Forces* 89.3 (2011): 733–762.

17 Kasinitz, Philip, John Mollenkopf, and Mary Waters (eds.). *Becoming New Yorkers: Ethnographies of the New Second Generation.* New York: Russell Sage, 2004; Kasinitz, Philip, Mary Waters, John Mollenkopf, and Jennifer Holdaway. *Inheriting the City: The Children of Immigrants Come of Age.* New York: Russell Sage, 2008.

18 Crul, Maurice and Jens Schneider. "Conclusions and Implications: The Integration Context Matters." In Maurice Crul, Jens Schneider and Frans Lelie, eds. *The European Second Generation Compared: Does the Integration Context Matter?* Amsterdam: Amsterdam UP, 2012.

19 Alba, Kasinitz, and Waters 2011; Haller, Portes, and Lynch 2011; Haller, William, Alejandro Portes, and Scott Lynch. "On the Dangers of Rosy Lenses: Reply to Alba, Kasinitz and Waters." *Social Forces* 89.3 (2011): 775–781.

20 Gans, Herbert. "Symbolic Ethnicity: The Future of Ethnic Groups and Cultures in America." *Ethnic and Racial Studies* 2.1 (1979): 1–20.

21 Vallejo, Jody. *Barrios to Burbs: The Making of the Mexican American Middle Class.* Stanford, CA: Stanford UP, 2012.

22 Lucassen, Leo. *The Immigrant Threat: The Integration of Old and New Migrants in Western Europe since 1850.* Urbana: U of Illinois, 2005, p. 73.

23 See for example, Caldwell, Christopher. *Reflections on the Revolution in Europe: Immigration, Islam, and the West.* London: Penguin, 2009.

24 Beaman, Jean. "But Madame, We Are French Also." *Contexts* 11.3 (2012): 46–51.

25 Crul and Schneider 2012, p. 378, op cit.

26 Ibid., pp. 381–383.

27 Ewa Morawska goes into much greater detail on this comparison than we have space for here. Morawska, Ewa. "Research on Immigration/Ethnicity in Europe and the US: A Comparison." *The Sociological Quarterly* 49.3 (2008): 465–482.

28 Crul, Maurice, and Jens Schneider. "Comparative Integration Context Theory: Participation and Belonging in New Diverse European Cities." *Ethnic and Racial Studies* 33.7 (2010): 1249–1268.

29 Harris, Judith. *The Nurture Assumption: Why Children Turn Out the Way They Do* New York: Simon and Schuster, 2009.

30 Ali, Syed. "Understanding Acculturation among Second-generation South Asian Muslims in the US." *Contributions to Indian Sociology* 42.3 (2008): 383–411; Ali, Syed, and Tineke Fokkema. "The Importance of Peers: Assimilation Patterns among Second-generation Turkish Immigrants in Western Europe." *Journal of Ethnic and Migration Studies,* forthcoming, DOI: 10.1080/1369183X.2014.921114.

31 Crosnoe, Robert. *Fitting In, Standing Out: Navigating the Social Challenges of High School to Get an Education.* Cambridge, MA: Cambridge UP, 2011; Crosnoe, Robert, and Monica Johnson. "Research on Adolescence in the Twenty-First Century." *Annual Review of Sociology* 37.1 (2011): 439–460; Faris, Robert, and Diane Felmlee. "Status Struggles: Network Centrality and Gender Segregation in Same- and

Cross-Gender Aggression." *American Sociological Review* 76.1 (2011): 48–73; Fletcher, Adam, Chris Bonell, and Annik Sorhaindo. "You Are What Your Friends Eat: Systematic Review of Social Network Analyses of Young People's Eating Behaviours and Bodyweight." *Journal of Epidemiology and Community Health* 65.6 (2011): 548–555; Harding, David. "Violence, Older Peers, and the Socialization of Adolescent Boys in Disadvantaged Neighborhoods." *American Sociological Review* 74.3 (2009): 445–464; Haynie, Dana, and D. Wayne Osgood. "Reconsidering Peers and Delinquency: How Do Peers Matter?" *Social Forces* 84.2 (2005): 1109–1130; Kandel, Denise. "On Processes of Peer Influences in Adolescent Drug Use: A Developmental Perspective." *Advances in Alcohol & Substance Abuse* 4.3–4 (1985): 139–162; Kreager, Derek. "Guarded Borders: Adolescent Interracial Romance and Peer Trouble at School." *Social Forces* 87.2 (2008): 887–910; Lee, Juliet, Robynn Battle, Brian Soller, and Naomi Brandes. "Thizzin'-Ecstasy Use Contexts and Emergent Social Meanings." *Addiction Research & Theory* 19.6 (2011): 528–541. Ream, Robert, and Russell Rumberger. "Student Engagement, Peer Social Capital, and School Dropout among Mexican American and Non-Latino White Students." *Sociology of Education* 81.2 (2008): 109–139; Ueno, Koji. "The Effects of Friendship Networks on Adolescent Depressive Symptoms." *Social Science Research* 34.3 (2005): 484–510; Warr, Mark, and Mark Stafford. "The Influence of Delinquent Peers: What They Think or What They Do?" *Criminology* 29.4 (1991): 851–866.

32 Haller, Portes and Lynch 2011; Zhou, Min, and Carl Bankston. *Growing Up American: How Vietnamese Children Adapt to Life in the US.* New York: Russell Sage Foundation, 1998; Zhou, Min, Jennifer Lee, Jody Vallejo, Rosaura Tafoya-Estrada, and Yang Sao Xiong. "Success Attained, Deterred, and Denied: Divergent Pathways to Social Mobility in Los Angeles's New Second Generation." *The ANNALS of the American Academy of Political and Social Science* 620.1 (2008): 37–61.

33 Zhou et al. 2008, p. 48, ibid.

34 Zhou et al. 2008, p. 49, ibid.

35 Bankston III, Carl, and Min Zhou. "The Social Adjustment of Vietnamese American Adolescents: Evidence for a Segmented-assimilation Approach." *Social Science Quarterly* (1997): 508–523, p. 521.

36 Gibson, Margaret. *Accommodation without Assimilation: Sikh Immigrants in an American High School.* Ithaca, NY: Cornell UP, 1988, p. 131; emphasis added.

37 Harris 2009, p. 250, op cit.

38 See Fordham, Signithia, and John Ogbu. "Black Students' School Success: Coping with the "Burden of 'Acting White'." *The Urban Review* 18.3 (1986): 176–206; Fryer, Roland. "'Acting White': The Social Price Paid by the Best and Brightest Minority Students." *Education Next* 6.1 (2006): 52–59. For a critique of the notion of "acting white," see Tyson, Karolyn. *Integration Interrupted: Tracking, Black Students, and Acting White after Brown.* New York: Oxford UP, 2011.

39 Interestingly, Gibson's earlier work on boys in St. Croix and later work on Mexican students in the United States more explicitly emphasize the effects of peers on educational outcomes. On the former, see Gibson, Margaret. "Reputation and Respectability: How Competing Cultural Systems Affect Students' Performance in School." *Anthropology & Education Quarterly* 13.1 (1982): 3–28; on the latter, see Gibson, Margaret, Patricia Gandara, and Jill Koyama, eds., *School Connections: US Mexican Youth, Peers, and School Achievement.* New York: Teachers College Press, 2004.

40 In her study, Waters' theoretical stance is closely aligned with segmented assimilation, though in later work, she is fully in the camp of new assimilation. Waters, Mary. "Ethnic and Racial Identities of Second-generation Black Immigrants in New York City." *International Migration Review* (1994): 795–820; Waters, Mary. *Black Identities: West Indian Immigrant Dreams and American Realities.* Cambridge, MA: Harvard UP, 1999.

41 Waters 1994: 807, ibid.

42 Harris 2009 op cit.; Milner, Murray, Jr. *Status and Sacredness: A General Theory of Status Relations and an Analysis of Indian Culture.* New York: Oxford UP, 1994; Milner, Murray, Jr. *Freaks, Geeks, and Cool Kids: American Teenagers, Schools, and the Culture of Consumption.* New York: Routledge, 2004.

43 Milner 1994, 2004, ibid.

44 Ali and Fokkema, forthcoming, op cit.

45 While most studies of second-generation assimilation largely ignore peer effects, there are a relatively small number of (mostly quantitative) studies that find peers to be critical for assimilation outcomes for the second generation. These studies have looked at a range of behaviors, such as binge drinking and substance abuse, dating and sexual behavior, age at which they get married, and whether they marry a native, a first-generation immigrant, or a second-generation immigrant. But they don't emphasize the theoretical importance of peers. See Cavanagh, Shannon. "Peers, Drinking, and the Assimilation of Mexican American Youth." *Sociological Perspectives* 50.3 (2007): 393–416; Prado, Guillermo, Shi Huang, Seth Schwartz, Mildred Maldonado-Molina, Frank Bandiera, Mario de la Rosa, and Hilda Pantin. "What Accounts for Differences in Substance Use Among US-born and Immigrant Hispanic Adolescents? Results from a Longitudinal Prospective Cohort Study." *Journal of Adolescent Health* 45.2 (2009): 118–125; King, Rosalind, and Kathleen Harris. "Romantic Relationships among Immigrant Adolescents." *International Migration Review* 41.2 (2007): 344–370; Huschek, Doreen, Aart Liefbroer, and Helga de Valk. "Timing of First Union among Second-generation Turks in Europe: The Role of Parents, Peers and Institutional Context." *Demographic Research* 22.16 (2010): 473–504; Huschek, Doreen, Helga de Valk, and Aart Liefbroer. "Does Social Embeddedness Influence Union Formation Choices among the Turkish and Moroccan Second Generation in The Netherlands?" *Journal of Comparative Family Studies* 42.6 (2011): 787–808.

46 Kalter, Frank. "The Second Generation in the German Labor Market: Explaining the Turkish Exception." In *The Next Generation: Immigrant Youth in a Comparative Perspective.* Alba, Richard and Mary Waters, eds. New York: NYU Press, 2011, p. 176.

47 Kalter, ibid., p. 180.

48 Gibson 1988, op cit.

49 Jiménez, Tomás, and Adam Horowitz. "When White Is Just Alright: How Immigrants Redefine Achievement and Reconfigure the Ethnoracial Hierarchy." *American Sociological Review* 78.5 (2013): 849–871.

50 A good starting point is Cohen, Robin. *Global Diasporas: An Introduction.* New York: Routledge, 2008.

51 Bierwirth, Chris. "The Lebanese Communities of Côte d'Ivoire." *African Affairs* 98.390 (1999): 79–99; Leichtman, Mara. "Migration, War, and the Making of a Transnational Lebanese Shi'i Community in Senegal." *International Journal of Middle East Studies* 42.2 (2010): 269–290.

52 Ali 2010, op cit.; Gardner, Andrew. *City of Strangers: Gulf Migration and the Indian Community in Bahrain*. Ithaca, NY: Cornell UP, 2010.

53 Ali, Syed. *Re-membering Selves: From Nobility and Caste to Ethnicity and Class in an Indian City*. Diss. University of Virginia, 2001.

54 Foner, Nancy. *From Ellis Island to JFK: New York's Two Great Waves of Immigration*. New Haven: Yale UP, 2000, pp. 9–10.

55 Rumbaut, Rubén. "Ages, Life Stages, and Generational Cohorts: Decomposing the Immigrant First and Second Generations in the US." *International Migration Review* 38.3 (2004): 1160–1205.

5

MALIGNED MIGRANTS

MUSLIMS IN THE UNITED STATES AND WESTERN EUROPE

Muslims are arguably the most maligned and despised migrants in the West today. And the reason for that is pretty clear: their perceived link to terrorism. You can't really talk about Muslims in the West without the topic of terrorism coming up.

So the question we need to ask is how much is terrorism by Muslims really a security issue? A quick way to gauge an answer is by the number of people killed by terrorists. From 1990 to 2011, terrorist acts committed by Muslims in Western Europe killed 263 people, including the victims of bombings in Madrid in 2004 and London in 2005. That's not an insignificant number. But during the same period, 249 people were killed by right-wing terrorism (or simply violence as the press usually refer to it), including the attacks by Anders Breivek in 2011 on a government building and teenage political youth camp of the Norwegian Labor Party. He killed 77 people.[1]

In the United States after 9/11 until 2013, there have been 21 people killed by Muslim terrorists. White, right-wing extremists (we don't call them terrorists in the United States) have killed 34.[2] In 2009, a report leaked from the Department of Homeland Security (DHS) warned of the threat posed by right-wing extremists to domestic security, and the possibility that former armed service members would join their ranks. Conservative politicians and media were livid, and the head of Homeland Security at the time, Janet Napolitano, was forced to backtrack and apologize. Since then, DHS has not released a single report on right-wing extremists, instead going back to focusing all its energy on Muslims. Bringing this up is not meant to downplay the heinous terrorist acts committed by Muslims in the West, but rather to put them into context.

Sociologist Charles Kurzman has studied terrorist acts committed by Muslims. He asks, with over a billion Muslims in the world, a great many of whom despise the West (including many who live in the West), and with easy access to lethal weaponry (even a car is a weapon), why don't we see more acts of terrorism? The short, simple answer is that, while terrorism globally is most definitely a real and deadly threat, there are actually very, very few terrorists among Muslims.[3] In other words, the fear of terrorism is far greater than the reality of terrorism. In fact, a national survey of law enforcement agencies in the United States has found that over half of all agencies feel there is little or no threat of al Qaeda-inspired extremism here, with only 2 percent reporting the threat as seriously "severe." Metropolitan forces were a bit more concerned, but still, only 7 percent felt the threat of al Qaeda-inspired extremism was severe. Overall, law enforcement agencies in the United States treat this risk as manageable.[4]

Statistically, terrorism, no matter who commits it, happens very infrequently. Of all the possible ways you could be killed, a terrorist attack is close to the bottom of the list. In the United States, the chance of being killed by a terrorist is one in three million—the same probability as being killed by a tornado. You are more likely to be killed by a toddler with a gun than by a terrorist.[5] Basically, if you fear for your health and life, there are many other things that should concern you before you worry about terrorism, which would be clear if you read nuanced, level-headed analyses of such things. But American and increasingly Western European media and politicians do not favor nuanced, levelheaded analyses, as that is not the way to gain audiences or votes. As sociologist Barry Glassner pointed out in his book *The Culture of Fear*, our perception of dangers around us has increased dramatically even if the risk of such things like child abductions hasn't.[6] Glassner's basic point is that there are "fear peddlers" in the media and government and elsewhere who benefit from trumpeting different types of social dangers.

So it is with terrorism and Muslims. There is now a cottage industry of media personalities and politicians who play off of the presence of Muslims in the West, constructing this population as a basic threat to personal safety and a certain way of life.[7] Since the fall of communism as the specter haunting Western Europe and the United States, Muslims have become the "go-to" bogeymen for Western politicians and pundits looking for someone to blame for any and all social ills. The fear and disdain of Muslims or Islam of the political right and parts of the left, especially in Europe, has become shrill, increasingly so since 9/11. As a result, Muslims in the United States and in parts of Western Europe are often seen and treated as the enemy within.

The loudest of these critics of Muslims living in the West are the "Eurabianists" who believe that Europe is being overrun by Muslim immigrants and that it is becoming an Arabian outpost. Their counterparts in the United States, the "Amerabianists," are saying much the same things. Essentially, their arguments boil down to the idea that Muslims and the West are like oil and water. Worse even, because they insist Muslims are inherently dangerous people, each one a potential terrorist.[8] (Glenn Beck, the highly influential American conservative TV and radio talk show host, says one out of ten Muslims globally are terrorists. With over one billion Muslims globally, that would be an awful lot of terrorists.) Anders Breivik was a big fan of many of these writers and politicians (including Bat Ye'or, who coined the term *Eurabia,* Dutch right-wing politician Geert Wilders, and the American anti-Muslim activists Pamela Gellar, Robert Spencer, and Daniel Pipes, among others). He name-checked them in his 1,500 page manifesto he released right before he went on his killing spree.[9] While most Eurabianists and Amerabianists found Breivik's actions deplorable, even the most even keeled among them believes some version of the above, and these views are widespread among politicians, academic and media pundits, and the general public.

There are three prominent perspectives when it comes to portraying Muslims in the popular press and academia. One is the notion that Muslim immigrants in the West, including those who were born and/or grew up in the West, are incapable of assimilating, as Islam is incompatible with Western values.[10] Another less inflammatory idea is that Muslims are becoming more insular and removed from Western societies.[11] A third vein of analysis is the idea that Muslims are integrating into their host societies, but distinctively as a Muslim community—conservative and religious.[12]

All three perspectives have elements that are true, but overall their arguments fall flat because they see Muslims *as a community*—unified, bounded, and with shared interests. There is some evidence for this in Islamic theology—the concept of the *ummah*, the global Muslim community that transcends tribe, nationality, class, etc. And at times, feelings of "Muslim-ness" do trump other identities, as when Muslims feel a sense of solidarity with and obligation to their oppressed brethren in places like Kosovo, Chechnya, and Palestine. But while it is convenient for analysts to use the *ummah* as a starting point, the vast majority of Muslims around the world see this concept more as an ideal to aspire to than a factual description of how Muslims actually live and relate to each other. Leaving aside obvious divisions of sect (Sunni, Shia, Alevi, etc.), Muslims are divided by ethnic and economic background, something easily seen by looking at who marries whom, and even who goes to which mosque. Muslims also vary with regard to social and religious behavior.

To write honestly and properly about Muslims in the West, one must take into account this great variation and disparity in how these folks live their lives. Using this insight as a starting point, the main question we ask in this chapter is, "How and to what degree are Muslims culturally and economically incorporating into the Western countries they live in, and how does this vary between them?"

Migration to the United States and Western Europe

Muslims have a long historical presence in the West. For instance, many Muslims had lived in Spain until the end of the 15th century when they were forced to choose between converting to Christianity, emigration, or death. There are stories that when Columbus sailed to the New World in 1492, there were Muslim sailors in his company. In 18th century England, some Indian Muslim sailors with the British East India Company settled in port towns and took local wives.[13] There was a great number of Muslim African slaves brought to the Americas, whose cultures were purposefully destroyed. In the United States, small numbers of Syrians, Jordanians, Lebanese, and Palestinians came in the late 19th-early 20th centuries. Most were Christians, but smaller numbers were Muslims.[14] There were also a small number of Bengali Muslim men who came in the late 19th-early 20th centuries, settling in US ghettoes like Harlem, West Baltimore, Treme in New Orleans, and Black Bottom in Detroit. Many of them married black, Creole, and Puerto Rican women.[15]

But these early migration patterns did not lead to the creation of lasting, sizeable Muslims communities, chain migrations, or sustaining networks of migrants. The migrant streams that actually were sustained happened in the mid-later parts of the 20th century. The United States (as did Canada and Australia around the same time) opened a legal channel for migrants, passing the Immigration and Nationality Act of 1965 (also known as the Hart-Cellar Act) that allowed for large-scale immigration to resume, which had largely been shut down due to the Immigration Act of 1924. The intention was to bring Europeans, but an unintended side effect was to open the door to professionals from third-world countries, especially doctors, nurses, and engineers. As they settled, they brought their families through reunification programs. Large numbers of Muslims from India and Pakistan came initially, as did others in smaller numbers from various Arab countries.

The Western European pattern was different. As their economies rebounded after World War II, almost across the board they required vast numbers of laborers. The immediate source for the larger economies of the United Kingdom, France, and Germany were Italians, Spanish, Polish, and Portuguese.[16] But they were not sufficient to meet the labor needs. In the United Kingdom, this demand was largely met in the 1950s and 1960s with workers from Jamaica (at the time still a British colony) and newly independent India and Pakistan (which included Bangladesh until it gained independence from Pakistan in 1971). Because of their colonial relations, workers from these places could travel and settle relatively freely, until the 1970s, when Britain put greater restrictions on movement and settlement. France also counted upon Algeria (its former colony) and Morocco and Tunisia (former protectorates) to supply a great amount of labor. Belgium, the Netherlands, and Germany were not colonial powers on the order of France and the United Kingdom, so they filled their labor demand by looking to Turkey and Morocco.

These labor migrants, mainly men who came alone, were assumed to be temporary (like today's laborers in the Persian Gulf). When the OPEC oil crisis of 1973 led to contracting economies throughout Europe and to the decline of manufacturing and closing of factories, it was assumed these migrants would go home. A funny thing happened though—many of them stayed. Not only did they stay, but they also brought their families, or went back and got married and returned to settle for good. So while Western European countries put great restrictions on further labor migration, the Muslim migrant population kept growing through family reunification, and in the 1990s, through the admission of refugees from the Balkans, Iraq, Somalia, and elsewhere. In 1950, there were fewer than 300,000 Muslims in the 27 countries that today make up the EU (European Union). Today they are close to 20 million of around 500 million, or 4 percent of the entire population.[17] This varies greatly from country to country, as you can see on Map 5.1. For instance, there are four million Muslims in Germany (approximately two-thirds of whom are Turkish), about 4 percent of the population.[18] Muslims in the Netherlands are about 6 percent of the population, mostly from Turkey and Morocco; in the United Kingdom, it's 3 percent—mainly South Asian. Spain's Muslim population is about 2 percent, and Italy's is around 1.5 percent.[19,20]

While Muslims migrating to Western Europe were mostly working class, in the United States, Muslim migrants initially, after the 1965 Immigration Act, were largely doctors and engineers and other professionals from South Asian and Arab countries. They mostly settled in typical immigrant receiving areas of metropolitan New York City, greater Los Angeles and Chicago, and pre-1965 areas of migration like Dearborn, Michigan, and Brooklyn. But they also established smaller communities in rural areas, such as Princeton, West Virginia. Ali's father was one of the early professional arrivals in 1971. He first came to rural Missouri, then moved to rural West Virginia (next door to one Filipino and two Pakistani families), before settling in New York City.

Unlike European Muslims who came in large numbers from the 1950s to 1970s, most foreign-born Muslims in the United States are

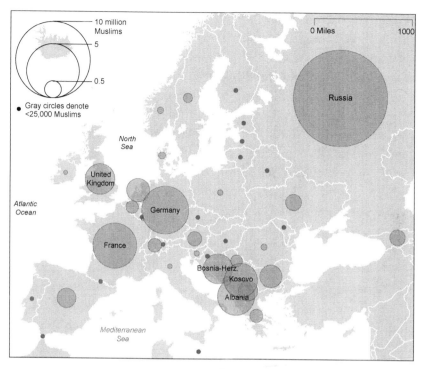

Map 5.1 Distribution of Muslim population in Europe.
Source: Pew Research Center, "Mapping the Global Muslim Population," 2009.

relatively recent arrivals. A recent Pew Research Center survey found that 40 percent came between 2000 and 2011, 31 percent in the 1990s, 16 percent came in the 1980s, and only 12 percent came before 1980.[21] While there are no reliable statistics, as the United States doesn't collect census information on religion, it's likely the bulk of recent arrivals came through family reunification. It's also likely that a large percentage of recent arrivals would have come much earlier if not for the fact that the backlog for processing family reunification "green cards" for permanent residency is often more than a ten-year wait.

The Muslim population in the United States compared to Western Europe is smaller in both absolute and relative terms. There are about 2.75 million Muslims in the United States; 1.8 million of them are adults. That's less than 1 percent of the total US population. Sixty-three percent of Muslims in the United States are first-generation immigrants, and 15 percent are second generation, while 22 percent are third generation, the majority of whom are African American (59 percent). A little more than two-thirds of African American Muslims are converts. Of the first generation, 41 percent come from the Middle East or North Africa, 26 percent from South Asia (Pakistan 14 percent, Bangladesh 5 percent, India 3 percent), 11 percent from sub-Saharan Africa, 7 percent from Europe, and 5 percent from Iran.[22] While 1.73 million foreign-born Muslims seems like a small number (out of a total population of 330 million), that would make Muslims the fifth-largest category of migrants, after Mexico, China, India, and the Philippines.

Economic Integration

In terms of income, American Muslims present an interesting picture. A 2011 survey by the Pew Research Center found that 14 percent of all American Muslims earn over $100,000 per year, roughly the same as the general population. But 45 percent earn less than $30,000 per year, compared to 36 percent of Americans overall. This shift though is correlated with the recession from 2008 onward. In the Pew Research Center's 2007 survey, 35 percent of Muslims reported earning less than $30,000 per year, compared to 33 percent of Americans generally.[23] Forty percent of Muslims have a college degree, compared to 29 percent of Americans overall.[24] Employment rates for Muslims in the United States are similar to other Americans: 70 percent say they are working (paid or unpaid) compared to 64 percent of Americans overall. Thirty percent of Muslims are professionals, compared to 26 percent of Americans overall.[25]

Muslims in Western Europe are not particularly well off. Poverty rates for Muslims there are far higher than the United States, owing in large part to the first generation's origins as low-level laborers. In Belgium, the proportion of Turks living below the poverty line is 59 percent and for Moroccans 56 percent. In Amsterdam, 32 percent of Turkish households and 37 percent of Moroccan households in 2006 lived on the minimum income compared with 13 percent of Dutch households. In the United Kingdom, 65 percent of Bangladeshis and 55 percent of Pakistanis were poor, compared with 20 percent of white Britons.

Of those who worked, half of Bangladeshis and a third of Pakistanis were paid less than 6.50 GBP in 2006 (minimum wage at the time was 6.08 GBP).[26]

Unemployment rates for European Muslims are also very high—twice the national average for second-generation Moroccan and Algerian immigrants in France and for Turkish nationals in Germany; in the Netherlands the unemployment rate among Moroccans and Turks is almost thrice the national average. In Belgium, the unemployment rate among Moroccans and Turks is five times the national unemployment rate of 7 percent.[27] In the United Kingdom, less than half of all Indian Muslim (41 percent), Pakistani (26 percent), and Bangladeshi (23 percent) adults have full-time jobs.[28]

Much of the labor-market disadvantage experienced by minority groups is due to low levels of education and skills. But with deindustrialization, a large proportion of manufacturing jobs disappeared. For Muslims throughout Western Europe, there is also an ethnic and religion penalty in the labor market—that is, if you compare them with natives throughout Europe with similar education backgrounds, skills, etc., they make less money and are less likely to be hired at every educational level.[29] Experiments that sent out matched resumes with Muslim and "European" (that is, white-sounding) names found that having a Muslim-sounding name dramatically decreases the possibility of being called for a job interview.[30] (This exactly mirrors experiments done in the United States that show that blacks face similar discrimination based simply on their names.[31]) Among Muslims, this penalty gets more pronounced if they're visibly religious. For instance women wearing the hijab (headscarf) are more often unemployed than women who don't, and they report experiencing discrimination twice as often when looking for a job.[32]

The situation for educated Muslims is different from working-class Muslims, as we would expect. For instance in the Netherlands, the employment rate of highly educated Turks and Moroccans (80 percent) is close to that of their Dutch peers (85 percent). But even if they're educated, Muslims are disproportionately unemployed or over-represented in lower-skilled jobs. Only 65 percent of Muslim university graduates are employed in higher skilled positions, compared with 85 percent of non-Muslim university graduates. Proportionally, non-Muslim university graduates are 1.6 times more likely than Muslim university graduates to be employed in modern professional occupations. However, Muslim and non-Muslim graduates also tend to be more equally distributed within traditional professional and clerical occupations, or as senior or middle managers.[33]

These numbers, even for the educated, show how Muslims in Europe are economically marginalized—this would seem to lend support to segmented assimilation theory. But these numbers mask change over time. For instance, in the Netherlands, the proportion of 15- to 65-year-olds in middle-to-higher-level jobs doubled from 1991 to 2002, leading to a fast-growing middle class among first- and second-generation Muslim immigrants there.[34] Indeed, while the public discussion surrounding Muslims focuses on poverty, unemployment, and poor educational outcomes, quietly a sizeable educated and professional middle-class second generation is growing throughout Europe, which actually supports new assimilation theory.[35]

Studies of economic mobility routinely show education is a critical variable. Among Western European Muslims, there is a great degree of variation depending on the place. A major result from the 2007–2008 TIES survey (which we discussed in Chapter 4) of second-generation Turks, Moroccans, and former Yugoslavs found that some Muslims perform quite well in schools, leading to good occupational and economic outcomes, such as with second-generation Turks in Stockholm and Paris. Some second-generation Turks in the Netherlands, Brussels, and Strasbourg, experienced fast upward mobility, but others quit their education too soon to qualify for a professional diploma. Second-generation Turks in Switzerland were upwardly mobile, but slowly. In Germany and Austria, however, there is little social mobility.[36]

Education on its own will not guarantee upward mobility or good jobs, especially for minorities. For instance, as we pointed out in Chapter 4, for second-generation Turks in Germany, the composition of their friendship networks may account for a significant part of the ethnic penalty they face in the labor market. That is, having too many Turks as friends works against you in the labor market. Conversely, having more native German friends led to better, and better paying, jobs.[37]

The experiences of Turkish Muslims vary greatly between countries. In Sweden, six times as many of the Turkish second generation
go on to higher education than in Germany. In both places, they are
the children of migrant workers, who sometimes even came from the
same villages. But in Sweden, they are poised to become professionals,
while in Germany they probably won't go into higher education. Differences in school systems across countries, especially with regard to
early childhood schooling, and different forms of tracking and access
to higher education, helps to explain why Turks do poorly academically
in Germany and Austria, but perform better in Sweden, Belgium, and
France.[38] For instance, in Sweden, as a good number of Turks go to
university, one in four young people from the Turkish second generation work in well-paid professional jobs, leading to the development of
a distinct Turkish-Swedish middle class in Stockholm.[39]

Cultural and Social Integration

If you get all your information about Muslims in the West from the
mainstream media, you probably think that Muslims largely keep to
themselves and either can't or won't integrate into their social surroundings. This is a common trope of the Eurabianists and Amerabianists
we discussed at the beginning of the chapter. But this is not so. Like
with economic integration, Muslims in the United States and Western
Europe do culturally integrate, though of course this varies.

Friends and Lovers

One way we can conceptualize social integration is having "native"
friends, or intermarriage with natives. Here we find interesting degrees
of variation. In France, Algerian immigrants are very much integrated.
In a 2005 survey, almost all Algerian-French Muslims said they had
non-Muslim friends and 62 percent said they had "many" French
friends. In terms of marriage, their attitudes are fairly liberal. Fifty-nine
percent of Algerian parents said they wouldn't object if their daughter
married a non-Muslim. In fact, of second-generation Algerian-French,
half of the men in the survey married native French women, and a quarter of women did as well.[40]

While in France there is a tendency toward inter-ethnic contact, this is not true across Western Europe. For instance, friendship patterns of Muslim first- and second-generation residents in the United Kingdom show a lower rate of social integration. Of Indian Muslims, 33 percent had only co-ethnic friends, while 25 percent had only interethnic friends. Pakistanis and Bangladeshis were a bit more insular with their friendships—43 percent of Pakistanis and 40 percent of Bangladeshis only had co-ethnic friends, while 17 percent of Pakistanis and 23 percent of Bangladeshis had only interethnic friends. But while nearly a majority of members of all second-generation groups in the United Kingdom had whites among their close friends, only a quarter of Indian Muslims, 30 percent of Bangladeshis, and 38 percent of Pakistanis did.[41]

Muslims in the United States fall somewhere in-between France and the United Kingdom in terms of friendship patterns. About half of American Muslims say they have only some or hardly any Muslim friends, while another half say all or most of their friends are Muslim. This varies by religiosity: Of the highly religious, 71 percent say most or all of their friends are Muslim, but among those with lower levels of religiosity, not surprisingly, only 30 percent say most or all of their friends are Muslim.[42]

Surveys that ask people who their friends are can be misleading, as one could say they have many interethnic friends, but they might just be schoolmates or coworkers who they're friendly with, but they don't necessarily hang out with. These could be more "professional" or less intimate relationships, rather than close and intimate ones. A better measure of social integration of individuals is marriage and dating.

In Western Europe, Christian immigrants intermarry with Europeans at far higher rates than people of non-European religions do, and that increases greatly from first-generation immigrants to the second generation. So people from the West Indies have far higher rates of intermarriage with native whites in the United Kingdom and Netherlands than Pakistanis or Turks do. Likewise in France, Portuguese intermarry with native French at more than twice the rate Algerians do. Interestingly, Algerians marry native French at a rate higher than any other Muslim group in Western Europe, and far higher than Indians (who are mostly Hindu, though a large minority is Muslim) in the United

Kingdom. And Muslims are not crossing ethnic/national boundaries either. That is, Turks do not marry Moroccans, and vice versa.[43]

So second-generation Turks and Moroccans throughout Europe tend not to marry native whites or other ethnics. They also more often find marriage partners from Turkey or Morocco, rather than other second-generation Turks or Moroccans. For instance, in the Netherlands and Belgium, two-thirds of second-generation Turks marry a partner from Turkey.[44]

Again, variation is the key theme here. One of the best studies of marriage patterns among second-generation Turks found that generally throughout Western Europe, except in Germany, second-generation Turks are more likely to marry a first-generation Turkish immigrant.[45] In Sweden, 41 percent of men and 45 percent of women marry first-generation Turkish immigrants. Elsewhere in Europe, the majority marries first-generation Turkish immigrants. More than a quarter of these marriages throughout Europe between second-generation resident and first-generation immigrants are between blood relations. But in Germany, which has the largest Turkish communities in Western Europe, less than 15 percent of second-generation men and women marry first-generation Turks. There, they overwhelmingly marry second-generation partners.

On the face of it, these patterns of marriage make it look like Turks in Western Europe are not socially integrating to their surroundings, as more than half of the married second-generation Turks had first-generation partners. But there are four very interesting results in this study that qualify this conclusion. The first is that having more contact with non–co-ethnic peers increases the likelihood of having a native partner. (Remember our discussion of peers and assimilation from Chapter 4.) Second, higher levels of education are associated with the higher likelihood of having a native partner, and lower levels of education lead to a greater likelihood that the person will marry a partner from Turkey. The third is that in the German cities of Berlin and Frankfurt, 65 percent of men and 70 percent of women had second-generation partners, and more second-generation Turks married native Germans than they did first-generation Turks. One obvious inference we can make is that size matters. That is, there is a bigger local marriage pool of second-generation Turks in Germany, making it easier for men and women to marry other second-generation Turks, who are German like them.

A fourth result that points to possible future integration patterns is that the younger of the second generation are more likely to choose a second-generation partner over a first-generation partner. They found that people of this age cohort (b. 1985–1990, between 18 and 23 years old at the time of the survey) were less likely to marry natives, but that could be because people who marry natives may marry them at later ages.[46]

We should note though that intermarriage with natives need not lead to upward economic mobility, and not marrying natives does not have to lead to downward economic mobility. For instance, in the United Kingdom, the Caribbean second generation marry native Britons in far greater number than Indians do, but they have far lower levels of education and lower incomes than Indians.[47]

Marriages between those of the Muslim second generation and someone from the home country—transnational marriages—are fairly common in Western Europe and in some places are the norm. Parents often prefer to have their sons and daughters marry someone from their city or village, oftentimes close kin, especially first cousins (which is Islamically legal and preferable). Some of these marriages are arranged, some are forced, and some look like dating, where the prospective bride or groom go to the home country, where they are set up with meetings with a handful of prospects whom they can evaluate—subject to their parents or relatives' approval. These are arranged meetings, rather than arranged marriages.[48]

In the United States, there are no data that can tell us to what degree such transnational marriages may be occurring, but it doesn't seem to be as common as in Western Europe. In Western Europe, it seems to be more common among working class rather than educated and professional second-generation Muslims. Anecdotally, Ali found during the course of his research on second-generation Muslims in New York that it would happen sporadically, but in the last two decades or so, parents did not push for it as much, as many of these relationships (though certainly not all) ended in divorce, in part because of the cultural divide.

It's likely that as parents have begun to acknowledge this cultural divide, they began to loosen restrictions on their children to allow *halal* (religiously acceptable) "dating." In the United States and United Kingdom, some parents and their children are working to make religiously compatible matches based on the individual's choice, but without long-term dating or sex (though it does happen). For the second generation, this is very important as they increasingly do not want to marry someone their parents choose, especially not a cousin from Pakistan or India.[49] Sometimes the parents make suggestions without forcing any one particular person, and sometimes siblings or friends act as matchmakers. Some second-generation Muslims have turned to websites such as Muslimmatrimonials.com and shaadi.com, but there's no real evidence, even anecdotal, to indicate to what degree these websites are effective for marriage. (But given that many non-Muslims in the United States are finding partners and spouses through websites like match.com, it wouldn't be surprising.) Even when choosing their own spouses in a halal manner, young Muslims tend to marry spouses that are acceptable to their parents—Muslims, usually of their same sect, and usually of their parents' ethnic and economic class background.

While most second-generation Muslims marry people of similar backgrounds, some go against the wishes and demands of parents and community and marry natives. Marrying a native is often seen as the ultimate indicator of social acceptance, but it also is sometimes seen as a repudiation of their parents and community. As we pointed out in Chapter 4, this is largely a function of peer group dynamics. Those who hang out with mostly natives are likely to marry natives; those with more of a mix of native and second-generation friends (especially of their parents' nationality) are more likely to marry a second-generation person. Ali found in research in New York that the very religious among the second generation often choose their own spouses, using their friends as intermediaries. There's no sex or dating, just a "sizing up" of the prospective spouse's Islamic tendencies (if in person with a chaperone, again often a friend, or else on the phone/text/email), and then marriage.[50]

One trend is that of young Muslims going to religious conferences, like ISNA (the Islamic Society of North America), which has its meeting with well over 30,000 attendees every Labor Day weekend (the first Monday in September). During one of the days there is a matrimonial "meet and greet," a kind of speed dating overpopulated with young women whose parents think they're old at 23. Full awkwardness ensues. At night, ISNA becomes "club ISNA," with young people circling the hotel lobby and later going to shisha cafes to mingle. But because these young adults are often quite uncomfortable around the other gender, usually nothing comes of it, though some may exchange emails or Facebook names.[51]

Religious Practice

Like dating and marriage, religious practices also vary between Western countries. In France, Muslims are not all that religious. Fewer than 5 percent attend mosque weekly, and 20 percent say they have no religion at all. Of those who said they have religion, 28 percent said they never pray, and 42 percent support a ban on hijab in the classroom. These numbers on religiosity are very similar to those for other French citizens.[52]

American Muslims on the other hard are largely religious. More than two-thirds (69 percent) say religion is very important to them (a very American thing—70 percent of American Christians overall say religion is very important to them). About half of Muslims attend mosque once a week (about the same rate as Christians), and about the same percentage say they pray the required five times a day. Another 18 percent say they pray less than five times a day, and 25 percent say they pray occasionally, or just on Eid (like Christmas and Easter for Christians). Only 8 percent say they never pray.[53]

While most US Muslims are religious, a surprisingly high number engage in *haram* (religiously forbidden) behaviors. A 2009 Gallup poll found that 14 percent of Muslims have had four to five alcoholic drinks at one time (binge drinking) in the past week (20 percent men, 6 percent women), and this did not vary much at all across age groups. And at 24 percent, they have the highest smoking rate among religious subgroups, and slightly higher than the American population overall (21 percent).[54]

Similarly, a 2001 national college survey found that for Muslim college students the prevalence of "risk behaviors" was 46 percent for alcohol, 25 percent for illicit drug use, 37 percent for tobacco use, and 30 percent for gambling (men gambled and smoked more, but alcohol and drug use and sexual activity were about the same).[55] Of the never married students, 54 percent reported having ever had sexual intercourse. Most Muslim students (58 percent) reported engaging in at least one risk behavior during the past year, three-quarters of whom engaged in two or more "risky" behaviors. However, the more religious the students were, the less likely they were to engage in such behaviors.[56]

While such behaviors are common, oftentimes Muslims are keen to keep up appearances that they're acting in a halal manner. For instance, one young Muslim college student insisted to Ali that while drinking alcohol and sex are clearly haram, smoking marijuana and oral sex are just fine, and halal. Ali said to her that maybe they weren't and that she was trying to skirt around the rules. But she was insistent.

While there are many Muslims in the West who engage in "Western" (and haram) behaviors of alcohol and drug consumption and premarital sex, there is one behavior you rarely find even among the most assimilated, atheistic Muslims—eating the pig. (Jews also aren't supposed to eat the pig, but aside from the very religious, a great many do.) No sociological study has ever, to our knowledge, addressed pig-eating behaviors among Muslims. And it's odd that this is the one thing that even straying Muslims will stay away from. Why? We're not sure. It could be that Muslims have it drummed into their heads that the pig is a filthy animal; indeed when you see the pig in its natural state in third-world countries, you will immediately understand the revulsion. The French Muslim journalist Khaleb Diab said after years of other haram behaviors he'd finally gotten over the hump and ate the pig. But only certain cuts![57] We gladly await the groundbreaking study of Muslim pork consumption in the West.

Acculturation on Their Own Terms

But you don't have to drink alcohol or eat the pig to be culturally assimilated, even if the French may insist on this.[58] In fact, many younger Muslims are insistent they can be Western and Muslim at the same time (which segmented assimilation theory sees as the best path). Where a couple of decades ago teenage and young adult Muslims might be religious but downplay their Muslim identity in public, today's young Muslims are almost defiant in proudly proclaiming their Muslimness.

American Mipsterz are a good example. (That would be a contraction of Muslims and hipsters—young Muslim women who wear hijab, or the headscarf.) According to the Mipsterz-Muslim Hipsters Facebook page, "A Mipster is someone at the forefront of the latest music, fashion, art, critical thought, food, imagination, creativity, and all forms of obscure everything."[59] A video of Mipster women made to Jay-Z's song "Somewhere in America" in December 2013 went viral.[60] They were on skateboards and climbing trees, in cool clothes doing everyday things. Like other Americans, except that they're wearing hijabs.

While this is a small (but perhaps growing) group of young Muslim women, it's an example of how Muslims are claiming space for themselves in public. Indeed, there is a noticeable change in how Muslims present themselves in public. Take the hijab. In the United States in the 1980s, few Muslim women of any age or immigration status wore hijab. One second-generation Arab Muslim woman interviewed in the mid-1980s said, "How women dress outside the mosque is their own private business. I don't want to go to university with my head covered, and wearing a short skirt does not make me a bad Muslim. I am a Muslim, and I am proud to say it, but I want to say it in ways other than dressing in obnoxious clothing. I want to blend in as far as my clothes go. I want to look normal."[61]

In the 1990s, as the United States began to accept multiculturalism as the social standard, looking like everyone else wasn't as critical. As the Muslim population grew rapidly in the cities, suburbs, high schools, and colleges, Muslim youth began to become more religious, and to visibly signal their Muslimness. Among young women, hijab-wearing became common. (Interestingly, their parents often opposed this, and sometimes would try to forbid it.) Specific events, like the first Gulf War (1990–1991), the first bombing of the World Trade Center (1993), and the Oklahoma City Federal Building bombing (1995) put Muslims in the spotlight. Well before 9/11, this forced many Muslims to think reflexively about the importance of Islam to themselves and to explain Islam to others. It was during this decade that younger Muslims became more religious, studying the Quran and religious commentaries themselves, often becoming more religious than their parents and older siblings who came of age in the United States in the 1970s and 1980s. Many scholars insist that 9/11 was a kind of tipping point for religiosity and young women wearing hijab, but they're not quite right; the social forces that brought those to the fore were already well under way.[62]

Today, young (and older) Muslim women wearing the hijab (and less frequently the jilbab, or full-length body cloak) are ubiquitous. About 60 percent of Muslim women in the United States in a 2011 survey said they always or mostly wear the hijab, while 40 percent never wear it. This is a sizeable shift from 2007, when about 48 percent said they never wear it. But interestingly, among native-born Muslims, which would include second-generation immigrants, 44 percent wear it all the time, while among first-generation immigrants, just 30 percent do.[63] Many immigrant women who came to the United States in the 1970s and 1980s never wore hijab in their countries of origin, but began to do so only in the United States, and some of them only did so many years after arriving.[64] For Muslims in the United States, the hijab is very much an American thing.

Like with religiosity, veiling among Muslim women varies across countries. For instance in France, only 14 percent of women wear the hijab. As France has been at the forefront of banning the hijab from public places, and in 2004 actually did ban it from public schools, you'd think the number of hijab-wearing women would be much higher. But you'd be wrong. The Netherlands has debated banning the jilbab, even though less than a hundred women in the entire country wear it. In the United Kingdom in 2006, the ex-foreign minister had called for banning the niqab, which covers the whole of a woman's face except for her eyes. Precious few women actually wore the niqab at the time.[65]

Basically, these Western European countries are making much ado about nothing. They are overreacting to a perceived threat these relatively small number of women pose to European culture. (Recall the discussion of the culture of fear from the beginning of the chapter.) Some writers insist the presence of Muslims who are asserting themselves publicly (as opposed the earlier generation who toiled silently, anonymously, and largely out of sight) has a direct, and adverse effect on natives. For instance, the conservative author Christopher Caldwell wrote that mass immigration to Western Europe generally, and of Muslims in particular, has made white Europeans feel "contemptible and small, ugly and asexual."[66] (And yes, he does use those words.) Interestingly in the United States, where hijabs and jilbabs and increasingly niqabs are ubiquitous, there is comparatively little discussion.

Mosques and Spies

In the summer of 2010, there was a huge controversy over the planned construction of a mosque in New York City. No, not the Park 51 Mosque near the World Trade Center that got all the global attention. This building was to be in the outer borough of Staten Island, a mostly insular area that feels more suburban than city.

A local chapter of the Muslim American Society (MAS) had quietly made plans to buy a disused convent from St. Margaret Mary's Roman Catholic Church for $750,000. The parish's priest had approved the sale, but then word spread that the Muslims were coming. For six weekends in a row, locals (white locals) protested the possibility of the mosque, alternating between concerns about traffic and parking in the Midland Beach residential neighborhood (which would bear the brunt of Hurricane Sandy two years later), and whether MAS had links with Hamas or the Muslim Brotherhood. One protestor said, "Mosques breed terrorism, I'm sorry." Another said, "We just want to leave our neighborhood the way it is—Christian, Catholic."[67]

The controversy was too much for the church's board of trustees, which included Archbishop Timothy Dolan, and they rejected the sale.[68] A year later, MAS opened a mosque a few miles away in the similar-looking residential neighborhood of Dongan Hills in Staten Island with barely any notice, and no public outcry.

What changed? Well, for one thing, 2010 was an election year, which often gives politicians cause to look for symbolic scapegoats. Also, the Dongan Hills property the Muslim group eventually bought—an inelegant pitched-roof orange rectangle—was formerly a Hindu temple, so locals were already accustomed to having people of "strange" religions in their midst. But something smaller, and more important changed: namely, the way local Muslims presented themselves in the local community. Before they finalized the purchase of the Dongan Hills mosque,

Muslim associated with the planned mosque went door-to-door in the neighborhood introducing themselves and their intentions. They allayed fears of parking overflow, told their neighbors they would not use the loudspeaker to announce prayers, and promised that the hall would be available as a community center for groups like the Boy Scouts. They also held an open-house reception for dozens of their neighbors.[69]

If we went just by survey data, we might not have expected the outreach to have done much. Only 30 percent of Americans have favorable views of Muslims and Islam.[70] However, of Americans who say they were not prejudiced toward Muslims, 53 percent said they knew a practicing Muslim, while 44 percent of those who said they had a great deal of prejudice toward Muslims knew a practicing Muslim. This is a 9-percentage point difference. It's not huge, but it is a difference. Simply knowing a Muslim does not endear them to you or make you much less prejudiced, but it can help.[71] Going door-to-door meant engaging with their neighbors in a meaningful way, having a conversation about substantial topics, talking about things that matter a lot to them (traffic, noise), and forcing them to see you as a person beyond the stereotype. One man said after meeting with the door-knocking Muslims, "They're nice people. They're my neighbors now."[72]

While this strategy may work at the neighborhood level, it's much tougher at broader levels. Muslims are scorned for being of a different religion and for being darker (American and Europeans generally still don't care for dark people). Even if they look white (like many Arabs and, well, white converts), their religion and sometimes dress (hijab, beards) marks them as different. The scorn is compounded by the blame that average Muslims in the West get for terrorist violence committed by other Muslims. Because Muslims are a small, relatively powerless minority, it is very difficult to counteract this at the level of government, or in the media. Because of the association with terrorism (like the association of blacks with crime), Muslims often find themselves being preemptively targeted by some police departments. For example, the Los Angeles Police Department allowed using cyber surveillance, informants, and unverified "tips" to spy on Muslims with hardly any transparency or oversight.[73] (This guilt by association is not something that white people faced when Timothy McVeigh blew up the Federal

Building in Oklahoma City in 1995, or when Anders Breivik killed 77 people in Norway in 2011.)

This was minor compared to the New York City Police Department's program. For years during Michael Bloomberg's mayoral administration (2002–2013), authorities would pay informants to "bait" Muslims into saying incriminating things, infiltrate Muslim organizations on college campuses, spy on mosques and Muslim-owned businesses, and spy on religious Muslims to see where they ate, prayed, and worked. Again, there was no prior cause or suspicion; being Muslim was reason enough. And this wasn't limited to New York; the NYPD spied on Muslims in Newark, New Jersey as well. The mayor at the time, Corey Booker, was never told about the spying program. When asked, he said, "Wow. This raises a number of concerns. It's just very, very sobering."[74]

Conclusion

Muslims have a long presence in the West going back hundreds of years. But it is only since the 1950s in Western Europe, and the 1960s in the United States, that they have formed sizeable communities and established a visible presence. As we saw, there is a great degree of variation in economic and cultural integration, often stemming from the conditions of their initial migration. In Western Europe, they came initially as uneducated laborers, often from rural backgrounds. In the United States, they came initially as professionals. Many people decry the pace at which Muslims in the United States and in Europe are integrating and feel that Islam is a "dangerous" and foreign religion, and that Muslims can't possibly integrate to the majority population.

But this is not a new story. Incorporation takes time, and people said the exact same things in the 19th and early 20th centuries about Irish Catholics in the United States and United Kingdom, Poles in Germany, and Italians in the United States and France.[75] These groups were thought to come from unusual religious backgrounds and hold political ideologies considered dangerous to the social fabric, and unassimilable. And, like Muslims today, all these groups were initially considered to be racially not white. But over time, they did assimilate. And they became white.

However—and this is a big however—the way Muslims are socially defined in the West today is not only dependent on internal dynamics within Western countries, but also international events. The Iranian Revolution in 1979, the two Gulf Wars (1990, 2003), 9/11, the bombings in Madrid (March 11, 2004) and London (July 7, 2005)—these events have all shaped Western understanding of Islam as a religious system, and the ways they approach Muslims living within their borders. This may ultimately affect the ability of Muslims, as a group, to assimilate.

Notes

1 Kundnani, Arun. "Blind Spot? Security Narratives and Far-right Violence in Europe." *ICCT Research Paper*, The Hague, 2012.
2 Bergen, Peter, and David Sterman. "U.S. Right Wing Extremists More Deadly than Jihadists." *CNN*. April 15, 2014. www.cnn.com/2014/04/14/opinion/bergen-sterman-kansas-shooting/ <retrieved April 22, 2014>
3 Kurzman, Charles. *The Missing Martyrs: Why There Are so Few Muslim Terrorists*. Oxford: Oxford UP, 2011. See also Mueller, John, and Mark Stewart. "The Terrorism Delusion: America's Overwrought Response to September 11." *International Security* 37.1 (2012): 81–110.
4 Schanzer, David, and Charles Kurzman. "Homegrown Terrorism Threat Was Overhyped." *NJ.com*. April 14, 2014. www.nj.com/opinion/index.ssf/2014/04/homegrown_terrorism_threat_was_overhyped_opinion.html <retrieved May 12, 2014>
5 Goldberg, J.J. "More Killed by Toddlers Than Terrorists in U.S." *The Jewish Daily Forward*. May 5, 2013. http://blogs.forward.com/jj-goldberg/176043/more-killed-by-toddlers-than-terrorists-in-us/ <retrieved June 2, 2014>
   Silver, Nate. "Crunching the Risk Numbers." *Wall Street Journal*. January 8, 2010. http://online.wsj.com/news/articles/SB10001424052748703481004574646963713065116 <retrieved June 9, 2014>
6 Glassner, Barry. *The Culture of Fear: Why Americans Are Afraid of the Wrong Things*. New York, NY: Basic, 1999.
7 A useful resource is a recent report by the Center for American Progress. Ali, Wajahat, Eli Clifton, Matthew Duss, Lee Fang, Scott Keyes, and Faiz Shakir. *Fear, Inc.: The Roots of the Islamophobia Network in America*. Washington, DC: Center for American Progress, 2011.
8 The most clear-minded, and rhetorically convincing, of all the Eurabianist and Amerabianist writers is Caldwell, Christopher. *Reflections on the Revolution in Europe: Immigration, Islam, and the West*. London: Penguin, 2009. See Ali's scathing review (Ali, Syed. "The Moslems Are Here—Be Afraid!" *Contexts* 9.4 [2010]: 72–73).
9 Archer, Toby. "Breivik's Swamp: Was the Oslo Killer Radicalized by What He Read Online." *Foreign Policy*. July 25, 2011. www.foreignpolicy.com/articles/2011/07/25/breivik s_swamp <retrieved June 2, 2014>
10 Again, the Eurabianists and Amerabianists. See Mishra, Pankaj. "A Culture of Fear." *The Guardian*. August 15, 2009. www.theguardian.com/books/2009/aug/15/eurabia-islamophobia-europe-colonised-muslims <retrieved May 2, 2014>

11 For example, Abdo, Geneive. *Mecca and Main Street: Muslim Life in America after 9/11*. Oxford: Oxford UP, 2006.

12 This is common among many ethnographies. See for instance, Keaton, Trica. *Muslim Girls and the Other France: Race, Identity Politics, and Social Exclusion*. Bloomington: Indiana UP, 2006; Peek, Lori. *Behind the Backlash: Muslim Americans after 9/11*. Philadelphia: Temple UP, 2011.

13 Fisher, Michael. *Counterflows to Colonialism: Indian Travellers and Settlers in Britain, 1600–1857*. Delhi: Permanent Black, 2004.

14 Smith, Jane. *Islam in America*. New York: Columbia UP, 2013.

15 Bald, Vivek. *Bengali Harlem and the Lost Histories of South Asian America*. Cambridge, MA: Harvard UP, 2013.

16 Lucassen, Leo. *The Immigrant Threat: The Integration of Old and New Migrants in Western Europe since 1850*. Urbana: U of Illinois, 2005.

17 Saunders, Doug. *The Myth of the Muslim Tide: Do Immigrants Threaten the West?* New York: Vintage, 2012, p. 40.

18 "Muslims in Germany." *SPIEGEL ONLINE*. n.d. www.spiegel.de/international/germany/bild-850607–127849.html <retrieved May 8, 2014>

19 Vaisse, Justin. *Muslims in Europe: A Short Introduction*. Center on the United States and Europe at Brookings, 2008.

20 Pew Research Center. "Mapping the Global Muslim Population." October 7, 2009. www.pewforum.org/2009/10/07/mapping-the-global-muslim-population/ <retrieved June 3, 2014>

21 Pew Research Center. *Muslim Americans: No Signs of Growth in Alienation or Support for Extremism*. Pew Research Center: Washington, DC, 2011, p. 14.

22 Pew Research Center 2011, p. 8, ibid.

23 Pew Research Center 2011, p. 17, ibid.

24 Mogahed, Dalia. *Muslim Americans: A National Portrait*. Washington, DC: Gallup, 2009, p. 23.

25 Mogahed, Dalia. *Muslim Americans: A National Portrait*. Washington, DC: Gallup, 2009, p. 11.

26 Saunders 2012, p. 74, op cit.

27 Open Society Institute. "Muslims in Europe: A Report on 11 EU Cities." New York: Open Society Institute, 2010, p. 110.

28 Mirza, Munira, Abi Senthilkumaran, and Zein Ja'far. *Living Apart Together: British Muslims and the Paradox of Multiculturalism*. London: Policy Exchange, 2007, p. 68.

29 Silberman, Roxane. "The Employment of Second Generations in France: The Republican Model and the November 2005 Riots." In Richard Alba and Mary Waters, eds., *The Next Generation: Immigrant Youth in a Comparative Perspective*. New York: NYU Press, 2011.

30 Crul, Maurice, Jens Schneider, and Frans Lelie. *Super Diversity: A New Perspective on Integration*. Amsterdam: VU University Press, 2013, p. 65.

31 Pager, Devah, and Bruce Western. "Identifying Discrimination at Work: The Use of Field Experiments." *Journal of Social Issues* 68.2 (2012): 221–237.

32 Crul et al. 2013, p. 65, op cit.

33 Open Society Institute 2012, p. 115, op cit.

34 Duyvendak, Jan, Trees Pels, and Rally Riijkschroeff. "A Multicultural Paradise? The Cultural Factor in Dutch Integration Policy." In Jennifer Hochschild and John Mollenkopf, eds., *Bringing Outsiders In: Transatlantic Perspectives on Immigrant Political Incorporation*. Ithaca, NY: Cornell UP, 2009, p. 133.

35 Beaman, Jean. *Liberte, Egalite, et Fraternite: Identity, Marginalization, and Second-Generation North African Immigrants in France*. Diss., Northwestern University, 2010.

36 Crul, Maurice, Philipp Schnell, Barbara Herzog-Punzenberger, Maren Wilmes, Marieke Slootman, and Rosa Gomez. "School Careers of Second-Generation Youth in Europe: Which Education Systems Provide the Best Chances for Success?" In Maurice Crul, Jens Schneider, and Frans Lelie, eds., *The European Second Generation Compared: Does the Integration Context Matter?* Amsterdam: Amsterdam UP, 2012, p.103.

37 Kalter, Frank. "The Second Generation in the German Labor Market: Explaining the Turkish Exception." In Richard Alba and Mary Waters, *The Next Generation: Immigrant Youth in a Comparative Perspective* (New York: NYU Press, 2011).

38 Crul, Schneider, and Lelie 2013, op cit.

39 Crul, Schneider, and Lelie 2013, op cit., p. 58.

40 Laurence, Jonathan, and Justin Vaïsse. *Integrating Islam: Political and Religious Challenges in Contemporary France*. Washington, DC: Brookings Institution, 2006, pp. 43–46.

41 Muttarak, Raya. "Generation, Ethnic and Religious Diversity in Friendship Choice: Exploring Interethnic Close Ties in Britain." *Ethnic and Racial Studies* 37.1 (2014): 71–98.

42 Pew Research Center 2011, op cit., p. 35.

43 Lucassen, Leo, and Charlotte Laarman. "Immigration, Intermarriage and the Changing Face of Europe in the Post War Period." *The History of the Family* 14.1 (2009): 52–68.

44 Ibid.

45 As mentioned earlier, TIES is not a country-by-country survey. Instead, they conducted their survey in 15 cities across 8 European countries.

46 Huschek, Doreen, Helga Valk, and Aart Liefbroer. "Partner Choice Patterns Among the Descendants of Turkish Immigrants in Europe." *European Journal of Population/ Revue Européenne De Démographie* 28.3 (2012): 241–268.

47 Safi, Mirna. "Intermarriage and Assimilation: Disparities in Levels of Exogamy among Immigrants in France." *Population* (English Edition) 63.2 (2008): 239–267.

48 Kibria, Nazli. "Transnational Marriage and the Bangladeshi Muslim Diaspora in Britain and the United States." *Culture and Religion* 13.2 (2012): 227–240; Lewis, Philip. *Young, British and Muslim*. London: Continuum, 2007; Santelli, Emmanuelle, and Beate Collet. "The Choice of Mixed Marriage among the Second Generation in France: A Lifetime Approach." *Papers: Revista de Sociologia* 97.1 (2012): 93–112; Selby, Jennifer. "Marriage-partner Preference among Muslims in France: Reproducing Tradition in the Maghrebian Diaspora." *Journal of the Society for the Anthropology of Europe* 9.2 (2009): 4–16.

49 Billaud, Julie. "Snapshots of British Islam (3): Halal Dating in London #ANTHROISLAM." *Allegra*. December 9, 2013. http://allegralaboratory.net/ snapshots-of-british-islam-3-halal-dating-in-london/ <retrieved March 12, 2014>

50 Ali, Syed. "Understanding Acculturation among Second-generation South Asian Muslims in the United States." *Contributions to Indian Sociology* 42.3 (2008): 383–411.

51 Kumar, Sujay. "Muslim, Single, Looking to Mingle." *The Daily Beast.* September 13, 2013. www.thedailybeast.com/witw/articles/2013/09/13/young-muslim-navigating-the-american-dating-gauntlet.html <retrieved March 28, 2014>; Siddiqui, Obaid. "Looking for Love and Finding Awkwardness at ISNA." *Altmuslim: Global Perspectives on Muslim Life, Politics, and Culture.* September 10, 2012. www.patheos.com/blogs/altmuslim/2012/09/looking-for-love-and-finding-awkwardness-at-isna/ <retrieved March 28, 2014>. Or you could just do a web search for "club ISNA."

52 Saunders 2012, p. 64, op cit.

53 Pew Research Center 2011, p. 9, op cit.

54 Mogahed 2009, p. 35, op cit.

55 This study was conducted by the Harvard School of Public Health. It has a small subsample of Muslims that show very interesting, and perhaps counterintuitive, results of how young Muslims in the United States behave. Of the 10,401 students surveyed, 135 (1.3 percent) reported they were raised in Muslim families. The sample of Muslim students consisted of 42.7 percent Other, 23.9 percent Asian American/Pacific Islander, 23.1 percent white, and 10.9 percent African American. Half of the participants (50.4 percent) were under 21 years of age, whereas 30 percent were between the ages of 22–23, and 19.3 percent of the participants were over 23 years. See Abu-Ras, Wahiba, Sameera Ahmed, and Cynthia L. Arfken. "Alcohol Use among US Muslim College Students: Risk and Protective Factors." *Journal of Ethnicity in Substance Abuse* 9.3 (2010): 206–220.

56 Abu-Ras et al. 2010, ibid.

57 Diab, Khaled. "Why Muslims Don't Pig Out." *The Guardian.* July 2, 2008. www.theguardian.com/commentisfree/2008/jul/02/islam.religion <retrieved March 12, 2014>

58 Marquand, Robert. "Facebook Draws 7,000 to Anti-Muslim Pork Sausage Party in Paris." *Christian Science Monitor.* June 17, 2010. www.csmonitor.com/World/Europe/2010/0617/Facebook-draws-7–000-to-anti-Muslim-pork-sausage-party-in-Paris <retrieved May 12, 2014>; see also Titley, Gavan. "Pork Is the Latest Front in Europe's Culture Wars." *The Guardian.* April 14, 2014. www.theguardian.com/commentisfree/2014/apr/15/le-pen-pig-whistle-politics?CMP=twt_gu <retrieved April 15, 2014>

59 Mipsterz—Muslim Hipsters. Facebook. https://www.facebook.com/Mipsterz/info <retrieved June 6, 2014>

60 Hafiz, Yasmine. "'Mipsterz' 'Somewhere In America' Video Showcases Muslim Hipster Swag; Sparks A Passionate Discussion." December 2, 2013. www.huffingtonpost.com/2013/12/02/mipsterz-somewhere-in-america-video_n_4374182.html <retrieved May 6, 2014>

61 Haddad, Yvonne, and Adair Lummis. *Islamic Values in the United States: A Comparative Study.* New York: Oxford UP, 1987, p. 132.

62 Ali, Syed. "Why Here, Why Now? Young Muslim Women Wearing Hijab." *The Muslim World* 95.4 (2005): 515–530.

63 Pew Research Center 2011, p. 31, op cit.

64 Ali found this to be fairly common among the older female relatives of people he interviewed and hung out while doing research among the South Asian Muslim second generation in New York City in the late 1990s-early 2000s.

65 Scott, Joan. *The Politics of the Veil*. Princeton, NJ: Princeton UP, 2010, p 3.

66 Caldwell, Christopher. *Reflections on the Revolution in Europe: Immigration, Islam, and the West*. London: Penguin, 2009, p. 85.

67 Del Signore, John. "Anti-Mosque Protesters On SI Bring Out NYC's Inner Bigot." Gothamist. June 21, 2010. http://gothamist.com/2010/06/21/anti-mosque_protesters_on_si_bring.php <retrieved May 1, 2014>

68 Del Signore, John. "Meeting To Discuss Mosque On Staten Island Ends Predictably." Gothamist. June 10, 2010. http://gothamist.com/2010/06/10/meeting_to_discuss_mosque_on_staten.php <retrieved April 30, 2014>; Padnani, Amy. "Midland Beach Mosque Voted Down by Church's Board of Trustees." Silive.com. July 22, 2010; www.silive.com/eastshore/index.ssf/2010/07/midland_beach_mosque_voted_dow.html <retrieved April 30, 2014>; Vitello, Paul. "Church Rejects Sale of Building for a Mosque." *New York Times*. July 22, 2010. www.nytimes.com/2010/07/23/nyregion/23mosque.html?sq=dolan%20mosque&st=cse&adxnnl=1&scp=6&adxnnlx=1313704711-xs4k3DQNo9xCYr5wLki9Yg <retrieved April 30, 2014>

69 Berger, Joseph. "Protests of a Plan for a Mosque? That Was Last Year." *New York Times*. August 18, 2011. <retrieved May 15, 2014> www.nytimes.com/2011/08/19/nyregion/mosque-opens-quietly-on-staten-island.html <retrieved May 15, 2014>; "Mosque Opens on SI Without Controversy." *The Real Deal*. August 19, 2011. http://therealdeal.com/blog/2011/08/19/mosque-opens-on-staten-island-without-controversy/ <retrieved May 15, 2014>

70 "Public Remains Conflicted Over Islam." *Pew Research Religion and Public Life Project*. August 24, 2010. www.pewforum.org/2010/08/24/public-remains-conflicted-over-islam/ <retrieved May 2, 2014>

71 "Islamophobia: Understanding Anti-Muslim Sentiment in the West." *Gallup World*. 2014. www.gallup.com/poll/157082/islamophobia-understanding-anti-muslim-sentiment-west.aspx <retrieved May 2, 2014>

72 Berger 2011, op cit. www.nytimes.com/2011/08/19/nyregion/mosque-opens-quietly-on-staten-island.html

73 Kolsy, Uzma. "LAPD Continues Controversial Anti-terrorism Spying Program with Little Oversight." *The Raw Story*. September 5, 2012. www.rawstory.com/rs/2012/09/05/lapd-continues-controversial-anti-terrorism-spying-program-with-little-oversight/ <retrieved May 6, 2014>

74 Goldman, Adam, and Matt Apuzzo. "NYPD Built Secret Files on Mosques Outside NY." *Associated Press*. February 22, 2012. www.ap.org/Content/AP-In-The-News/2012/NYPD-built-secret-files-on-mosques-outside-NY <retrieved May 6, 2014>. For a full compilation of the articles the Associated Press reporters Matt Apuzzo and Adam Goldman wrote on the NYPD spying program, see www.ap.org/Index/AP-In-The-News/NYPD <retrieved May 6, 2014>.

75 Gottschalk, Peter. *American Heretics: Catholics, Jews, Muslims, and the History of Religious Intolerance*. Palgrave Macmillan, 2013; Lucassen, *The Immigrant Threat*, 2005, op cit.

6

How Migration
Impacts Societies

In the spring of 2014, a high school senior named Kwasi Enin made headlines in the United States (or lit up the Internet depending upon your source of news), when he got accepted to all eight Ivy League schools on the basis of a stellar class rank and a 2250 SAT score. Actually, it wasn't just this accomplishment, wonderful and impressive as it may have been, that made the story newsworthy. It was the fact that Enin was a first-generation immigrant from Ghana.

For some, Enin's scholarly success was a cause for celebration—a symbol of migrant mobility and accomplishment as well as of the openness and inclusiveness of American society with respect to migrants and minorities more generally. In other quarters, Enin's case was seen as more problematic, and in fact provoked a fair bit of controversy and angst. The controversy did not come from the usual sources such the Tea Party set that has emerged in opposition to immigration in the United States over the past few years or even more right-wing racial nativists. Concern came, instead, from the other end of the political and social spectrum—those who are interested in and committed to projects of racial equity and justice for disadvantaged racial minorities. The basic problem for racial justice advocates was that it was believed that immigrants like Enin were benefiting from "affirmative action" programs designed and intended not for immigrants but for other, "native" American minorities who had been historically disadvantaged and marginalized by racism and discrimination in the United States.

Though it was not entirely clear that Enin had benefited from such admission policies, the concerns clearly had some basis in the social facts of American migration and racial demography. A 2007 study by Doug Massey and his colleagues, for example, found that black students of recent immigrant origin were significantly over-represented among students at elite-level American colleges and universities.[1] A little over a quarter of black freshman in their study were first- and second-generation immigrants, with upwards of 35 percent of student admits at the most select institutions in their study. (To put this in context, consider that the 3.3 million foreign-born blacks in the country represent approximately 8 percent of all black Americans, and 12 percent of all black children—large numbers perhaps, but nowhere near the proportion being accepted into American institutions of higher learning.) And Enin's story is not only about the distribution of resources between and among various immigrant and minority communities in the United States. It also reminds us of how migrants like Enin and his family are changing the basic population demographics of immigrant-receiving societies like the United States.[2]

Though unique in many respects, Enin's case and experience are illustrative of the larger theme of this chapter: the broader societal impacts and implications of migration. Who, besides migrants themselves, are impacted by immigration—and in what ways?

The bulk of this book so far has been focused on the experience of migrants—their motives, the larger social, economic, and political factors that shape and determine their movements, as well as the environmental forces that shape their incorporation (or lack thereof) in their new communities. But we haven't really addressed head on the issues, questions, and topics that make immigration and migration such a hotly contested issue in contemporary societies all over the world today—namely, how migrants impact the societies they enter, what kinds of contributions they make, what changes they occasion, and the extent to which they take resources and opportunities away from others. The reason that immigration is often so controversial in political culture is less about migrants themselves than it is about the changes—both real and perceived, intentional, and unintentional—that they bring in the countries they are moving to and those from which they are departing. And this is not just a story that impacts individuals or particular social groups. This is a broad, societal level story about the impacts and implications—ranging from changing population profiles and racial demographics to economics and culture—that increased migration and diversity present in the countries sending and receiving them.

The Economic Question

Perhaps no immigration "impact issue" is more widely debated and hotly contested than the economic one. For those who are supportive of immigration, the financial benefits of migration are clear and obvious both for the migrants themselves and for the societies they enter: Migrants work hard, often at jobs natives are not interested in or trained for, they pay taxes, and allow goods and services to be cheaper and more available than they would be otherwise. For those who are more critical, immigration may or may not be an economic boon for migrants, but it is definitely believed to be a drain on social services such as education, health care, welfare, etc.

Both economists and policy makers have done a great deal of research on these questions. It is beyond the scope of this chapter to try to adjudicate these debates and competing economic models once and for all. However, there are a few basic points that we can offer.

First and most basically, it is pretty clear that migration is generally a positive economic force for migrants themselves. This is not always true for every migrant in all social contexts; indeed, some of the case studies and stories we've presented in the previous chapters make that clear. However, overall we believe this to be true basically because migration in the contemporary world usually involves people moving from a poorer place to a richer one. And this is not just speculation. One recent overview found that migrants from the poorest countries experience on average a "15-fold increase" in income after migrating.[3]

The main economic issue of migration is the financial costs and consequences for sending and receiving societies. Let's start with the former, the countries that migrants are leaving in order to move to a new place.

You might assume that sending nations are negatively impacted by these departures—after all, they are losing people, potential workers and laborers, and creative capacity—what many people call "brain drain."

However, although migrants may be leaving a place physically, they typically do not leave it behind altogether. That is, they become transnationals (which we discussed in Chapter 1). Transnationalism is often thought of as a new and unique historical development. In fact, there has always been a good deal of transnational interaction and exchange historically.[4] Not all migrants come wanting citizenship and incorporation. In fact, many come with quite different hopes and expectations. Some want to work and return. Many migrants who move to a place do so with the intent of both gathering resources that can be sent back home and one day returning to their country of origin. Others maintain extensive contacts and connections with friends and family in the countries they came from. There is typically much more movement back and forth than is often realized (though less than what many researchers claim). And it also appears to be the case that these connections and exchanges are even easier to support and maintain in the contemporary era because of all the new technologies of communication, transportation, and cultural exchange that now mark the worlds that we inhabit.

As migrants make more money in their new contexts and improve their standards of living, they typically not only save more money, but they send surprisingly large chunks of that money—remittances— back to people in the societies that they initially came from. How much? Estimates vary but with remittances and other transfers of resources and support, a conservative estimate is that migrants provide upwards of 10 percent of total GDP for some countries.[5] This is why many sending countries have actually established policies and programs to organize and support it. It is also why many of these countries have begun to craft new laws for citizenship, to allow and encourage voting, political participation, and cultural exchange with their citizens living abroad. For instance, many more countries today allow dual citizenship, rather than forcing their citizens to choose between their old countries and new.

What, then, of the receiving countries and nations? What are the financial impacts and consequences for them? Here we come to the issue that is by far the most complicated and contested aspect of the economic impact question—and the one that is probably the most studied, not only by sociologists but also by economists, political scientists, geographers, and public policy specialists.

Much of the debate over the economic costs and benefits of migration is focused on the poorest migrants, refugees, and those immigrants whose status is most questionable in terms of formal laws and policies. On the one hand, there is no question that this group of immigrants and their children present receiving countries with significant economic costs in terms of the need to provide government benefits and social services.[6] On the other hand, there are extensive debates among researchers and policy makers about how to calculate these expenses. For example, should education for the children of these immigrants—the vast majority of whom are or will become citizens—count? And what are often minimized (or missed altogether, partly because it is difficult to document) are the contributions that they make to local economies via taxes and their own consumer spending. It is worth pointing out that low-skilled immigrant workers tend to take jobs in service-sector industries ranging from agriculture to fast food to custodial work and hospitality that are highly needed, but difficult for employers to fill.

Another point that is often missing from cost-benefit analyses of immigrant labor is a systemic consideration of the benefits of richer, more highly educated migrants. Doctors, scientists and researchers, engineers, software developers, and other technical experts not only make obvious economic contributions, but they bring a high level of cultural, social, and economic capital with them upon moving into a new country.

All things considered, most scholars believe that migrant workers have a neutral if not slightly positive impact on per capita income and economic productivity. Perhaps it isn't surprising, then, that immigration is usually supported by big business and those in favor of free markets and unfettered economic growth more generally.[7]

This isn't to say that everyone in a country benefits economically from migration. Quite the contrary, some industries and businesses benefit more than others, and the social and administrative costs of migration are more likely to fall upon states or regions with larger numbers of migrants. These facts help explain why communities with adverse economic conditions are often particularly sensitive to the economic challenges that can be posed by immigrants.[8] Workers are another group whose material interests may be compromised by migration. While it is true that migrants typically take jobs that are far less attractive to natives, migrant labor can and often does drive down wages and benefits, especially for the lower-skilled, less educated workers in the job market. In point of fact, numerous studies have shown that American employers discriminate against African Americans in favor of immigrants for entry-level jobs.[9] And on the other end of the spectrum, American engineers complain constantly (and with good reason) that technology companies are using the H1B visa program to undermine the former by bringing in highly educated but underpaid Asian engineers.[10]

Suffice it to say, this competition and unevenness is part of the reason the economic question is so controversial: The benefits and costs are not equally distributed, and those who don't reap its benefits are less likely to be supportive, or are more likely to focus on other social or cultural drawbacks that they may perceive. But often these competing interests and motivations get mixed up. Some of the most pointed criticisms of American migration policy from sociologists are how naïve, inefficient, and even contradictory American laws and policies have been when it comes to the economic dynamics that drive the relocation of people from one place to another.[11] When there are limited economic opportunities in one place and jobs in another, people in the poorer place are going to find ways to come and take advantage of those opportunities. And industries and employers who need this labor will find a way to find them, especially if these workers are willing to work harder and cheaper than other potential workers in their communities. Yet the problem is that Americans have wanted the material benefits of migrant labor without being willing to assume any of the attendant social costs and responsibilities. They have wanted to have their cake and eat it too.

Demographics: Population Growth and Racial Reconfiguration[12]

As any student of demography knows, population trends are determined by three basic factors: births, deaths, and—drum roll, please—migration. A great deal of the research we have covered in previous chapters— indeed of migration itself—can be seen in a very basic and fundamental sense as the study of population and demography. And there is no greater evidence of the demographic importance of migration than contemporary American society.

With a population of 300 million and growing, the United States is a rarity among the most industrialized, developed nations of the world—especially compared to those of Western Europe. In Western European countries, population growth has slowed to a crawl, leveled out, or even begun to decline altogether. There are many reasons for this, but at the most basic level, it's because as older people are dying, young people are delaying family formation, having fewer children, and are less and less likely to even have babies at all.[13] Birth rates, in short, are not replacing the deaths, leading to zero or even negative population growth. The United States is the clear exception to this trend, and the reason for this is not so much stable or expanding birth rates, but because of its high levels of immigration over the past several decades.[14]

Though it has leveled off a bit in recent years, the sheer numbers of migrants who have entered into the United States since the 1960s is astounding. As we detailed in the introduction, there are approximately 40 million foreign born people in the United States today—which is about 12–13 percent of the total population or one in eight Americans. This is one of the highest rates in American history, and a decisive contributor to continued population growth.

The implications of demographic growth via migration are not limited to overall population numbers in a given country. Migration and changing population dynamics also can reshuffle and reshape large-scale social categories like race and ethnicity.

According to official Census projections and other sources, the United States will soon be a "majority-minority" society by 2050 (if not earlier). That is, those who are not white in the very near future will outnumber the white majority. This transition is well underway, and in many states and cities, this has already happened. Nearly a quarter of states have already achieved majority-minority status or will soon get there, and within 35 years or so, the proportion of Hispanics in the United States will nearly double (from 16 to 30 percent of the population), and 8 percent of Americans will be of Asian origin (up from about 5 percent currently). And the important point, at least in the context of this book, is that international migration accounts for the bulk of this racial re-composition and reordering.[15] This happens in both direct and indirect ways. On the one hand, large numbers of immigrants from diverse countries and cultures and with a wide range of skin tones have come into the country in the last few decades. On the other hand, there is a new baby boom among new immigrant groups and other communities of color—all while native, non-Hispanic white women are experiencing significant declines in birth rates.

The implications of these demographic shifts are profound—and we will come to some of the cultural impacts (or potential impacts) shortly—but demographics are not, in and of themselves, destiny.

Sociologists who study race and demographics envision a wide range of scenarios for American's racial future. For example, Richard Alba (who we discussed in Chapter 4) believes that mass immigration is leading to a "blurring" of racial categories and boundaries in the United States. That is, changing demographics will break down color lines and racial barriers and open up the possibility of a more integrated society.

Alba's vision of a less racialized America stems from two main sources. One is the characteristics and behaviors of new immigrant groups—their overall socio-economic upward mobility, increasing rates of intermarriage, residential integration, and how quickly immigrants learn English and accommodate themselves to American culture. Because of their continuing assimilation, new immigrants are fundamentally challenging prevailing racial hierarchies and stereotypes and diversifying mainstream culture in the process.[16]

The second reason for Alba's optimism is his understanding and analysis of the opportunities presented by current economic projections and demographics. An expanding global economy, the exit of baby boomers from the labor force, and the declining birth rates of the majority-white group together create conditions in which individuals of immigrant minorities can move up without affecting the life chances of natives.[17] This is "non-zero-sum mobility"—mobility that doesn't provoke the competitive backlash that new immigrants often encounter—and it essentially describes the situation for ethnic European immigrants in the United States who came earlier. Although Irish, Italian, and other Southern and Eastern European migrants to the United States were initially seen as racially inferior, they benefited from a booming post-World War II economy that led to mass economic mobility and also benefited from restrictive policies that sharply curtailed immigration after their arrival. Over time, these once "different" immigrants were able to assimilate—or "become white"—and thus overcome and indeed reconfigure the boundaries and barriers of race.

Other sociologists are less optimistic than Alba. These critics believe that migration and the dynamics of incorporation (or the lack thereof) will bring either the reinforcement—or "hardening"—of existing racial barriers or the emergence of new racial lines.

One of these sociologists is Eduardo Bonilla-Silva.[18] In coming years, Bonilla-Silva believes the most prominent and problematic racial boundaries and barriers—especially those associated with privilege and power—will calcify. Bonilla-Silva sees race as a system of relationships between advantaged and disadvantaged groups, in which those who benefit from existing racial systems are unlikely to acknowledge or unwilling to relinquish the privileges that go along with being white. More than a few sociological (and non-sociological) analysts agree. But what makes Bonilla-Silva's approach unique is his belief that the reproduction of racial categories and inequalities are driven less by old-fashioned prejudice than, ironically, by the colorblind ideals to which Americans of all racial backgrounds adhere. Basically, he believes that the adherence to abstract, individualist ideals will blind Americans to the persistent social barriers that stand in the way of migrant and minority mobility and incorporation.[19]

Alongside the entrenchment of current racial lines, Bonilla-Silva also predicts the emergence of new racial categories that go beyond black and white. In particular, he sees the explosion of Latino immigration, the evolving status of immigrant groups like Asian Americans, and increases in interracial dating and mixed-race children as evolving from a bi-racial system of "white" and "non-white" to a tri-racial system of "white," "honorary white," and "collective black." This scheme resembles the hierarchy in many Latin American countries.

Just as many Latin American countries tend to downplay the colonial legacies of privilege for those with lighter skin tones, Bonilla-Silva suggests we will do the same in the United States. Even those at the bottom of this racial stratification system will refuse to identify in racialized terms, preferring instead to claim national or ethnic unity—"We are all Puerto Rican," for example. But such ideals and identifications will obscure the deeper realities of race. A new racial landscape will *appear* more fluid and multicultural, but Bonilla-Silva argues that it will actually be more tilted toward white privilege in that it will discourage talking about race at all. It will quietly encourage non-black racial minorities (including African and West Indian immigrants) in their struggle to become "white," or at least "whiter."

Ethnicity and Cultural Change

So far we have been talking mainly about racial demographics and classifications, but there are obviously many other forms of social distinction and collective identification. One that is closely related to race and central to the study of migration is ethnicity. In contrast to race, which is typically predicated on some kind of perceived difference in genetics or biology, ethnicity is a claim to collective identification based upon descent and homeland, upon kinship, common culture, and national origin. It also tends to be more elective or within the control of those who claim the identity (or disavow it). Ethnic affiliations are not unrelated to racial groups. As Hartmann has stressed in his work with Stephen Cornell, any single group or population can be both a race and an ethnic group at the same time, or at least exhibit both racial and ethnic characteristics.[20] The Irish immigrants who came to the United States in the early part of the 20th century are a good example. Upon entry, these migrants were seen as non-white and racially inferior, but they also carved out for themselves a distinctive ethnic identity and community based upon common kinship, cultural customs, and traditions.[21]

What is most important about ethnicity for us is that its emphasis on culture and self-assertion signals a whole other, hugely important set of questions about the impacts and consequences of immigration—namely, how migrants shape and reshape the culture and overall way of life of the communities and societies they are entering into. For example, when the Irish and other Southern and Eastern European immigrants came to the United States from the mid-1800s to the early 1900s, they encountered cities and communities that were dominated by white, Anglo-Saxon, and Protestant (WASP) culture. These migrants brought with them different cultural customs, traditions, religious practices and beliefs. These new cultures and customs were not always tolerated and smoothly accepted by the native WASP majority. The Prohibition movement can be read as an attempt by WASPs to reclaim a more traditional vision of recreation and leisure in American culture and society.[22] But ultimately, the Prohibition movement lost steam, and a new set of practices and traditions prevailed.

Given the large number of immigrants we are talking about and their commitment to their ethnic culture and traditions, American culture itself became over the course of the 20th century less and less Anglo and Protestant, and more Catholic and Jewish, with more Southern and Eastern European influences—new foods and music, new holidays, customs, and cultural traditions. The change that came with migration, in other words, wasn't just a one-way street of assimilation and accommodation on the part of migrants; it was a two-way street where a new blend of cultures and ethnic customs, traditions, and beliefs emerged.[23]

In the first half of the 20th century, Americans talked about this phenomenon as cultural pluralism.[24] Today, it is typically discussed under the heading of multiculturalism, and it isn't just the United States that is grappling with its effects. It is all societies that are receiving migrants in large numbers, especially those with strong cultural commitments and traditional national identities.

Multiculturalism and Diversity

In Chapter 4, we talked about segmented assimilation, a theoretical framework proposed by Alejandro Portes and Min Zhou to explain how the incorporation of young immigrants in any society is dependent on factors like race, parental capital, and how the migrant group was received in the United States legally and socially. One of the things that is important about segmented assimilation is that it captures a shift or "turn" in assimilation studies in recent decades: Namely, the realization that there are many different, highly diverse pathways of incorporation in the contemporary world, and that incorporation is a population-level process wherein the "unit within which change occurs—the unit that undergoes assimilation—is not the person but a multi-generational population."[25]

This is perhaps clearest if you think about co-ethnic enclaves—communities where immigrants of particular backgrounds live and work in relatively high concentrations—as a kind of middle road in the United States between traditional assimilation and the newer and more problematic downward mode of incorporation. On the one hand, an ethnic enclave can be seen as a transitional step for individuals on the way to fuller economic incorporation and even eventual fuller cultural incorporation, a way that migrants are incorporated into their new economic and social environments. On the other hand, this pathway implies and is basically dependent upon the existence of a distinctive ethnic group and community. This group may indeed help individuals in their transition to American culture. However, it can also be—or become—an end or entity in and of itself, a community, culture, and distinctive way of life for those who make it up. And these groups, depending upon their size and public visibility, can have significant consequences for the countries and societies within which they take shape.

Hmong refugees in the United States are one migrant group who, for a variety of reasons, have tended to settle in such enclaves or co-ethnic communities. In a study of Hmong immigrants living in enclaves in St. Paul, Minnesota, Hartmann, along with Teresa Swartz and Pao Lee, found that second-generation Hmong Americans were hoping to carve out for themselves and their children a distinctive social niche and cultural community, one where Hmong cultural traditions and practices—including spiritual beliefs, origin stories, kinship networks, and language—were protected and preserved.[26] Their experience begins to suggest some of the broader impacts migrant populations can have in a place, in a community, or on a culture. Let us explain.

As second-generation Hmong—American citizens all—move from high school and adolescence into young adulthood, they come to exhibit the traits and characteristics reminiscent of the bicultural, ethnic pathway of segmented assimilation. On the one hand, they have been leveraging their educational ambitions into relatively high rates of college attendance and educational attainment. Many have moved into good jobs and promising careers, and most have established families and homes of their own. At the same time, Hmong American young adults continue to live in fairly tight, intergenerational communities and households, where they help their parents with translation and negotiating American institutions and their parents help them with childcare, housework, food preparation, and the like. In this context, Hmong language is still spoken and the unique cultural traditions and customs associated with ties of kinship and clan membership are maintained. Moreover, these new Americans continue to think of themselves as different and distinct from other Americans, occupying a unique bicultural status. Rather than completely shedding Hmong culture and completely embracing an imagined "American" culture, they are convinced that they will be the generation carving out a new Hmong culture and community in their new country. In other words, the more established Hmong young adults are becoming in socio-economic terms *and* the more secure in their own hybrid, bicultural American identity, the more they express a commitment to securing traditional Hmong culture and customs. This is less about them personally, than about the future of Hmong culture and community especially with regards to their children.

One second-generation Hmong woman put it this way. "When you are younger, you think, 'Oh, come on. We're in America. We're Americans. We're in America.' But then as you start getting older, you're kind of like it's not, it's not about 'Hmong pride.' It's more about maintaining, it's your heritage. You want to be proud of what you have [and] where you came from and things like that. And you just want to maintain some of it. You want to remember some of it, instead of just, 'Oh, we have to go to a museum to see it.'"

Food, clothes, rituals, family stories—these were all things this woman and many others said were essential to pass on to the next generation. Several of the young adults in this study had taken on active leadership roles in Hmong cultural and community organizations, in efforts to preserve and pass on Hmong culture, and/or influence its form in the US context. Others had begun to take on leadership roles in their own clans and kinship networks.

This new Hmong American culture and community is a "work in progress," with the second generation seeing themselves as cultural bridges, preserving traditional Hmong culture and forging new hybrid forms in America for the future. But what we really want to highlight are some of the broader implications of their vision of themselves as an ethnic community as well as their role in and vision of American society.

The first and most basic point is the vision of society and culture we see through the eyes of these new immigrants—not just a melting pot of assimilating individuals, but a more pluralist, multicultural collection of distinctive ethnic cultures and communities. The new cultural identities and co-ethnic communities created by immigrant groups like the Hmong in the United States and elsewhere is not just about themselves, but about creating expanded and more diverse visions of the communities, cultures, and nations within which they live and reside. This is the notion that is typically thought of as multiculturalism—nations or communities defined not by having a singular, unified culture, but those composed of multiple and relatively discrete customs, lifestyles, values, and beliefs.[27]

One of the features that distinguishes contemporary multiculturalism from its earlier pluralist cousin is the level of acceptance and celebration that it enjoys in communities and societies all over the world. In contrast to previous eras, many people in various countries now see the expansion and diversification of their national cultures as positive and productive. They see migrants and the new ethnic, cultural, and religious traditions and practices they bring with them as making their communities and societies more multifaceted, interesting, creative, heterogeneous places to live. Ethnic and other forms of cultural diversity brought by migrants are not just tolerated; they are actively encouraged and celebrated. There is perhaps no better illustration of this point than the celebration of difference and diversity that has emerged across racial, religious, ethnic, and political lines in the United States. As Nathan Glazer sardonically put it for Americans, "We are All Multiculturalists, Now."[28]

Here, we should also highlight the role that visible, vibrant, and expanding ethnic-immigrant communities can play in bridging the gaps between communities of color and other, more traditionally privileged groups. Among the many examples that can be given, New York City, with its amazing array of diverse ethnic communities and neighborhoods, is probably the most obvious and well-researched example. [29] Granted, the Big Apple occupies a very unique place in US society and our history of racial, ethnic, and immigrant relations, and is not without its own tensions and challenges. Nonetheless, the city is notable for its relative success in integrating all these diverse elements and ingredients into a vibrant and highly functioning mix of cultures. Much of this success is based on the existence, and perhaps even New Yorkers' active promotion and empowerment, of its ethnic neighborhoods and how all the different cultural communities ultimately form a common identity.

For all of the appeal of cultural diversity *and* in spite of the important role that ethnic-immigrant communities can play in bridging boundaries within a society, the cultural changes and challenges that come with the increased size and visibility of migrant enclaves must also be taken into account. Multiculturalism is still far from universally accepted. It is that resistance and indeed backlash that we turn to next.

Cultural Backlash and Response

Not everyone is happy with the rise of multiculturalism, and a great deal of backlash has occurred. Much of the backlash against the ethnic diversification and multiculturalism that typically accompany international migration has come from the political Right. White nativism and anti-immigrant backlash and other types of xenophobia are nothing new—in the United States or elsewhere. Jews, Irish, Japanese, and others have all endured varyingly levels of social and political oppression. But the resistance to migration and multiculturalism is changing in some important respects as well. In the United States and Western Europe, as we touched upon in the last chapter, the backlash to immigration and multiculturalism more generally has focused more around issues of culture and religion—and in particular anti-Muslim sentiment, which has ramped up in the post-9/11 era.

Fear and disdain for Muslims as a people and Islam as a religion predates 9/11. In the United States, we can trace it back to the 1979 Iranian revolution. This really became a public issue around the time of the 1991 Gulf War, and was amplified after the 1993 World Trade Center bombing, and the 1995 Oklahoma City federal building bombing. In Europe, the disdain for Muslims as a group developed over the course of the 1980s, largely spurred on by increasing migration and the shift in the Muslim population from single laborers to families with children. But it was also events such as anti-racism protests in the early 1980s in the United Kingdom and France, book burnings and riots in the United Kingdom over Salman Rushdie's novel, *The Satanic Verses* in 1989, and in France controversies surrounding Muslim women veiling in public in the 1990s that made Muslims visible.

So what is new? Anti-Muslim sentiment is no longer confined to the fringe, but now is firmly ensconced among mainstream politicians in Western Europe and the United States. The terrorist attacks of 9/11 made racist anti-Muslim attitudes and pronouncements legitimate. While the most vitriolic politicians are on the far right in Europe, such as Jean-Marie Le Pen (and his daughter Marie Le Pen) in France and Pim Fortuyn in the Netherlands, American politicians of the right have left behind George W. Bush's pronouncements post-9/11 that Islam is a religion of peace and that the United States is not at war with Muslims, and now echo the kinds of speech that is common in Europe. This sentiment grew rapidly during the Obama presidency.

What is underlying the overt and subtle hostility to Muslim and other stigmatized immigrant groups such as Mexican Americans in the United States is more than just old-fashioned racism and prejudice. It is also the conviction that traditional national cultures are under threat. This reaction is not only motivated by a nostalgic harking to the "good old days," but also because many feel a reversal of multiculturalism will be for the political and social good of the nation. And they sort of have a point. Many of the world's migrants are not only lower-skilled and less educated, they are moving into societies with large differences in lifestyle, language, and religion. Migration and multiculturalism are, in other words, bringing about genuine cultural change, and change can be challenging and often destabilizing, bringing both benefits but also certain costs and consequences. (Again, many other migrant groups, like Jews, Germans, and Italians in the United States, Irish in the United Kingdom, and Poles in Germany were treated similarly to Muslim migrants.)

For example, some conservatives in the United States and Western Europe are genuinely convinced that their societies were founded on certain principles that will be tarnished by a too culturally disparate nation. Even among (white) citizens in the West who harbor no conscious racial anxiety, the coming demographic changes require a shift in thought. And the key questions here are the following: What will be the

basis for solidarity and unity for a nation in the context of the prolifera-
tion of ethnic cultures and migrant traditions? What kinds of cultures
will emerge? Will multiculturalism continue, or will new cultural forms
and practices solidify? What will be the basis of social solidarity in
this context? And what does this imply for how we engage and treat
people from new and different societies that come into our midst? These
are very real questions and challenges.

In previous generations, the answer to these dilemmas was relatively
simple: assimilation—that is, ensuring that newcomers were socialized
into the norms and practices of their new countries and contexts. The
costs and consequences of the changes wrought by migration, in other
words, were borne by migrants themselves. Indeed, it was they who were
expected to change. With the onset of multiculturalism, however, and the
large immigrant enclaves and communities that have emerged in many
places, this impetus to change migrants is much less viable or compelling.
New policies and approaches must be worked out, and it is societies that
are increasingly being forced to adapt and change as a result.

Working with sociological theorist Joseph Gerteis, Hartmann
has pointed out three basic alternatives to dealing with the diversity
that international migration and multiculturalism have created.[30] The
first is what they call cosmopolitanism. This is where, in the liberal-
individualist tradition, societies basically acknowledge and allow new
cultural practices and traditions in their midst. But they focus on creating laws, institutions, and cultural norms that would treat individuals
as equitably and fairly as possible regardless of race, religion, ethnicity,
nationality, or other culturally distinctive characteristics. In this cosmopolitan vision, the new cultural traditions and practices brought by
immigrants would be recognized and perhaps even celebrated—a new,
more pluralist national culture acknowledged—but in terms of laws and
policies the group-specific differences would be downplayed in order to
bring out the commonalities all citizens share. Put differently, different
cultural groups would be allowed and perhaps even privately celebrated,
but not formally encouraged or supported at a collective level. With its
emphasis on individualism and expansive citizenship, this ideal is one
that appeals, for example, to Americans of a range of cultural and political persuasions as well as to many in Great Britain.

The other two approaches to establishing solidarity in the face of cultural diversity focus more on the existence of different ethnic groups and cultures within a given society, seeing them not as something to be overcome or transcended but as social and cultural units to build solidarity around. In the first and most extreme version, "segmented pluralism," multicultural societies would basically create a separate and distinct place for different social groups and cultural communities. The society as a whole would thus be a collection of largely isolated if more or less equal communities, more of a union or republic of separate cultures and communities. The old Soviet Union, with its collection of ethnic and national communities unified under a federated system of governance and culture, was an example of this. A more contemporary example is Belgium, which has recognized its various immigrant communities both legally and in the public culture.

In contrast to this segmented or confederated vision, Hartmann and Gerteis also envision a more interactive, collaborative brand of multiculturalism. Instead of maintaining order and solidarity by remaining isolated and independent, the diverse cultural groups that make up a particular society or nation would recognize and communicate with one another for the purposes of creating a new, more vibrant and interactive shared culture. This new cultural solidarity would not only be accepting of individuals from different backgrounds (as with cosmopolitanism), but would actively recognize and indeed try to encourage, sustain, and actively support some set of diverse cultural groups and communities. In contrast to the segmented approach, however, this approach puts the emphasis on interaction, communication, and exchange between various communities and cultures. In this framework, perhaps best expressed in Charles Taylor's visions for Canada as a meeting place of French, English, and Aboriginal practices, a nation or society would be not be defined by a single national culture, but a collection of equally recognized, valued, and contributing cultural traditions.[31]

It is difficult to say which of these various options will or should take hold in any given country in the years to come. These options can also co-exist at different levels and times and places within a country. For instance, the way New York City at the local level deals with immigrants is vastly different from how the state of Arizona does. Similarly, Great

Britain deals with migrants and diversity very differently than France or Germany.[32] These are political and ideological projects as much as anything. But there are at least two empirical factors that will shape and determine these outcomes to some extent that should be considered— and these bring us back to a consideration of ethnicity and immigration.

One has to do with the future of distinctive social groups in an ostensibly multicultural context. The literature on ethnicity in the United States suggests that the strength and persistence of ethnic ties and their contribution to cultural diversity more generally depend on an ongoing relation to immigration. That is, ethnic ties are richer, thicker, and more likely to be reproduced when ethnic communities are constantly reinvigorated by continuing in-migration of new community members who bring with them the culture and customs from their countries of origin thus continuing the cultural distinctiveness and traditions of the community.

The literature on immigration and American ethnicity has been the basis of much of this thinking because the potential loss of native culture and identity is a familiar challenge confronting all immigrant ethnic groups. Indeed, the challenge of maintaining ethnic identities and communities is the essence of the "third generation" problem, where the children of immigrants and the children of children of immigrants become fascinated with and nostalgic for traditional culture even as they become assimilated and quite removed from it.[33] But if third or fourth generation white ethnic immigrants in the United States and Western Europe are less likely to have strong ties with co-ethnics, because of intermarriage and the dissolution of ethnic neighborhoods, more recent first or second-generation (mostly non-white these days like the Hmong Americans we discussed earlier) immigrants are likely to be more strongly involved in ethnic networks. However, given all of the economic and political and social forces we have discussed in previous chapters, it could also be that these identities will "thin out" and become symbolic, divorced from any ethnic community. Or they may not. As we showed in Chapter 4, some Mexicans by the third generation became white, while others maintained links with a broader Mexican immigrant community, and identify themselves as Mexican, Latino, or Hispanic.

In this context, we realize that the future of multiculturalism will likely have less to do with the scale and scope of migration than it does with the conditions of incorporation and treatment of migrants—and especially their children—in the years and generations after their initial relocation and settlement. In other words, the future of migration, ethnic affiliation, and multiculturalism may well be less about questions of culture and national solidarity than about the structure and organization of economic opportunities, access to public facilities and resources, and the existence (or lack thereof) of cultural tolerance and acceptance for those who are new or different or with fewer resources and opportunities.

This brings us to another, final set of concerns about multiculturalism and diversity: the concerns of equity, opportunity, social support, and even social justice. These concerns about multiculturalism are fundamentally different from those of the more conservative backlash we have already described. These concerns, often from the Left, about multiculturalism are not driven by perceived threats of disunity or disorder that can come with excessive cultural diversity. Rather, they are about the problems of inequality and injustice that can come down upon communities that are somehow different and distinct from those who are largest or have the most power in any given society. So we are talking about a certain resistance to multiculturalism, but a different kind of resistance, one that is a less active backlash against migrants than an argument that migrants and those who are different are often in need of social assistance and support.

According to these more politically progressive critics, one of the biggest problems with most multiculturalist policies and programs is that they are rarely able or willing to create the conditions and opportunities that would allow for the success and full incorporation of migrants and others who are different or disadvantaged in contemporary societies. The further problem with multiculturalism, in this view, is that it often makes things worse.

One such example comes from Alana Lentin and Gavan Titley. In a book called *The Crises of Multiculturalism: Racism in a Neoliberal Age*, they argue that multiculturalism has actually "become a central site for coded debates about belonging, race, legitimacy, and social futures in a globalized, neoliberal era."[34] The empirical material that is the basis of

Lentin and Titley's claims comes mostly from Western Europe, and is focused far more on cultural politics—head scarves, minarets, cartoons, and campaign speeches—than actual laws, social programs, or public policies. But the key point here is that "multiculturalism," as it tends to be understood in many contemporary societies, is actually associated with and thus helps to reproduce racism, intolerance, xenophobia, and Islamophobia—again in a somewhat less overt, actively oppositional way and more akin to the kind of colorblind racism Eduardo Bonilla Silva talked about for American racial demographics.

Lentin and Titley explain, for example, how in a supposedly post-racial, colorblind era, much public talk about difference and multiculturalism reduces problems of migrant incorporation and mobility (or lack thereof) to questions of "culture." Such a cultural frame both minimizes the challenges of establishing and maintaining a truly multicultural society and reduces its inherent problems to the agency and choice of otherwise marginalized, disempowered groups. In other words, it blames migrants themselves for whatever difficulties and shortcomings they experience and which they present to their new countries and cultures.

Scholarly analysts like Lentin and Titley also criticize the conventional attack on multiculturalism for its supposed misplaced emphasis on tolerance and excessive catering to group separatism, which, among other things, misses the conditions of social and economic inequality that should accompany concerns about solidarity. They suggest that media coverage of immigration and integration debates gets caught up in other political issues and agendas. They also suggest that distinctions between "good diversity" and "bad diversity" actually serve to produce and reinforce subtler, new commonsense distinctions and hierarchies. Additionally, they assert that the now common mainstream critique of various "integrationist policies" depends on an exaggerated, stylized, and fundamentally inaccurate vision of multiculturalism's orientation to various cultural differences, identities, affiliations, and practices.

Taken as a whole, this more progressive criticism of multiculturalism is not about the challenges that migration and diversity present in contemporary societies, it is more about the difficulties that contemporary societies present for migrants and others who may be different or unique. And again, perhaps the key point here is that it is not just the culture and identity of migrants that matter when we are thinking of the cultural consequences of migration and multiculturalism, it is the conditions of incorporation that may be most decisive. And all too often when rich multicultural communities and cultures can be found, they come at the cost of the persistent social inequalities encountered by those who are actually the source of that very creativity, excitement, and innovation that we believe comes with diversity.

Conclusion

Migration is all about change—and change can be difficult and unsettling, just as it can benefit some, at the expense of others. This statement is obvious to the point of being banal for migrants themselves whose lives are typically upended in ways and to an extent that are often even more extreme than they might have expected. But it is a bit less expected in communities and countries that are relatively stable and self-satisfied, and which may be only partially or incompletely committed to allowing significant migration in their midst. And it is in these contexts and for these people that the economic, demographic, and cultural (and other) transformations wrought by immigration may be the most difficult to realize and deal with. In this chapter, we have highlighted just a few of the most obvious of these impacts in the hopes of helping to show that the migration story is, ultimately, not just about migrants but about all of us.

Notes

1 Massey, Douglas, Margarita Mooney, Kimberly Torres, and Camille Charles. "Black Immigrants and Black Natives Attending Selective Colleges and Universities in the US." *American Journal of Education* 113 (2007): 243–271.

2 For additional background, see: Waters, Mary, Philip Kasinitz, and Asad L. Asad. "Immigrants and African Americans." *Annual Review of Sociology* 40 (2014): 369–390.

3 Waldinger, Roger. "Crossing Borders: International Migration in the New Century." *Contemporary Sociology* 42.3 (2013): 349–363.

4 Foner, Nancy. *From Ellis Island to JFK: New York's Two Great Waves of Immigration.* New Haven: Yale UP, 2000.

5 World Bank. "Migrants from Developing Countries to Send Home $414 Billion in Earnings in 2013." October 2, 2013. www.worldbank.org/en/news/feature/2013/10/02/Migrants-from-developing-countries-to-send-home-414-billion-in-

earnings-in-2013 <retrieved November 22, 2013>; see also: Taylor, Edward. "The New Economics of Labour Migration and the Role of Remittances in the Migration Process." *International Migration* 37 (1999): 63–88.

6 Portes, Alejandro. *The Economic Sociology of Immigration.* New York: Russell Sage Foundation, 1995; Bean, Frank, and Stephanie Bell-Rose. *Immigration and Opportunity: Race, Ethnicity, and Employment in the US.* New York: Russell Sage Foundation, 1999.

7 World Bank. *Global Economic Prospects: Economic Implications of Remittances and Migration.* Washington, DC: The World Bank, 2006.

8 Skrentny, John, and Micah Gell-Redman. "Japan, the US, and the Philosophical Basis of Immigration Policy." *American Behavioral Scientist* 56.8 (2012): 995–1007.

9 Bean, Frank, and Dan Hammermesh. *Help or Hindrance? The Economic Implications of Immigration for African Americans.* New York: Russell Sage, 1998.

10 Moss, Philip, and Chris Tilly. *Stories Employers Tell: Race, Skill, and Hiring in America.* New York: Russell Sage Foundation, 2001.

11 Massey, Douglas, Jorge Durand, and Nolan Malone. *Beyond Smoke and Mirrors: Mexican Immigration in an Era of Economic Integration.* New York: Russell Sage Foundation, 2002.

12 Portions of this section are based upon a chapter Hartmann originally wrote with Kia Heise. Hartmann, Douglas and Kia Heise, "The Uncertain Future of Race in a Changing America." In Doug Hartmann and Chris Uggen, *Color Lines and Racial Angles* (pp. 3–19). New York: W.W. Norton, 2014. Our thanks go to Heise for allowing us to adapt and incorporate this material.

13 Balbo, Nicoletta, Francesco Billari, and Melinda Mills. "Fertility in Advanced Societies: A Review of Research." *European Journal of Population/Revue Européenne de Démographie* 29.1 (2013): 1–38.

14 Cherlin, Andrew. "Demographic Trends in the United States: A Review of Research in the 2000s." *Journal of Marriage and Family* 72.3 (2010): 403–419.

15 Lee, Jennifer, and Frank Bean. *The Diversity Paradox: Immigration and the Color Line in the 21st Century.* New York: Russell Sage Foundation, 2010.

16 Alba, Richard, and Victor Nee. *Remaking the American Mainstream: Assimilation and Contemporary Immigration.* Cambridge, MA: Harvard UP, 2003.

17 Alba, Richard. *Blurring the Color Line: The New Chance for a More Integrated America.* Cambridge, MA: Harvard UP, 2009, p. 15.

18 Bonilla-Silva, Eduardo. "From Bi-racial to Tri-racial: Towards a New System of Racial Stratification in the USA." *Ethnic and Racial Studies* 27.6 (2004): 931–950.

19 Bonilla-Silva, Eduardo. *Racism without Racists: Color-blind Racism and the Persistence of Racial Inequality in the US.* Lanham, MD: Rowman & Littlefield, 2003.

20 Cornell, Stephen, and Douglas Hartmann. *Ethnicity and Race: Making Identities in a Changing World,* 2nd ed. Thousand Oaks, CA: Pine Forge, 2007.

21 Barrett, James, and David Roediger. "Inbetween Peoples: Race, Nationality and the 'New Immigrant' Working Class." *Journal of American Ethnic History* (1997): 3–44.

22 Gusfield, Joseph. *Symbolic Crusade: Status Politics and the American Temperance Movement.* Urbana: University of Illinois Press, 1963.

23 Glazer, Nathan, and Daniel Moynihan. *Beyond the Melting Pot: The Negroes, Puerto Ricans, Jews, Italians, and Irish of New York City,* 2nd ed. Cambridge, MA: MIT, 1970.

24 Kallen, Horace. "Democracy Versus the Melting-Pot: A Study of American Nationality." *The Nation*. February 25, 1915.

25 Brubaker, Rogers. "The Return of Assimilation? Changing Perspectives on Immigration and Its Sequels in France, Germany, and the US." *Ethnic and Racial Studies* 24.4 (2001): 531–548, p. 543.

26 Swartz, Teresa Toguchi, Douglas Hartmann, and Pao Lee. "Immigrant Incorporation in Qualitative, Lifecourse Perspective: The Hmong American Case." Unpublished manuscript, University of Minnesota, Minneapolis.

27 Kymlicka, Will. *Multicultural Odysseys: Navigating the New International Politics of Diversity*. Oxford: Oxford UP, 2007.

28 Glazer, Nathan. *We Are All Multiculturalists Now*. Cambridge, MA: Harvard UP, 1997. See also Kivisto, Peter. "We Really Are All Multiculturalists Now." *The Sociological Quarterly* 53 (2012): 1–24.

29 Kasinitz, Philip, John Mollenkopf, Mary Waters, and Jennifer Holdaway. *Inheriting the City: The Children of Immigrants Come of Age*, Cambridge, MA: Harvard UP, 2008. See also Smith, Robert. *Mexican New York*. Berkeley: University of California Press, 2006; and Lee, Jennifer. *Civility in the City: Blacks, Jews, and Koreans in Urban America*. Cambridge, MA: Harvard UP, 2002.

30 Hartmann, Douglas, and Joseph Gerteis. "Dealing with Diversity: Mapping Multiculturalism in Sociological Terms." *Sociological Theory* 23.2 (2005): 218–240.

31 Taylor, Charles. *Multiculturalism: Examining the Politics of Recognition*. Princeton, NJ: Princeton University Press, 1994.

32 For further examples and more extensive discussions see: Joppke, Christian. *Selecting by Origin: Ethnic Migration in the Liberal State*. Cambridge, MA: Harvard UP, 2005; and Kymlicka, Will. *Multicultural Odysseys: Navigating the New International Politics of Diversity*. Oxford: Oxford UP, 2007.

33 Gans, Herbert. "Symbolic Ethnicity: The Future of Ethnic Groups and Cultures in America." *Ethnic and Racial Studies* 2.1 (1979): 1–20.

34 Lentin, Alana, and Gavan Titley. *The Crises of Multiculturalism: Racism in a Neoliberal Age*. London: Zed, 2011, p. 12.

CONCLUSION
FACTORS AND ACTORS THAT WILL SHAPE THE FUTURE

The number of international migrants, as we discussed in the introduction, is rather small, roughly 3 percent of the global population. The vast majority of those are settled. The year-by-year flow of migrants is far, far smaller. For all the attention focused on global migration, relatively few people actually pick up and leave their homes to try their luck in a new land.

But for those who do migrate, things change and often quite dramatically—for them, their families and others back home, and for the natives in their new countries. And in an increasingly interconnected and diverse world, these transformations are more visible, meaningful, and revealing than ever before.

We began the book by asking these four questions: Why do people leave their homes for a new land? Where do they go and how do they get there? What do they do once they get there? And what about their children, what happens to them?

Our goal in this book has been twofold. We aimed to answer these questions by giving you a broad overview of the state of research in the field. And we wanted to expose you to cutting edge work we feel have not gotten their due in other textbooks in the field. To that end, we gave in-depth attention to such topics as human trafficking, Muslim migrants in the West, migrant laborers, and professional expatriates. We looked at how migrants move through the use of brokers. And we looked at the culture of migration and the effects of peers on assimilation, two under-used theoretical approaches that examine why migrants move and how assimilation happens.

Obviously we hope that these explorations will help students and scholars of migration better understand the migrant experiences and impacts that are so prominent and prevalent in the contemporary world. But what about the future? What can the theories and analyses and facts we have assembled contribute to our understanding and engagement with migration and incorporation?

For all of our big talk and bold analyses, we sociologists are often scared to make predictions about the future. The worlds we live in are complicated, and it is difficult to say how all of these different forces will combine together and what other, unexpected new forces and trends will emerge in the future.

Migration is no different. It is difficult, if not impossible to predict how local and global economies may shift, how current birth rates will change, and what kinds of public policies and political movements may take shape. But if we don't want to make specific predictions, we do feel fairly confident about the underlying factors and key actors that will drive and shape the future of migration, immigration, and incorporation in a global society.

Economy

As we made clear, getting better and/or better paying jobs is a prime factor for migrants. That's the economic pull. The push is when the local job market doesn't have enough good or good paying jobs. In the early 20th century, the United States was most definitely the land of economic opportunity. By the late 20th century this was still true, but other lands of opportunity emerged as well. Western European countries were sending migrants in the 19th and early 20th centuries; by the end of the 20th century, Germany, Ireland, France, the Netherlands and other countries had become countries of immigration. The resource-rich Persian Gulf countries also began to attract large numbers of migrants, as did Russia, Singapore, and Taiwan.

As has happened before, as the economic fortunes of countries wax and wane, some other migrant-sending countries may become migrant-receiving countries. Could Brazil, India, and China end up being migrant-receiving countries? Their economies have been expanding rapidly and they already attract some high-end professional expatriates. As their economies expand, wages will go up for lower-level workers, and it's very possible, perhaps even likely, that they will attract workers from poorer countries. It's also possible that, as the middle class in the United States shrinks, many Americans will migrate in search of greener pastures. Maybe they'll go to Canada, which now has a bigger middle class proportionally than the United States.[1]

Economic factors are also important in determining patterns of incorporation. The path to assimilation for European migrants to the United States in the early mid-20th century was made with relatively high-paying blue-collar jobs, and later with educational and financial benefits (like free education for returning military veterans and subsidized loans for housing in the suburbs), which made movement to the middle class relatively easy for a great number second- and third-generation European-Americans. For a variety of reasons (not least of which is a volatile economy and a compartmentalized job market), today's minority migrants often face a worse job market and have far fewer benefits than did yesteryear's migrants and their children, something segmented assimilation theorists have stressed. And all of these jobs and financial benefits are themselves driven and determined by the economy itself—the broader economic climate in local, national, and international terms.

Again, economies are uncertain and unpredictable. We don't know exactly where economic growth will continue to expand in coming years, where it will flatten out, or where it might do something even more extreme. However, we can be sure that whatever happens, the economy will be a major factor in both determining migrant flows all over the world as well as in shaping the incorporation experiences of migrants wherever they land.

Networks and Brokers

Personal networks funnel migrants to certain places. Once a stream of migration begins to be established, more and more people from the sending areas will go. It's not a risky prediction to say that the population of Mexicans in New York City will increase. That's a no brainer. But will would-be migrants strike out in new paths to new places? For years, sociologists who study migration have seen that the initial costs of migration are high, financially, socially, and psychologically. But it could be that with increased cultural globalization that the social "distance" between most places has shrunk so much that the psychological "cost" perhaps has come down. If so, we would expect new networks to develop in new countries.

One way that might happen is through the actions of brokers. For example, Ali has a cousin in Hyderabad who was trying to get to the United States in the late 1990s. Because he was straight out of college with little work experience, the United States was going to be too difficult—the United States consular officials would certainly have rejected his application without a second thought. Saudi Arabia was a popular option, but he wasn't interested in going to Saudi Arabia. His broker suggested Malaysia. Getting a visa was easy, the pay was good (comparable to wages in the Persian Gulf, but lower than the United States), and it was fairly close by. Ali was a big fan of this plan, but his cousin turned it down, as he had no information on Malaysia, no contacts, and basically was not the adventurous type. It was a risk. The point here is that brokers could play a role in shaping new patterns of migration to emerging hotspots for work, finding places where visas are relatively easy and cheap to get, and where wages are high enough to justify a move.

Law and Policy

Throughout the book we've stressed that governmental policies directly shape both patterns of immigration and migrant incorporation experiences. Sometimes what governments want happens; sometimes it doesn't, and sometimes there are unintended consequences. But no matter what, political leaders and government officials make the rules, and potential migrants—as well as those who want to encourage and facilitate immigration—have to follow them or figure out ways around them. The United States was a country of mass immigration in the 19th and 20th centuries until the Immigration Act of 1924, which dramatically limited the number of migrants arriving. In 1910, over one million people gained legal permanent residence; by 1935 that number dropped to about 35,000. The political tide had turned again in the early 1960s, and the United States once again became a country of mass immigration due to the passage of the Immigration and Nationality Act of 1965.

Immigration policies and programs also have important impacts on the experiences that migrants have once they settle in a new place, how migrants and their children adapt to their new surroundings. We have mentioned how important education—in particular, public education—was to that huge mass of European immigrants who came to the United States in the late 19th and early 20th centuries, and have seen many different examples of this over the course of this book. If migrants come to new countries looking for opportunities for themselves and their children, many of the most important avenues for mobility require education and training. Without proper—and probably better—education and job training, migrants and their children will not be able to fill the positions potentially available to them. This stagnation would reinforce, rather than challenge, existing racial categories and hierarchies and would further stand in the way of their economic assimilation. In other words, even if the economy is strong, migrants must have the proper education, skills, and training to fill the jobs that may be available to them. And such programs and policies do not just happen; they are not just shaped by the invisible hand of the market. They are enacted and implemented through law and policy.

It is also important to point out that changes in policies regarding migration don't happen in a vacuum. Often there are economic concerns, as when countries face labor shortages. Economic downturns can also cause native workers to be resentful of immigrant workers, and politicians may placate them by restricting migration. At other times, politicians may ignore the concerns of workers in favor of the desires of "big business." And sometimes, politics is politics, driven by interests and agendas that have little or nothing to do with markets and the economy. We have seen this in recent years in the United States with government debates over immigration reform since President Obama took office in 2008. The recession has given way to a slight recovery, but the US Congress has done nothing of substance about immigration reform.

Our point is that there is no one-to-one correlation between the politics of immigration and the economy—and, moreover, that immigration and settlement policies are swayed in large part by the shifting winds of public opinion. In the recent past in the United States, in Europe, and all over the world, immigration policy has been a very politically controversial issue. Immigration has its supporters as well as its critics, some of whom, as we discussed in Chapter 6 under the heading of multiculturalism, are virulent in their backlash. It is not clear if or how these different attitudes and positions will evolve in the near future. But there is no reason to expect that immigration will become any less of an issue than it already is. Quite the contrary, as migration flows continue, as migrants are incorporated in new and different ways, and as new countries get impacted by all of these dynamics, there is every reason to expect that migration will continue to be a contested and controversial public issue.

In a recent article on the philosophical bases of immigration policy, John Skrentny and Micah Gell-Redman identify three different perspectives through which attitudes about migrants and immigration policy itself are filtered in public debates.[2] One is the utilitarian or economic point of view, often taken by national experts and lawmakers interested in maximizing their country's overall position and power. The second is a more rights-oriented approach. Advocates interested in social justice, human dignity, and equal protections typically emphasize it for migrant workers and residents. The third position is the one that they say is the most popular (that is, held by most ordinary citizens) and most consequential, if also the most misunderstood—the "traditional community" perspective. In this view, stable communities are seen as a primary value, and the concern is that this stability and continuity is often put at risk by the change and uncertainty that can come with migration.

Skrentny and Gell-Redman believe it is important to understand all three of these different perspectives on migrants and migration more generally, if we are to understand and contribute to better immigration policies and programs. But they believe it is especially challenging to grasp the complexities of the traditional community perspective. In their view, we must understand that many regular citizens in places all over the world are viscerally committed the communities that they live in, and their fear of the changes that could come with migrant cannot be simply dismissed as racism, prejudiced, or xenophobia. But while these folks must be taken seriously, their fears and concerns are also often easily manipulated by elites. The politics of immigrations are obviously complex and multifaceted, as difficult to predict or anticipate as the economy. But, extrapolating from Skrentny and Gell-Redman, there may be at least one general, take-away point: that the greater the cultural differences in lifestyle, language, or religion between migrants and native populations, the more challenging the public debates about immigration policy will be.

Migrants Themselves

How do migrants identify and understand themselves in a new place? What do they do? What choices will they make, or actions will they take? In formal, theoretical terms, these questions are all about agency—that is, the ability of migrants themselves to shape their lives and the worlds around them. Sociologists are often dismissive of agency, preferring instead to focus on social structures, external conditions, broad historical forces, and factors like the economy or public policy. And, truth be told, we've put a lot of emphasis on these contextual forces and factors throughout this book (not to mention in this concluding chapter). But it is important to recognize that agency plays a role in determining the migration and incorporation experience of both individual migrants (what kinds of jobs an individual may find, who he or she marries, whether they have kids, etc.) as well as collectively—how large any particular co-ethnic enclave may be, what kinds of resources they are able to assemble, whether they are able to work together and help each other out (or not).

The demographics of race and population growth more generally in the United States present one interesting, if open-ended, example. As we discussed in Chapter 6, immigration has obvious consequences for population growth no matter what the context or time period. And the important point in the context of this discussion of agency is that these impacts are driven not only by the fact of new folks entering into a country or community, but also by how these migrants marry and reproduce. These behaviors and practices are not uniform or fully determined, but vary according to different groups, communities, and contexts. This point certainly applies to Hispanics, one of the largest and fastest growing groups in the United States today. Indeed, according to several recent estimates, Hispanic population growth in the United States isn't driven so much by simple migration as it is by what experts call "natural increase"—which is to say, reproduction, the fact that folks from this community are having babies. In 2012, immigrants accounted for only a little over one-third (35 percent) of the Hispanic population. Hispanic Americans are distinguished by other unique and often unappreciated behavioral patterns as well: For example, over two-thirds (68 percent) speak English fluently, high school graduates are more likely than whites to enroll in college, and they are becoming more liberal on social issues such as abortion and gay rights.[3] All of this is to highlight the ways in which Hispanic migrants and the larger Hispanic community is actively shaping itself and its role in American society.

Increases in interracial dating and mixed-race children among both migrants and natives further complicate any predictions on the future of the racial composition of the United States (not to mention elsewhere). The percentage of people in interracial marriages more than doubled from 1980 to 2010. Currently, 8.4 percent of US marriages are interracial. In states with larger populations of Hispanic and Asian immigrants, people are more likely to marry outside of their race, and they are most likely to marry whites: 43 percent of interracial marriages were white-Hispanic couples, 14 percent were white-Asian couples, and 12 percent were white-black couples.

According to the 2010 Census, there are nine million mixed-race individuals in the United States. But the future is far from clear. We don't know how they or their children will identify—whether it's with an existing racial category or with newly emergent "mixed race" classifications (or even some other, emerging labels). And we don't know how new generations of migrants and their children will identify or establish families either. Many demographic projections assume people of color will continue to identify in the same ways they have in previous decades. Yet this is not necessarily the case. For example, the increase in the Native American population in the 1960s and 1970s resulted not from demographic changes, but from identity changes: More Americans named and claimed a Native American identity. Alternately, first-generation African immigrants see American racial hierarchies and are resisting being lumped in with African Americans (though members of the second and third generations exhibit much different patterns).

There are many other examples of migrant agency that we could give—about the extent to which various immigrant groups take advantage of whatever education and training is offered to them; about what kinds of jobs they gravitate to; about how migrants assemble themselves into communities or not, and the extent to which they understand themselves as communities willing to work together or individuals who are largely on their own. But the key point here is that if we are to understand the immigration experience at any given time or in any given context, one of the factors we must pay attention to are the activities and understandings of migrants themselves.

Race, Class, and Gender

It is easy to talk about migrants as a homogeneous, unified group, or migration and immigration as a singular, coherent process and set of patterns, but nothing could be further from the truth. If there is one lesson we hope has come through loud and clear throughout all of the cases and examples that compose the chapters of this book, it is that there are many different factors driving migration and many different types of migrants. Migrants move for many different reasons, encounter many different kinds of societies and social conditions, and bring with them many different kinds of resources, interests, and limitations.

Realizing the existence of such variation and diversity is a crucial insight, whether you are trying to make sense of the migration experience of any individual migrant or any larger community of migrants. Yet insisting on the diversity and variation of the migrant experience is not to suggest that each and every migration story is unique and exceptional. There are patterns and regularities, commonalities across cases, and generalities that hold across different groups, countries, and contexts. Many of these patterns are structured by broad social and historical forces such as the economy, laws and public policy, and public opinion. But they are also structured by the social qualities and characteristics shared by different migrants and migrant communities. And the most basic and fundamental of these, at least in the sociological lexicon, are those associated with race, class, and gender.

Class, of course, is deeply implicated with the economy, which we have talked about extensively in this book. Simply put, migrants who are richer and more educated have a much different—and usually more advantaged—experience than those who have lower skills or less material resources at their disposal. In the last chapter, we talked about multiculturalism, which typically highlights issues of race, ethnicity, nationality, and religion. One basic takeaway point from this is that whether there is a match in terms of race and ethnicity or whether there are differences and whether a population confronts racial stigmas or finds themselves associated with those who are already privileged and empowered in a society matters a great deal in terms of the migrant experience in any given place. And we have presented several case studies that suggest how radically different migration policies and the migration experience can be depending upon whether it is focused upon male or female migrants.

As with all of the other factors and forces we have identified in this chapter, we are reluctant to specify just exactly how race or class or gender may matter overall, whether these social differences would be positive or negative, or how they might impact migration patterns or incorporation experiences. But what we would suggest—indeed insist upon—is that race, class, and gender will be among the most important and decisive social variables that shape and determine the migration experience. Look for them and how they play out and you will be well on your way to a rich and thoroughly sociological understanding of migration.

Notes

1 Leonhardt, David, and Kevin Quealy. "The American Middle Class Is No Longer the World's Richest." *New York Times*. April 22, 2014. www.nytimes.com/2014/04/23/upshot/the-american-middle-class-is-no-longer-the-worlds-richest.html?_r=0 <retrieved June 24, 2014>
2 Skrenty, John, and Micah Gell-Redman. "Japan, the United States, and the Philosophical Bases of Immigration Policy." *American Behavioral Scientist* 56.6 (2012): 995–1007.
3 Casselman, Ben. "Immigration Isn't Driving Hispanic Population Growth." *FiveThirtyEight*. July 9, 2014. http://fivethirtyeight.com/datalab/immigration-isnt-driving-hispanic-population-growth/ <retrieved July 10, 2014>

BIBLIOGRAPHY

Abdo, Geneive. *Mecca and Main Street: Muslim Life in America after 9/11*. Oxford: Oxford UP, 2006.

Abel, Guy, and Nikola Sander. "Quantifying Global International Migration Flows." *Science* 343 (2014): 1520–1522.

Abu-Ras, Wahiba, Sameera Ahmed, and Cynthia L. Arfken. "Alcohol Use among US Muslim College Students: Risk and Protective Factors." *Journal of Ethnicity in Substance Abuse* 9.3 (2010): 206–220.

Agustín, Laura. "The Disappearing of a Migration Category: Migrants Who Sell Sex." *Journal of Ethnic and Migration Studies* 32.1 (2006): 29–47.

Alba, Francisco. "Mexico: The New Migration Narrative." *Migration Information Source*. April 24, 2013. www.migrationpolicy.org/article/mexico-new-migration-narrative/ <retrieved May 12, 2014>

Alba, Richard. *Blurring the Color Line: The New Chance for a More Integrated America*. Cambridge, MA: Harvard UP, 2009.

Alba, Richard, and Victor Nee. *Remaking the American Mainstream: Assimilation and Contemporary Immigration*. Cambridge, MA: Harvard UP, 2003.

Ali, Syed. *Dubai: Gilded Cage*. New Haven: Yale UP, 2010.

Ali, Syed. "'Go West Young Man': The Culture of Migration among Muslims in Hyderabad, India." *Journal of Ethnic and Migration Studies* 33.1 (2007): 37–58.

Ali, Syed. "Going and Coming and Going Again: Second-Generation Migrants in Dubai." *Mobilities* 6.4 (2011): 553–568.

Ali, Syed. "The Moslems Are Here—Be Afraid!" *Contexts* 9.4 (2010): 72–73.

Ali, Syed. *Re-membering Selves: From Nobility and Caste to Ethnicity and Class in an Indian City*. Diss. University of Virginia, 2001.

Ali, Syed. "Understanding Acculturation among Second-generation South Asian Muslims in the US." *Contributions to Indian Sociology* 42.3 (2008): 383–411.

Ali, Syed. "Why Here, Why Now? Young Muslim Women Wearing Hijab." *The Muslim World* 95.4 (2005): 515–530.

Ali, Syed, and Tineke Fokkema. "The Importance of Peers: Assimilation Patterns among Second-generation Turkish Immigrants in Western Europe." *Journal of Ethnic and Migration Studies*, forthcoming, DOI: 10.1080/1369183X.2014.921114.

Ali, Wajahat, Eli Clifton, Matthew Duss, Lee Fang, Scott Keyes, and Faiz Shakir. *Fear, Inc.: The Roots of the Islamophobia Network in America*. Washington, DC: Center for American Progress, 2011.

Anderson, Bridget, and Blanka Hancilová. "Migrant Labour in Kazakhstan: A Cause for Concern?" *Journal of Ethnic and Migration Studies* 37.3 (2011): 467–483.

Arango, Joaquin. "Explaining Migration: A Critical View." *International Social Science Journal* 52.165 (2000): 283–296.

Archer, Toby. "Breivik's Swamp: Was the Oslo Killer Radicalized by What He Read Online." *Foreign Policy*. July 25, 2011. www.foreignpolicy.com/articles/2011/07/25/breivik_s_swamp <retrieved June 2, 2014>

Balbo, Nicoletta, Francesco Billari, and Melinda Mills. "Fertility in Advanced Societies: A Review of Research." *European Journal of Population/Revue Européenne de Démographie* 29.1 (2013): 1–38.

Bald, Vivek. *Bengali Harlem and the Lost Histories of South Asian America*. Cambridge, MA: Harvard UP, 2013.

Bankston III, Carl, and Min Zhou. "The Social Adjustment of Vietnamese American Adolescents: Evidence for a Segmented-assimilation Approach." *Social Science Quarterly* (1997): 508–523.

Barrett, James, and David Roediger. "Inbetween Peoples: Race, Nationality and the 'New Immigrant' Working Class." *Journal of American Ethnic History* (1997): 3–44.

Basch, Linda, Nina Glick Schiller, and Cristina Szanton Blanc. *Nations Unbound: Transnational Projects, Postcolonial Predicaments, and Deterritorialized Nation-States*. Staten Island, NY: Gordon and Breach, 1994.

Beaman, Jean. "But Madame, We Are French Also." *Contexts* 11.3 (2012): 46–51.

Beaman, Jean. *Liberte, Egalite, et Fraternite: Identity, Marginalization, and Second-Generation North African Immigrants in France*. Diss., Northwestern University, 2010.

Bean, Frank, and Stephanie Bell-Rose. *Immigration and Opportunity: Race, Ethnicity, and Employment in the US*. New York: Russell Sage Foundation, 1999.

Bean, Frank, and Dan Hammermesh. *Help or Hindrance? The Economic Implications of Immigration for African Americans*. New York: Russell Sage, 1998.

Beaverstock, Jonathan. "Lending Jobs to Global Cities: Skilled International Labour Migration, Investment Banking and the City of London." *Urban Studies* 33.8 (1996): 1377–1394.

Beaverstock, Jonathan. "Servicing British Expatriate 'Talent' in Singapore: Exploring Ordinary Transnationalism and the Role of the 'Expatriate' Club." *Journal of Ethnic and Migration Studies* 37.5 (2011): 709–728.

Benson, Michaela, and Karen O'Reilly. *Lifestyle Migration: Expectations, Aspirations and Experiences*. Farnham, England: Ashgate, 2009.

Bergen, Peter, and David Sterman. "U.S. Right Wing Extremists More Deadly than Jihadists." *CNN*. April 15, 2014. www.cnn.com/2014/04/14/opinion/bergen-sterman-kansas-shooting/ <retrieved April 22, 2014>

Berger, Joseph. "Protests of a Plan for a Mosque? That Was Last Year." *New York Times*. August 18, 2011. www.nytimes.com/2011/08/19/nyregion/mosque-opens-quietly-on-staten-island.html <retrieved May 15, 2014>

Bierwirth, Chris. "The Lebanese Communities of Côte d'Ivoire." *African Affairs* 98.390 (1999): 79–99.

Billaud, Julie. "Snapshots of British Islam (3): Halal Dating in London #ANTHROISLAM." *Allegra*. December 9, 2013. http://allegralaboratory.net/snapshots-of-british-islam-3-halal-dating-in-london/ <retrieved March 12, 2014>

Bonilla-Silva, Eduardo. "From Bi-racial to Tri-racial: Towards a New System of Racial Stratification in the USA." *Ethnic and Racial Studies* 27.6 (2004): 931–950.

Bonilla-Silva, Eduardo. *Racism without Racists: Color-blind Racism and the Persistence of Racial Inequality in the US*. Lanham, MD: Rowman & Littlefield, 2003.

Borjas, George. *Friends or Strangers: The Impact of Immigrants on the American Economy*. New York: Basic, 1990.

Brennan, Denise. "Life Beyond Trafficking." *Contexts* 13.1 (2014): 20–21.

Brennan, Denise. *Life Interrupted: Trafficking into Forced Labor in the United States*. Durham, NC: Duke UP, 2014.

Brennan, Denise. *What's Love Got to Do with It? Transnational Desires and Sex Tourism in the Dominican Republic*. Durham, NC: Duke UP, 2004.

Brubaker, Rogers. "The Return of Assimilation? Changing Perspectives on Immigration and Its Sequels in France, Germany, and the US." *Ethnic and Racial Studies* 24.4 (2001): 531–548.

Busza, Joanna, Sarah Castle, and Aisse Diarra. "Trafficking and Health." *British Medical Journal*, June 5, 2004, 328 (7452): 1369–1371.

Caldwell, Christopher. *Reflections on the Revolution in Europe: Immigration, Islam, and the West*. London: Penguin, 2009.

Casas, Laura Oso. "Money, Sex, Love and the Family: Economic and Affective Strategies of Latin American Sex Workers in Spain." *Journal of Ethnic and Migration Studies* 36.1 (2010): 47–65.

Casselman, Ben. "Immigration Isn't Driving Hispanic Population Growth." *FiveThirtyEight*. July 9, 2014. http://fivethirtyeight.com/datalab/immigration-isnt-driving-hispanic-population-growth/ <retrieved July 10, 2014>

Cassim, Shezanne. "I Went to Jail for Posting a Comedy Skit on YouTube. Is This the Modern UAE?" *The Guardian*. February 9, 2014. www.theguardian.com/commentisfree/2014/feb/09/shezanne-cassim-jail-uae-youtube-video <retrieved February 12, 2014>

Cavanagh, Shannon. "Peers, Drinking, and the Assimilation of Mexican American Youth." *Sociological Perspectives* 50.3 (2007): 393–416.

Cherlin, Andrew. "Demographic Trends in the United States: A Review of Research in the 2000s." *Journal of Marriage and Family* 72.3 (2010): 403–419.

Cohen, Jeffrey. *The Culture of Migration in Southern Mexico*. Austin: U of Texas Press, 2004.

Cohen, Jeffrey, and İbrahim Sirkeci. *Cultures of Migration: The Global Nature of Contemporary Mobility*. Austin: U of Texas Press, 2011.

Cohen, Robin. *Global Diasporas: An Introduction*. New York: Routledge, 2008.

Colic-Peisker, Val. "Free Floating in the Cosmopolis? Exploring the Identity-belonging of Transnational Knowledge Workers." *Global Networks* 10.4 (2010): 467–488.

Colwell, Jessica. "China Census: Foreign Demographics in Shanghai." *Shanghaiist*. September 23, 2011. http://shanghaiist.com/2011/09/23/china_census_foreigners _make_up_1_o.php <retrieved March 8, 2014>

Constable, Nicole. *Romance on a Global Stage: Pen Pals, Virtual Ethnography, and "Mail-order" Marriages.* Berkeley: U of California, 2003.

Cornell, Stephen, and Douglas Hartmann. *Ethnicity and Race: Making Identities in a Changing World,* 2nd ed. Thousand Oaks, CA: Pine Forge, 2007.

Crosnoe, Robert. *Fitting In, Standing Out: Navigating the Social Challenges of High School to Get an Education.* Cambridge, MA: Cambridge UP, 2011.

Crosnoe, Robert, and Monica Johnson. "Research on Adolescence in the Twenty-First Century." *Annual Review of Sociology* 37.1 (2011): 439–460.

Crul, Maurice, and Jens Schneider. "Comparative Integration Context Theory: Participation and Belonging in New Diverse European Cities." *Ethnic and Racial Studies* 33.7 (2010): 1249–1268.

Crul, Maurice, and Jens Schneider. "Conclusions and Implications: The Integration Context Matters." In Maurice Crul, Jens Schneider, and Frans Lelie, eds., *The European Second Generation Compared: Does the Integration Context Matter?* Amsterdam: Amsterdam UP, 2012.

Crul, Maurice, Jens Schneider, and Frans Lelie. *Super Diversity: A New Perspective on Integration.* Amsterdam: VU University Press, 2013.

Crul, Maurice, Philipp, Schnell, Barbara Herzog-Punzenberger, Maren Wilmes, Marieke Slootman, and Rosa Gomez. "School Careers of Second-Generation Youth in Europe: Which Education Systems Provide the Best Chances for Success?" In Maurice Crul, Jens Schneider, and Frans Lelie, eds., *The European Second Generation Compared: Does the Integration Context Matter?* Amsterdam: Amsterdam UP, 2012.

de Haas, Hein. "Migration and Development: A Theoretical Perspective." *International Migration Review* 44.1 (2010): 227–264.

Del Signore, John. "Anti-Mosque Protesters On SI Bring Out NYC's Inner Bigot." Gothamist. June 21, 2010. http://gothamist.com/2010/06/21/anti-mosque _protesters_on_si_bring.php <retrieved May 1, 2014>

Del Signore, John. "Meeting to Discuss Mosque On Staten Island Ends Predictably." Gothamist. June 10, 2010. http://gothamist.com/2010/06/10/meeting_to_discuss_mosque_on_staten.php <retrieved April 30, 2014>

DeParle, Jason. "A Good Provider Is One Who Leaves." *The New York Times.* April 22, 2007. http://query.nytimes.com/gst/fullpage.html?res=9D04E7D6113FF931A1 5757C0A9619C8B63&ref=jasondeparle&pagewanted=all <retrieved March 30, 2013>

Diab, Khaled. "Why Muslims Don't Pig Out." *The Guardian.* July 2, 2008. www. theguardian.com/commentisfree/2008/jul/02/islam.religion <retrieved March 12, 2014>

Doward, Jamie. "Qatar World Cup: 400 Nepalese Die on Nation's Building Sites since Bid Won." *The Observer.* February 16, 2014. www.theguardian.com/football/2014/feb/16/qatar-world-cup-400-deaths-nepalese <retrieved March 28, 2014>

Duyvendak, Jan, Trees Pels, and Rally Riijkschroeff. "A Multicultural Paradise? The Cultural Factor in Dutch Integration Policy." In Jennifer Hochschild and John Mollenkopf, eds., *Bringing Outsiders In: Transatlantic Perspectives on Immigrant Political Incorporation.* Ithaca, NY: Cornell UP, 2009.

Ehrenreich, Barbara, and Arlie Russell Hochschild, "Introduction." In Barbara Ehrenreich and Arlie Russell Hochschild, eds., *Global Woman: Nannies, Maids, and Sex Workers in the New Economy.* New York: Metropolitan, 2003.

Faris, Robert, and Diane Felmlee. "Status Struggles: Network Centrality and Gender Segregation in Same- and Cross-Gender Aggression." *American Sociological Review* 76.1 (2011): 48–73.

Farrer, James. "Global Nightscapes in Shanghai as Ethnosexual Contact Zones." *Journal of Ethnic and Migration Studies* 37.5 (2011): 747–764.

Farrer, James. "'New Shanghailanders' or 'New Shanghainese': Western Expatriates' Narratives of Emplacement in Shanghai." *Journal of Ethnic and Migration Studies* 36.8 (2010): 1211–1228.

Favell, Adrian. *Eurostars and Eurocities: Free Movement and Mobility in an Integrating Europe.* Malden, MA: Blackwell, 2008.

Fechter, Anne-Meike. "From 'Incorporated Wives' to 'Expat Girls': A New Generation of Expatriate Women?" In Anne Coles and Anne-Meike Fechter, eds., *Gender and Family among Transnational Professionals.* New York: Routledge, 2007.

Fechter, Anne-Meike, and Heather Hindman. *Inside the Everyday Lives of Development Workers: The Challenges and Futures of Aidland.* Sterling, VA: Kumarian, 2011.

Finnegan, William. "A Reporter at Large: The Countertraffickers." *The New Yorker.* May 5, 2008. www.newyorker.com/reporting/2008/05/05/080505fa_fact_finnegan? currentPage=all <retrieved May 30, 2013>

Fisher, Michael. *Counterflows to Colonialism: Indian Travellers and Settlers in Britain, 1600–1857.* Delhi: Permanent Black, 2004.

Fletcher, Adam, Chris Bonell, and Annik Sorhaindo. "You Are What Your Friends Eat: Systematic Review of Social Network Analyses of Young People's Eating Behaviours and Bodyweight." *Journal of Epidemiology and Community Health* 65.6 (2011): 548–555.

Fokkema, Tineke, Laurence Lessard-Phillips, James Bachmeier, and Susan Brown. "The Link Between the Transnational Behaviour and Integration of the Second Generation in European and American Cities." *Nordic Journal of Migration Research* 2.2 (2012): 111–123.

Foner, Nancy. *From Ellis Island to JFK: New York's Two Great Waves of Immigration.* New Haven: Yale UP, 2000.

Fordham, Signithia, and John Ogbu. "Black Students' School Success: Coping with the "Burden of 'Acting White'." *The Urban Review* 18.3 (1986): 176–206.

Freeman, Caren. *Making and Faking Kinship: Marriage and Labor Migration between China and South Korea.* Ithaca: Cornell UP, 2011.

Fryer, Roland. "'Acting White': The Social Price Paid by the Best and Brightest Minority Students." *Education Next* 6.1 (2006): 52–59.

Gallagher, Anne. "Trafficking for Organ Removal." *Contexts* 13.1 (2014): 18–19.

Gans, Herbert. "Second-generation Decline: Scenarios for the Economic and Ethnic Futures of the Post-1965 American Immigrants." *Ethnic and Racial Studies* 15.2 (1992): 173–192.

Gans, Herbert. "Symbolic Ethnicity: The Future of Ethnic Groups and Cultures in America." *Ethnic and Racial Studies* 2.1 (1979): 1–20.

Gardner, Andrew. *City of Strangers: Gulf Migration and the Indian Community in Bahrain.* Ithaca, NY: Cornell UP, 2010.

Gibson, Margaret. "Reputation and Respectability: How Competing Cultural Systems Affect Students' Performance in School." *Anthropology & Education Quarterly* 13.1 (1982): 3–28.

Gibson, Margaret, Patricia Gandara, and Jill Koyama (eds.). *School Connections: US Mexican Youth, Peers, and School Achievement.* New York: Teachers College Press, 2004.

Gibson, Margaret. *Accommodation Without Assimilation: Sikh Immigrants in an American High School*. Ithaca, NY: Cornell UP, 1988.

Gibson, Margaret. "Reputation and Respectability: How Competing Cultural Systems Affect Students' Performance in School." *Anthropology & Education Quarterly* 13.1 (1982): 3–28.

Gibson, Owen. "More than 500 Indian Workers Have Died in Qatar since 2012, Figures Show." *The Guardian*. February 18, 2014. www.theguardian.com/world/2014/feb/18/qatar-world-cup-india-migrant-worker-deaths <retrieved March 28, 2014>

Glassner, Barry. *The Culture of Fear: Why Americans Are Afraid of the Wrong Things*. New York: Basic, 1999.

Glazer, Nathan. "On Beyond the Melting Pot, 35 Years After." *International Migration Review* 34.1 (2000): 270–279.

Glazer, Nathan. *We Are All Multiculturalists Now*. Cambridge, MA: Harvard UP, 1997.

Glazer, Nathan, and Daniel Moynihan. *Beyond the Melting Pot: The Negroes, Puerto Ricans, Jews, Italians, and Irish of New York City*, 2nd ed. Cambridge, MA: MIT, 1970.

Goldberg, Eleanor. "Super Bowl Is Single Largest Human Trafficking Incident in U.S.: Attorney General." *The Huffington Post*. February 3, 2013. www.huffingtonpost.com/2013/02/03/super-bowl-sex-trafficking_n_2607871.html <retrieved Jan 12, 2013>

Goldberg, J. J. "More Killed by Toddlers Than Terrorists in U.S." *The Jewish Daily Forward*. May 5, 2013. http://blogs.forward.com/jj-goldberg/176043/more-killed-by-toddlers-than-terrorists-in-us/ <retrieved June 2, 2014>

Goldman, Adam, and Matt Apuzzo. "NYPD Built Secret Files on Mosques Outside NY." *Associated Press*. February 22, 2012. www.ap.org/Content/AP-In-The-News/2012/NYPD-built-secret-files-on-mosques-outside-NY <retrieved May 6, 2014>

Gonzales, Roberto, and Leo Chavez. "Awakening to a Nightmare." *Current Anthropology* 53.3 (2012): 255–281.

Gordon, Milton. *Assimilation in American Life: The Role of Race, Religion, and National Origins*. New York: Oxford UP, 1964.

Gordon, Milton. "Assimilation in America: Theory and Reality." *Daedalus* 90.2 (1961): 263–285.

Gottschalk, Peter. *American Heretics: Catholics, Jews, Muslims, and the History of Religious Intolerance*. Palgrave Macmillan, 2013.

Granovetter, Mark. "The Strength of Weak Ties." *American Journal of Sociology* 78.6 (1973): 1360.

Gusfield, Joseph. *Symbolic Crusade: Status Politics and the American Temperance Movement*. Urbana: University of Illinois Press, 1963.

Haddad, Yvonne, and Adair Lummis. *Islamic Values in the United States: A Comparative Study*. New York: Oxford UP, 1987.

Hafiz, Yasmine. "'Mipsterz' 'Somewhere in America' Video Showcases Muslim Hipster Swag; Sparks A Passionate Discussion." December 2, 2013. www.huffingtonpost.com/2013/12/02/mipsterz-somewhere-in-america-video_n_4374182.html <retrieved May 6, 2014>

Haller, William, Alejandro Portes, and Scott Lynch. "Dreams Fulfilled, Dreams Shattered: Determinants of Segmented Assimilation in the Second Generation." *Social Forces* 89.3 (2011): 733–762.

Haller, William, Alejandro Portes, and Scott Lynch. "On the Dangers of Rosy Lenses: Reply to Alba, Kasinitz and Waters." *Social Forces* 89.3 (2011): 775–781.

Ham, Julie. *What's the Cost of a Rumour? A Guide to Sorting out the Myths and the Facts about Sporting Events and Trafficking*. Bangkok: GAATW, 2011.

Harding, David. "Violence, Older Peers, and the Socialization of Adolescent Boys in Disadvantaged Neighborhoods." *American Sociological Review* 74.3 (2009): 445–464.

Harkinson, Josh. "How H1-B Visas Are Screwing Tech Workers." *Mother Jones*. February 22, 2013. www.motherjones.com/politics/2013/02/silicon-valley-h1b-visas-hurt-tech-workers <retrieved April 3, 2013>

Harris, Judith. *The Nurture Assumption: Why Children Turn Out the Way They Do*. New York: Simon and Schuster, 2009.

Hartmann, Douglas, and Joseph Gerteis. "Dealing with Diversity: Mapping Multiculturalism in Sociological Terms." *Sociological Theory* 23.2 (2005): 218–240.

Hartmann, Douglas, and Kia Heise. "The Uncertain Future of Race in a Changing America." In Doug Hartmann and Chris Uggen, eds., *Color Lines and Racial Angles*, New York: W.W. Norton, 2014.

Haynie, Dana, and D. Wayne Osgood. "Reconsidering Peers and Delinquency: How Do Peers Matter?" *Social Forces* 84.2 (2005): 1109–1130.

Hoang, Kimberly. "Transnational Gender Vertigo." *Contexts* 12.2 (2013): 22–26. www.worldbank.org/en/news/feature/2013/10/02/Migrants-from-developing-countries-to-send-home-414-billion-in-earnings-in-2013 <retrieved November 22, 2013>

Human Rights Watch. *Building Towers, Cheating Workers: Exploitation of Migrant Construction Workers in the United Arab Emirates*. New York: Human Rights Watch, 2006. www.hrw.org/reports/2006/11/11/building-towers-cheating-workers <accessed June 4, 2014>

Human Rights Watch. *"The Island of Happiness": Exploitation of Migrant Workers on Saadiyat Island, Abu Dhabi*. New York: Human Rights Watch, 2009. www.hrw.org/reports/2009/05/18/island-happiness <retrieved June 1, 2013>

Human Rights Watch. *Swept under the Rug: Abuses against Domestic Workers around the World*. New York: Human Rights Watch, 2006. www.hrw.org/reports/2006/07/27/swept-under-rug <retrieved June 1, 2013>

Huschek, Doreen, Helga de Valk, and Aart Liefbroer. "Does Social Embeddedness Influence Union Formation Choices among the Turkish and Moroccan Second Generation in the Netherlands?" *Journal of Comparative Family Studies* 42.6 (2011): 787–808.

Huschek, Doreen, Helga de Valk, and Aart Liefbroer. "Partner Choice Patterns among the Descendants of Turkish Immigrants in Europe." *European Journal of Population/ Revue Européenne De Démographie* 28.3 (2012): 241–268.

Huschek, Doreen, Aart Liefbroer, and Helga de Valk. "Timing of First Union among Second-generation Turks in Europe: The Role of Parents, Peers and Institutional Context." *Demographic Research* 22.16 (2010): 473–504.

International Organization for Migration. *World Migration Report 2013: Migrant Well-being and Development*. Geneva: International Organization for Migration, 2013.

"Islamophobia: Understanding Anti-Muslim Sentiment in the West." *Gallup World*. 2014. www.gallup.com/poll/157082/islamophobia-understanding-anti-muslim-sentiment-west.aspx <retrieved May 2, 2014>

Jiménez, Tomás, and Adam Horowitz. "When White Is Just Alright: How Immigrants Redefine Achievement and Reconfigure the Ethnoracial Hierarchy." *American Sociological Review* 78.5 (2013): 849–871.

Joppke, Christian. *Selecting by Origin: Ethnic Migration in the Liberal State.* Cambridge, MA: Harvard UP, 2005.

Kallen, Horace. "Democracy Versus the Melting-Pot: A Study of American Nationality." *The Nation*, February 25, 1915.

Kalter, Frank. "The Second Generation in the German Labor Market: Explaining the Turkish Exception." In Richard Alba and Mary Waters, eds., *The Next Generation: Immigrant Youth in a Comparative Perspective.* New York: NYU Press, 2011.

Kandel, Denise. "On Processes of Peer Influences in Adolescent Drug Use: A Developmental Perspective." *Advances in Alcohol & Substance Abuse* 4.3–4 (1985): 139–162.

Kandel, William, and Douglas Massey. "The Culture of Mexican Migration: A Theoretical and Empirical Analysis." *Social Forces* 80.3 (2002): 981–1004.

Kasinitz, Philip, John Mollenkopf, and Mary Waters (eds.). *Becoming New Yorkers: Ethnographies of the New Second Generation.* New York: Russell Sage, 2004.

Kasinitz, Philip, Mary Waters, John Mollenkopf, and Jennifer Holdaway. *Inheriting the City: The Children of Immigrants Come of Age.* New York: Russell Sage, 2008.

Keaton, Trica. *Muslim Girls and the Other France: Race, Identity Politics, and Social Exclusion.* Bloomington: Indiana UP, 2006.

Keefe, Patrick. "The Snakehead: The Criminal Odyssey of Chinatown's Sister Ping." *The New Yorker.* April 24, 2006. www.newyorker.com/archive/2006/04/24/060424fa_fact6?currentPage=all <retrieved June 19, 2013>

Khimm, Suzy. "Do We Need More Skilled Foreign Workers?" *The Washington Post.* March 21, 2013. www.washingtonpost.com/blogs/wonkblog/wp/2013/03/21/do-we-need-more-skilled-foreign-workers/ <retrieved April 1, 2013>

Kibria, Nazli. "Transnational Marriage and the Bangladeshi Muslim Diaspora in Britain and the United States." *Culture and Religion* 13.2 (2012): 227–240.

King, Rosalind, and Kathleen Harris. "Romantic Relationships among Immigrant Adolescents." *International Migration Review* 41.2 (2007): 344–370.

King, Russell, and Anastasia Christou. "Of Counter-Diaspora and Reverse Transnationalism: Return Mobilities to and from the Ancestral Homeland." *Mobilities* 6.4 (2011): 451–466.

Kivisto, Peter. "We Really Are All Multiculturalists Now." *The Sociological Quarterly* 53 (2012): 1–24.

Kolsy, Uzma. "LAPD Continues Controversial Anti-terrorism Spying Program with Little Oversight." *The Raw Story.* September 5, 2012. www.rawstory.com/rs/2012/09/05/lapd-continues-controversial-anti-terrorism-spying-program-with-little-oversight/ <retrieved May 6, 2014>

Korpela, Mari. "A Postcolonial Imagination? Westerners Searching for Authenticity in India." *Journal of Ethnic and Migration Studies* 36.8 (2010): 1299–1315.

Kreager, Derek. "Guarded Borders: Adolescent Interracial Romance and Peer Trouble at School." *Social Forces* 87.2 (2008): 887–910.

Krissman, Fred. "Sin Coyote Ni Patrón: Why the 'Migrant Network' Fails to Explain International Migration." *International Migration Review* 39.1 (2005): 4–44.

Kumar, Sujay. "Muslim, Single, Looking to Mingle." *The Daily Beast.* September 13, 2013. www.thedailybeast.com/witw/articles/2013/09/13/young-muslim-navigating-the-american-dating-gauntlet.html <retrieved March 28, 2014>

Kundnani, Arun. "Blind Spot? Security Narratives and Far-right Violence in Europe." ICCT Research Paper, The Hague, 2012.

Kurien, Prema. *Kaleidoscopic Ethnicity: International Migration and the Reconstruction of Community Identities in India.* New Brunswick, NJ: Rutgers UP, 2002.

Kurzman, Charles. *The Missing Martyrs: Why There Are so Few Muslim Terrorists.* Oxford: Oxford UP, 2011.

Kyle, David, and Rey Koslowski. "Introduction." In David Kyle and Rey Koslowski, eds., *Global Human Smuggling: Comparative Perspectives,* 2nd ed. Baltimore: Johns Hopkins UP, 2011.

Kymlicka, Will. *Multicultural Odysseys: Navigating the New International Politics of Diversity.* Oxford: Oxford UP, 2007.

Lan, Pei-Chia. "Legal Servitude and Free Illegality: Migrant 'Guest Workers' in Taiwan." In Parreñas, Rhacel Salazar, and Lok Siu, eds., *Asian Diasporas: New Formations, New Conceptions.* Stanford, CA: Stanford UP, 2007.

Lan, Pei-Chia. "New Global Politics of Reproductive Labor: Gendered Labor and Marriage Migration." *Sociology Compass* 2.6 (2008): 1801–1815.

Lan, Pei-Chia. "White Privilege, Language Capital and Cultural Ghettoisation: Western High-Skilled Migrants in Taiwan." *Journal of Ethnic and Migration Studies* 37.10 (2011): 1669–1693.

Laurence, Jonathan, and Justin Vaïsse. *Integrating Islam: Political and Religious Challenges in Contemporary France.* Washington, DC: Brookings Institution, 2006.

Lee, Jennifer. *Civility in the City: Blacks, Jews, and Koreans in Urban America,* Cambridge, MA: Harvard UP, 2002.

Lee, Jennifer, and Frank Bean. *The Diversity Paradox: Immigration and the Color Line in the 21st Century.* New York: Russell Sage Foundation, 2010.

Lee, Juliet, Robynn Battle, Brian Soller, and Naomi Brandes. "Thizzin'-Ecstasy Use Contexts and Emergent Social Meanings." *Addiction Research & Theory* 19.6 (2011): 528–541.

Leichtman, Mara. "Migration, War, and the Making of a Transnational Lebanese Shi'i Community in Senegal." *International Journal of Middle East Studies* 42.2 (2010): 269–290.

Lentin, Alana, and Gavan Titley. *The Crises of Multiculturalism: Racism in a Neoliberal Age.* London: Zed, 2011.

Leonard, Karen. "Guests in the Gulf: South Asian Expatriates." In Richard Warren Perry and Bill Maurer, *Globalization under Construction: Governmentality, Law, and Identity.* Minneapolis: U of Minnesota, 2003.

Leonhardt, David, and Kevin Quealy. "The American Middle Class Is No Longer the World's Richest." *New York Times.* April 22, 2014. www.nytimes.com/2014/04/23/upshot/the-american-middle-class-is-no-longer-the-worlds-richest.html?_r=0 <retrieved June 24, 2014>

Levitt, Peggy. "Roots and Routes: Understanding the Lives of the Second Generation Transnationally." *Journal of Ethnic and Migration Studies* 35.7 (2009): 1225–1242.

Levitt, Peggy. "Social Remittances: Migration Driven Local-Level Forms of Cultural Diffusion." *International Migration Review* 32.4 (1998): 926–948.

Levitt, Peggy. *The Transnational Villagers.* Berkeley: U of California, 2001.

Levitt, Peggy, and B. Nadya Jaworsky. "Transnational Migration Studies: Past Developments and Future Trends." *Annual Review of Sociology* 33.1 (2007): 129–156.

Levitt, Peggy, and Deepak Lamba-Nieves. "Social Remittances Revisited." *Journal of Ethnic and Migration Studies* 37.1 (2011): 1–22.

Levitt, Peggy, and Nina Glick Schiller. "Conceptualizing Simultaneity: A Transnational Social Field Perspective on Society." *International Migration Review* 38.3 (2004): 1002–1039.

Levitt, Peggy, and Mary Waters. *The Changing Face of Home: The Transnational Lives of the Second Generation.* New York: Russell Sage Foundation, 2002.

Lewis, Philip. *Young, British and Muslim.* London: Continuum, 2007

Lindquist, Johan. "The Elementary School Teacher, the Thug and His Grandmother: Informal Brokers and Transnational Migration from Indonesia." *Pacific Affairs* 85.1 (2012): 69–89.

Lindquist, Johan, Biao Xiang, and Brenda Yeoh. "Opening the Black Box of Migration: Brokers, the Organization of Transnational Mobility and the Changing Political Economy in Asia." *Pacific Affairs* 85.1 (2012): 7–19.

Lucassen, Leo. *The Immigrant Threat: The Integration of Old and New Migrants in Western Europe since 1850.* Urbana: U of Illinois, 2005.

Lucassen, Leo, and Charlotte Laarman. "Immigration, Intermarriage and the Changing Face of Europe in the Post War Period." *The History of the Family* 14.1 (2009): 52–68.

Marquand, Robert. "Facebook Draws 7,000 to Anti-Muslim Pork Sausage Party in Paris." *Christian Science Monitor.* June 17, 2010. www.csmonitor.com/World/Europe/2010/0617/Facebook-draws-7-000-to-anti-Muslim-pork-sausage-party-in-Paris <retrieved May 12, 2014>

Massey, Douglas. "America's Immigration Policy Fiasco: Learning from Past Mistakes." *Daedalus* 142.3 (2013): 5–15.

Massey, Douglas. "Why Does Immigration Occur? A Theoretical Synthesis." In Charles Hirschman, Philip Kasinitz, and Josh DeWind, eds., *The Handbook of International Migration: The American Experience.* New York: Russell Sage Foundation, 1999.

Massey, Douglas, Jorge Durand, and Nolan Malone. *Beyond Smoke and Mirrors: Mexican Immigration in an Era of Economic Integration.* New York: Russell Sage Foundation, 2002.

Massey, Douglas, Margarita Mooney, Kimberly Torres, and Camille Charles. "Black Immigrants and Black Natives Attending Selective Colleges and Universities in the US." *American Journal of Education,* 113 (2007): 243–271.

Massey, Douglas, and Magaly Sanchez. *Brokered Boundaries: Creating Immigrant Identity in Anti-Immigrant Times.* New York: Russell Sage Foundation, 2010.

Massey, Douglas et al. *Worlds in Motion: Understanding International Migration at the End of the Millenium.* Oxford: Clarendon, 1998.

Mathews, Gordon. *Ghetto at the Center of the World: Chungking Mansions, Hong Kong.* Chicago, IL: U of Chicago, 2011.

Matloff, Norman. "Are Foreign Students the 'Best and Brightest'?" *Economic Policy Institute.* February 28, 2013. www.epi.org/publication/bp356-foreign-students-best-brightest-immigration-policy/ <retrieved April 3, 2013>

Mckeown, Adam. "How the Box Became Black: Brokers and the Creation of the Free Migrant." *Pacific Affairs* 85.1 (2012): 21–45.

Milner, Murray, Jr. *Freaks, Geeks, and Cool Kids: American Teenagers, Schools, and the Culture of Consumption.* New York: Routledge, 2004.

Milner, Murray, Jr. *Status and Sacredness: A General Theory of Status Relations and an Analysis of Indian Culture.* New York: Oxford UP, 1994.

Mipsterz—Muslim Hipsters. Facebook. www.facebook.com/Mipsterz/info <retrieved June 6, 2014>

Mirza, Munira, Abi Senthilkumaran, and Zein Ja'far. *Living Apart Together: British Muslims and the Paradox of Multiculturalism.* London: Policy Exchange, 2007.

Mishra, Pankaj. "A Culture of Fear." *The Guardian.* August 15, 2009. www.theguardian.com/books/2009/aug/15/eurabia-islamophobia-europe-colonised-muslims <retrieved May 2, 2014>

Mogahed, Dalia. *Muslim Americans: A National Portrait.* Washington, DC: Gallup, 2009.

Molland, Sverre. "'I Am Helping Them': 'Traffickers', 'Anti-traffickers' and Economies of Bad Faith." *The Australian Journal of Anthropology* 22.2 (2011): 236–254.

Molland, Sverre. "Safe Migration, Dilettante Brokers and the Appropriation of Legality: Lao-Thai 'Trafficking' in the Context of Regulating Labour Migration." *Pacific Affairs* 85.1 (2012): 117–136.

Morawska, Ewa. "Research on Immigration/Ethnicity in Europe and the US: A Comparison." *The Sociological Quarterly* 49.3 (2008): 465–482.

Moss, Philip, and Chris Tilly. *Stories Employers Tell: Race, Skill, and Hiring in America.* New York: Russell Sage Foundation, 2001.

Mosse, David. *Adventures in Aidland: The Anthropology of Professionals in International Development.* New York: Berghahn, 2011.

"Mosque Opens on SI Without Controversy." *The Real Deal.* August 19, 2011. http://therealdeal.com/blog/2011/08/19/mosque-opens-on-staten-island-without-controversy/ <retrieved May 15, 2014>

Mueller, John, and Mark Stewart. 2012. "The Terrorism Delusion: America's Overwrought Response to September 11." *International Security* 37(1): 81–110.

"Muslims in Germany." *SPIEGEL ONLINE.* n.d. www.spiegel.de/international/germany/bild-850607-127849.html <retrieved May 8, 2014>

Muttarak, Raya. "Generation, Ethnic and Religious Diversity in Friendship Choice: Exploring Interethnic Close Ties in Britain." *Ethnic and Racial Studies* 37.1 (2014): 71–98.

Ong, Aihwa. *Flexible Citizenship: The Cultural Logics of Transnationality.* Durham, NC: Duke UP, 1999.

Open Society Institute. "Muslims in Europe: A Report on 11 EU Cities." New York: Open Society Institute, 2010.

Padnani, Amy. "Midland Beach Mosque Voted Down by Church's Board of Trustees." Silive.com. July 22, 2010. www.silive.com/eastshore/index.ssf/2010/07/midland_beach_mosque_voted_dow.html <retrieved April 30, 2014>

Pager, Devah, and Bruce Western. "Identifying Discrimination at Work: The Use of Field Experiments." *Journal of Social Issues* 68.2 (2012): 221–237.

Parreñas, Rhacel Salazar. *Illicit Flirtations: Labor, Migration, and Sex Trafficking in Tokyo.* Stanford, CA: Stanford UP, 2011.

Peek, Lori. *Behind the Backlash: Muslim Americans after 9/11.* Philadelphia: Temple UP, 2011.

Pew Research Center. "From Germany to Mexico: How America's Source of Immigrants Has Changed Over a Century." May 27, 2014. www.pewresearch.org/fact-tank/2014/05/27/a-shift-from-germany-to-mexico-for-americas-immigrants/ <retrieved June 2, 2014>

Pew Research Center. "Mapping the Global Muslim Population." October 7, 2009. www.pewforum.org/2009/10/07/mapping-the-global-muslim-population/ <retrieved June 3, 2014>

Pew Research Center. *Muslim Americans: No Signs of Growth in Alienation or Support for Extremism.* Washington, DC: Pew Research Center, 2011.

Poros, Maritsa. *Modern Migrations: Gujarati Indian Networks in New York and London.* Stanford, CA: Stanford UP, 2011.

Portes, Alejandro. "Conclusion: Theoretical Convergencies and Empirical Evidence in the Study of Immigrant Transnationalism." *International Migration Review* 37.3 (2003): 874–892.

Portes, Alejandro. *The Economic Sociology of Immigration.* New York: Russell Sage Foundation, 1995.

Portes, Alejandro, Patricia Fernández-Kelly, and William Haller. "The Adaptation of the Immigrant Second Generation in America: A Theoretical Overview and Recent Evidence." *Journal of Ethnic and Migration Studies* 35.7 (2009): 1077–1104.

Portes, Alejandro, and Rubén Rumbaut. *Legacies: The Story of the Immigrant Second Generation.* Berkeley: U of California, 2001.

Portes, Alejandro, and Min Zhou. "The New Second Generation: Segmented Assimilation and Its Variants." *The ANNALS of the American Academy of Political and Social Science* 530.1 (1993): 74–96.

Prado, Guillermo, Shi Huang, Seth Schwartz, Mildred Maldonado-Molina, Frank Bandiera, Mario de la Rosa, and Hilda Pantin. "What Accounts for Differences in Substance Use Among US-born and Immigrant Hispanic Adolescents? Results from a Longitudinal Prospective Cohort Study." *Journal of Adolescent Health* 45.2 (2009): 118–125.

"Public Remains Conflicted Over Islam." *Pew Research Religion and Public Life Project.* August 24, 2010. www.pewforum.org/2010/08/24/public-remains-conflicted-over-islam/ <retrieved May 2, 2014>

Rahman, Md Mizanur. "Gendering Migrant Remittances: Evidence from Bangladesh and the United Arab Emirates." *International Migration* 51.S1 (2013): e159–e178.

Ratha, Dilip et al. "Migration and Remittance Flows: Recent Trends and Outlook, 2013–2016." *Migration and Development Brief* 21 (2013): 2.

Ream, Robert, and Russell Rumberger. "Student Engagement, Peer Social Capital, and School Dropout among Mexican American and non-Latino White Students." *Sociology of Education* 81.2 (2008): 109–139.

Rumbaut, Rubén. "Ages, Life Stages, and Generational Cohorts: Decomposing the Immigrant First and Second Generations in the US." *International Migration Review* 38.3 (2004): 1160–1205.

Rytina, Nancy. 2013. "Estimates of the Legal Permanent Resident Population in 2012." *Population Estimates* (July). Washington, DC: Office of Immigration Statistics, US Department of Homeland Security.

Safi, Mirna. "Intermarriage and Assimilation: Disparities in Levels of Exogamy among Immigrants in France." *Population* (English Edition) 63.2 (2008): 239–267.

Sander, Nikola, Guy Abel, and Ramon Bauer. "The Global Flow of People." www.global-migration.info/ <retrieved July 8, 2014>

Santelli, Emmanuelle, and Beate Collet. "The Choice of Mixed Marriage among the Second Generation in France: A Lifetime Approach." *Papers: Revista de Sociologia* 97.1 (2012): 93–112.

Sassen, Saskia. *A Sociology of Globalization.* New York: W.W. Norton, 2007.

Saunders, Doug. *The Myth of the Muslim Tide: Do Immigrants Threaten the West?* New York: Vintage, 2012.

Schanzer, David, and Charles Kurzman. "Homegrown Terrorism Threat Was Overhyped." *NJ.com*. April 14, 2014. www.nj.com/opinion/index.ssf/2014/04/homegrown_terrorism_threat_was_overhyped_opinion.html <retrieved May 12, 2014>

Schlosser, Eric. "In the Strawberry Fields." *The Atlantic*. November 1, 1995. www.theatlantic.com/magazine/archive/1995/11/in-the-strawberry-fields/305754/ <retrieved Jan 22, 2013>

Scott, Joan. *The Politics of the Veil*. Princeton, NJ: Princeton UP, 2010.

Selby, Jennifer. "Marriage-partner Preference among Muslims in France: Reproducing Tradition in the Maghrebian Diaspora." *Journal of the Society for the Anthropology of Europe* 9.2 (2009): 4–16.

Siddiqui, Obaid. "Looking for Love and Finding Awkwardness at ISNA." *Altmuslim: Global perspectives on Muslim Life, Politics, and Culture*. September 10, 2012. www.patheos.com/blogs/altmuslim/2012/09/looking-for-love-and-finding-awkwardness-at-isna/ <retrieved March 28, 2014>

Silberman, Roxane. "The Employment of Second Generations in France: The Republican Model and the November 2005 Riots." In Richard Alba and Mary Waters, eds., *The Next Generation: Immigrant Youth in a Comparative Perspective*. New York: NYU Press, 2011.

Silver, Nate. "Crunching the Risk Numbers." *Wall Street Journal*. January 8, 2010. http://online.wsj.com/news/articles/SB10001424052748703481004574646963713065116 <retrieved June 9, 2014>

Skinner, E. Benjamin. "South Africa's New Slave Trade and the Campaign to Stop It." *Time*. January 18 2010. http://content.time.com/time/magazine/article/0,9171,1952335,00.html <retrieved March 22, 2013>

Skrentny, John, and Micah Gell-Redman. "Japan, the US, and the Philosophical Basis of Immigration Policy." *American Behavioral Scientist*, 56.8 (2012): 995–1007.

Slack, Jeremy, Daniel Martinez, Scott Whiteford, and Emily Peiffer. "In the Shadow of the Wall: Family Separation, Immigration Enforcement and Security." Center for Latin American Studies, The University of Arizona, March, 2013.

Smith, Jane. *Islam in America*. New York: Columbia UP, 2013.

Smith, Robert. *Mexican New York: Transnational Lives of New Immigrants*. Berkeley: U of California, 2006.

Solomon, Anna. *The Little Bride*. New York: Riverhead, 2011.

Stanley, Phiona. *A Critical Ethnography of "Westerners" Teaching English in China: Shanghaied in Shanghai*. Milton Park, Abingdon and New York: Routledge, 2013.

Stark, Oded. *The Migration of Labor*. Cambridge, MA: Blackwell, 1991.

Stirrat, Roderick. "Mercenaries, Missionaries and Misfits: Representations of Development Personnel." *Critique of Anthropology* 28.4 (2008): 406–425.

Swartz, Teresa Toguchi, Douglas Hartmann, and Pao Lee. "Immigrant Incorporation in Qualitative, Lifecourse Perspective: The Hmong American Case." Unpublished manuscript, University of Minnesota, Minneapolis.

Taylor, Charles. *Multiculturalism: Examining the Politics of Recognition*. Princeton, NJ: Princeton UP, 1994.

Taylor, Edward. "The New Economics of Labour Migration and the Role of Remittances in the Migration Process." *International Migration* 37.1 (1999): 63–88.

Terrazas, Aaron. "Mexican Immigrants in the United States." *Migration Policy Institute*. February 22, 2010. www.migrationpolicy.org/article/mexican-immigrants-united-states-0#11 <retrieved July 17, 2013>

Thibodeau, Patrick, and Sharon Machlis. "The Data Shows: Top H-1B Users Are Offshore Outsourcers." *Computerworld*. February 14, 2013. www.computerworld.com/s/article/9236732/The_data_shows_Top_H_1B_users_are_offshore_outsourcers <retrieved January 17, 2014>

Titley, Gavan. "Pork Is the Latest Front in Europe's Culture Wars." *The Guardian*. April 14, 2014. www.theguardian.com/commentisfree/2014/apr/15/le-pen-pig-whistle-politics?CMP=twt_gu <retrieved April 15, 2014>

Toyota, Mika. "Editorial Introduction: International Marriage, Rights and the State in East and Southeast Asia." *Citizenship Studies* 12.1 (2008): 1–7.

Tseng, Yen-Fen. "Shanghai Rush: Skilled Migrants in a Fantasy City." *Journal of Ethnic and Migration Studies* 37.5 (2011): 765–784.

Tyson, Karolyn. *Integration Interrupted: Tracking, Black Students, and Acting White after Brown*. New York: Oxford UP, 2011.

Ueno, Koji. "The Effects of Friendship Networks on Adolescent Depressive Symptoms." *Social Science Research* 34.3 (2005): 484–510.

US Bureau of the Census. "B05005. Year of Entry by Nativity and Citizenship Status in the United States—Universe: Population Born Outside the United States." *2011 American Community Survey 1-Year Estimates*. Washington, DC: US Bureau of the Census, 2012. http://factfinder2.census.gov/faces/tableservices/jsf/pages/productview.xhtml?pid=ACS_11_1YR_B05005&prodType=Table <retrieved October 9, 2014>

Vaisse, Justin. *Muslims in Europe: A Short Introduction*. Washington, DC: Center on the United States and Europe at Brookings, 2008.

Vallejo, Jody. *Barrios to Burbs: The Making of the Mexican American Middle Class*. Stanford, CA: Stanford UP, 2012.

Vasta, Ellie. "Immigrants and the Paper Market: Borrowing, Renting and Buying Identities." *Ethnic and Racial Studies* 34.2 (2011): 187–206.

Vitello, Paul. "Church Rejects Sale of Building for a Mosque." *New York Times*. July 22, 2010. www.nytimes.com/2010/07/23/nyregion/23mosque.html?sq=dolan%20mosque&st=cse&adxnnl=1&scp=6&adxnnlx=1313704711-xs4k3DQNo9xCYr5wLki9Yg <retrieved April 30, 2014>

Waldinger, Roger. "Crossing Borders International Migration in the New Century." *Contemporary Sociology: A Journal of Reviews* 42.3 (2013): 349–363.

Waldinger, Roger, and David Fitzgerald, "Transnationalism in Question." *American Journal of Sociology* 109.5 (2004): 1177–1195.

Walsh, Katie. "'Dad Says I'm Tied to a Shooting Star!' Grounding (Research on) British Expatriate Belonging." *Area* 38.3 (2006): 268–278.

Wang, Horng-Luen. "Regulating Transnational Flows of People: An Institutional Analysis of Passports and Visas as a Regime of Mobility." *Identities* 11.3 (2004): 351–376.

Warner, W. Lloyd, and Leo Srole. *The Social Systems of American Ethnic Groups*. New Haven: Yale UP, 1945.

Warr, Mark, and Mark Stafford. "The Influence of Delinquent Peers: What They Think or What They Do?" *Criminology* 29.4 (1991): 851–866.

Waters, Mary. *Black Identities: West Indian Immigrant Dreams and American Realities*. Cambridge, MA: Harvard UP, 1999.

Waters, Mary. "Ethnic and Racial Identities of Second-generation Black Immigrants in New York City." *International Migration Review* 28.4 (1994): 795–820.

Waters, Mary, Philip Kasinitz, and Asad L. Asad. "Immigrants and African Americans." *Annual Review of Sociology* 40 (2014): 369–390.

Weiner, Myron. "International Migration and Development: Indians in the Persian Gulf." *Population and Development Review* 8.1 (1982): 1–36.

Weitzer, Ronald. "Macro Claims Versus Micro Evidence." *Contexts* 13.1 (2014): 24–25.

Weitzer, Ronald. "The Social Construction of Sex Trafficking: Ideology and Institutionalization of a Moral Crusade." *Politics and Society* 35.3 (2007): 447–475.

World Bank. *Global Economic Prospects: Economic Implications of Remittances and Migration*. Washington, DC: The World Bank, 2006.

World Bank. "Migrants from Developing Countries to Send Home $414 Billion in Earnings in 2013." October 2, 2013. www.worldbank.org/en/news/feature/2013/ 10/02/Migrants-from-developing-countries-to-send-home-414-billion-in-earnings-in-2013 <retrieved November 22, 2013>

Xiang, Biao. *Global "Body Shopping": An Indian Labor System in the Information Technology Industry*. Princeton, NJ: Princeton UP, 2007.

Xiang, Biao. "Predatory Princes and Princely Peddlers: The State and International Labour Migration Intermediaries in China." *Pacific Affairs* 85.1 (2012): 47–68.

Yeoh, Brenda, and Weiqiang Lin. "Rapid Growth in Singapore's Immigrant Population Brings Policy Challenges." *Migration Information Source*. April 3, 2012. www. migrationpolicy.org/article/rapid-growth-singapores-immigrant-population-brings-policy-challenges/ <retrieved June 5, 2014>

Yeoh, Brenda, and Katie Willis. "Negotiating 'Home' and 'Away': Singaporean Professional Migrants in China." In David W. Haines, Keiko Yamanaka, and Shinji Yamashita, *Wind over Water: Migration in an East Asian Context*. New York: Berghahn, 2012.

Yeoh, Brenda, and Katie Willis. "Singaporeans in China: Transnational Women Elites and the Negotiation of Gendered Identities." *Geoforum* 36.2 (2005): 211–222.

Yinbi, Ni. "Shanghai Reports 6.7% Rise in Expat Population." *ShanghaiDaily.com*. January 9, 2013. www.shanghaidaily.com/Metro/expat-community/Shanghai-reports-67-rise-in-expat-population/shdaily.shtml <retrieved March 8, 2014>

Zhou, Min, and Carl Bankston. *Growing Up American: How Vietnamese Children Adapt to Life in the US*. New York: Russell Sage Foundation, 1998.

Zhou, Min, Jennifer Lee, Jody Vallejo, Rosaura Tafoya-Estrada, and Yang Sao Xiong. "Success Attained, Deterred, and Denied: Divergent Pathways to Social Mobility in Los Angeles's New Second Generation." *The ANNALS of the American Academy of Political and Social Science* 620.1 (2008): 37–61.

Zoepf, Katherine. "Where the Boys Are, at Least for Now, the Girls Pounce." *New York Times*. November 2, 2006. www.nytimes.com/2006/11/02/world/middleeast/ 02beirut.html <retrieved January 2, 2014>

INDEX

Note: Page numbers with *m* indicate maps; those with *t* indicate tables.

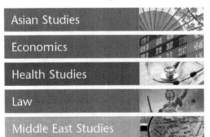

Printed by PGSTL